PRASE

Julie Tully's memoir, *Dispatches from the Cowgirl*, opens with a literal bang. It's a frantic, exciting and very well written opening to this story of one woman's experience of raising a family in Sub-Saharan Africa, while her husband worked as a foreign area officer for the US Navy.

One of the most engaging qualities of the book is the reader's opportunity in seeing a child adapt and thrive in different, occasionally difficult, circumstances.

With so much traveling and relocating going on, Tully often found herself being asked if she didn't miss home to which she was able to answer "Where is home?" As the book illuminates Tully and her family began to think of home as an abstract concept. And she writes, "Home took two forms: the physical and the emotional. Home was where our belongings were. Home was also our family and friends. Home was food. Home was a song. Home was a rainstorm. Home was a favorite vista. Home was becoming bigger and bigger the more we moved. Most of all, home was when and where we felt at ease." —*IndieReader*

Tully's memoir captures her extraordinary experience of living in Africa as the spouse of a naval diplomat in vivid detail.

A genuine interest in people and the culture of the host nation make Tully's memoir heartwarming. Despite the challenges of settling into a place and culture alien to her, she is forever willing and excited to meet new people, embraces learning about their lives and challenges, and possesses the self-awareness to remember that her position is a privileged one, with minor problems in comparison to the larger world. As life progresses, Tully enthusiastically takes on more responsibilities, such as planning, organizing, and attending social events in addition to her roles of mother and wife. She's charming, as is the book, which emphasizes the unpaid and often unrecognized labor and sacrifices of women in similar positions worldwide.

Tully's uncomplicated and clean prose, laced with gentle humor, narrates in engaging detail the travails of their frequent moves, describing their sometimes exotic and sometimes mundane life in Africa...this is a fascinating account of one woman's journey around the earth. —*BookLife/Publisher's Weekly*

Great for fans of:
Brigid Keenan's *Diplomatic Baggage: The Adventures of a Trailing Spouse*, Cherry Denman's *Diplomatic Incidents*

How I wish I had Julie Tully's *Dispatches from the Cowgirl* to prepare me for my own military family adventures overseas! Tully's light touch, startling humor, and keen insights are a joy to read. From calculating how many jars of peanut butter to pack for a year, to juggling worries about deadly snakes, potential terrorist attacks, and police shakedowns, Tully's memoir will resonate with all readers, both civilian and military, wherever they might find themselves in this far-flung world. —Siobhan Fallon, author of *You Know When the Men are Gone* and *The Confusion of Languages*

Dispatches
from the
Cowgirl

a memoir

Dispatches from the Cowgirl

Through the Looking Glass with a Navy Diplomat's Wife

Julie Tully

W. Brand Publishing

NASHVILLE, TENNESSEE

j.brand@wbrandpub.com

W. Brand Publishing

www.wbrandpub.com

Cover design by JuLee Brand / designchik.net

Dispatches from the Cowgirl / Julie Tully –1st ed.

Available in Hardcover, Paperback, Kindle, and eBook formats.

Hardcover ISBN: 978-1-956906-25-7

Paperback ISBN: 978-1-956906-26-4

eBook ISBN: 978-1-956906-27-1

Library of Congress Control Number: 2022936507

Contents

part four: Djibouti

For John and Quinn

. . . and Cat Two.

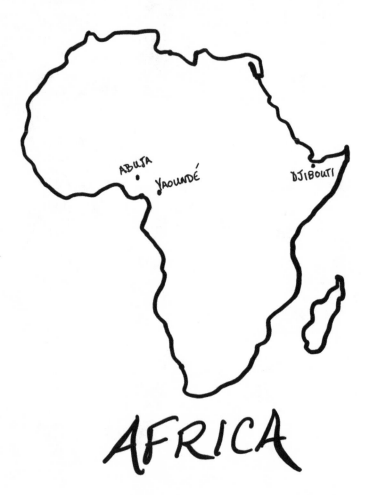

ABUJA

Yaoundé

DJIBOUTI

AFRICA

Actually, the best gift you could have given her
was a lifetime of adventures.

— Lewis Carroll, *Alice in Wonderland*

I can't go back to yesterday,
for I was a different person then.

— Lewis Carroll, *Alice in Wonderland*

acknowledgments

This book has been a journey, and I would like to thank those who made the journey both possible and enjoyable.

To JuLee Brand, my publisher at W. Brand Publishing: Like I said, it was serendipity—same name, same outlook. Through stories we can change the world. Thank you for taking a chance on mine.

To my incredible editor Brunella Costagliola at The Military Editor® Agency: Wow, where do I even begin? I stumbled upon you by chance, not knowing you were a Neapolitan. You are proof positive that speaking with an accent is a superpower—you are incredible, and I am lucky to have you in my corner.

To the friends I've made along the way—some that I've written about in this book, others I have not: Thank you. A life lived far away from home can be lonely, but you've helped to make it a happy and fulfilling one and have become part of our extended family.

To Catie, a fellow FAO spouse and kindred spirit: We've walked Africa together yet separately. You make living this lifestyle brighter. Thank you for helping to bring it forward.

To Dawn: We were meant to meet. The bad one and the evil one. Writers who see the world through a different lens. Love you.

To my family, the original storytellers: All those years of listening to tales at the dinner table, on long car rides, and around the campfire—they rubbed off. Thanks for allowing me to wander the world while still welcoming me home.

To Quinn, who had no say about being born into this circus: Thanks for being so awesome, for being so you. The world is a better place with you in it. And thank you for being my most wonderful cheerleader. My heart melts every time you say you're proud of me.

And finally, to John, my handsome sailor, without whom this book would have never happened: Thank you for being brave enough to ask for this cowgirl's address all those years ago. Thank you for believing in me. Thank you for being a willing first editor. But most of all, thank you for putting up with me— it's been a wild ride, and I can't wait to see what's next.

introduction

Hi. I'm Julie.

If we ever meet in real life, that's probably how I'll introduce myself, having never been one for formalities or titles. It's not that I don't answer to them; it's just that I feel more comfortable with the basics—my name is Julie, end of story. All very ironic considering how I've spent much of my adult life, as a trailing spouse in the military and diplomatic world, and especially ironic given the part I write about in this book. But before you get to that, there are a few things I think you should know about me, a bit of background to help the book make more sense.

First of all, I was born into the fifth generation of a cattle ranching family in northern California. I spent the first three decades of my life either working cattle or marketing the beef that came from them. I identify as a cowgirl because that is where I began, my original imprint. Am I still a cowgirl? Yes, but only in the same sense that a marine is always a marine.

Second of all, for the past two-plus decades, my life has also been tied to the sea through my husband, an officer in the United States Navy. A rather improbable plot twist considering how I started—a girl of the land marrying a man of the sea—but one that has suited me well. It is because of my husband's position as a foreign area officer that I called Sub-Saharan Africa home from February 2011 to July 2018.

Something else you should know about me is that I love stories and storytelling. Stories are what make life beautiful and compelling. Stories keep life interesting because you never know what lies beneath someone's surface. And most importantly, stories connect us—sometimes showing us how big the world is and at other times how very small it can be. The travelogue aspect of this book grew from stories I sent home to family and friends, sharing with them glimpses of what my life was like far from home, far from where I began as a cowgirl—a view of places they may never see for themselves.

What I didn't expect was that those short vignettes of life in Africa would also grow into the memoir of a woman rediscovering herself. While writing about the world around me, I inadvertently told the story of how I found purpose again after leaving my career to become a full-time mom and trailing spouse. Those stories combined with my personal diaries from that time told a larger tale—one where I was a real-life Alice in Wonderland, eventually returning from my rabbit hole forever changed.

And while I tell true stories of things that happened to me, of people I met, and the events I experienced, I need to clarify something: what I write in this book is solely from my perspective, things that happened to me during my time living as a military spouse in Africa. I do not speak for my husband, our government, or any of the others I encountered along the way. These are simply my observations. I have taken the liberty of changing the names within the book for the same reason; this is my story to tell, not theirs, and I respect their privacy.

The time I spent in Africa was eye-opening and enlightening. I moved to the continent unsure of what my place was in the world and left it stronger and more confident; yet with the understanding that not having all of life's answers was perfectly fine and completely human. Africa showed me the importance of being myself. And it's all of this—the place, the lifestyle, the people—that I am sharing with you.

While I bleed navy blue and am still very much an American cowgirl at heart, I miss Africa every day.

Julie
Italy, 2021

prologue

June 25, 2014

The bomb went off while I was on the phone with my mom. The violent, *whip crack boom* broke the glorious normality of the moment, rattling our living room windows.

I froze.

My son, Quinn, who was busy playing with Legos on the coffee table, also froze.

"Wow!" I said to my mom, improvising quickly, knowing the boom had also been loud enough for her to hear. "That lightning was close."

Quinn, clearly puzzled by my deception, opened his mouth to correct me, but I put a finger to my lips and shushed him quiet. "Must be a storm coming in," I continued telling my mom. It wasn't unusual for strong thunderstorms to suddenly roll through that time of year in Nigeria, so I figured it was a good enough bluff to buy me some time. I don't remember my mom's response or much of our conversation after that—I was too busy scanning my other phone that had been sitting on the end table next to me, trying to find news alerts that would tell me what happened. Like the locals, I had learned that having two cell phones with different service providers was a necessity, not a luxury, in a country like Nigeria where things worked well until they didn't—you always needed a backup. On that afternoon, my second phone offered undisrupted access to the news—of which there was, curiously, none at that moment. I refocused my attention back to my mom and told her as brightly as possible, that I should go but that I would talk to her soon.

"Okay, honey, love you," her words floating over the thousands of miles between us—her in California and me nine time zones away. "Tell your guys that I love them too."

"I will," I assured her, then hit the end call button, wondering if she had believed any of what I just said, because like all moms she had a sixth sense about things.

Quinn, on the other hand, was having none of it.

"Mom," he pleaded after I hung up, expressing his frustration and confusion, "you lied to Grandma!" Lying was a big no-no in our house.

I sat there on the sofa, a million thoughts going through my head. A bomb. *Boko Haram must have finally hit the heart of Abuja,* I thought. *But where? How close? Was it the embassy? Was my husband okay? Would he be able to get home? Were we safe in our compound? Would we be evacuated? We were due to fly out for our R&R to the United States the following week, would we be coming back?* My mind was quickly spiraling out of control, and I knew better than to let it happen.

I had to calm down, but it took a lot of effort; I had never faced anything like this before. I stopped and took a breath. *Come on, Julie, get a hold of yourself.* I refocused, blocking the frenzied emotions trying to break the surface. Those feelings had to wait. I had to work through what came next.

I turned back to Quinn, who was staring at me intently, looking for an answer, for reassurance. "I know, I told a lie," I confessed while making sure my embassy-issued handheld emergency radio, also sitting on the end table, was on. I got up, walked to the windows, and scanned the compound outside, then checked that the front door was locked and bolted. "Honey, I don't know for sure what happened, but it does no good to worry Grandma until we know what's going on." I struggled to keep my voice as light as possible.

Satisfied with my answer, he finally asked, "What *was* that?"

"I don't know, but I think it was a bomb," were the words that came out of my mouth as I sat back down next to him in the living room. Words I never thought I would have to say to my child. While he knew such things were a very real possibility in our life, actually saying them out loud to him sent a chill up my spine. I rested my hand on his shoulder. "Just stay away from the windows and wait for me to see what I can find out."

I looked at the radio and phones again—full signal but still silent. Outside was quiet. I couldn't hear anything unusual, but then again, I couldn't hear much at all, which wasn't normal for Abuja. No cars honking on the road next to us. No chatter from the housekeepers and gardeners walking around the compound. Nothing.

Finally, an electronic bird chirp broke the silence. A text from my husband, John, who was working at our embassy on the other side of town: Just heard about a possible bomb in Abuja, heard anything?

Thankfully, John's text at least assured me it wasn't the embassy and that he was okay.

Another text from John: Wuse? Banex Plaza?

No sooner had I read the second text, I found the first news story. Headline: "Bomb Blast at Abuja Mall."

"Crap," I said out loud, garnering another look of disapproval from Quinn for crude language. *No wonder it shook the house.* The mall in question, Banex Plaza in the Wuse district, was only a little over a mile away. Our favorite pizza place was next door to it. Quinn's best friend lived just down the street from it. We had driven by there only the day before. The bomb had been, literally and figuratively, very close to home.

I texted John back: Yes. Radio on. Checking house. Waiting for information. There was nothing more to say at that point.

Sirens began wailing in the background. I guessed they were most likely from ambulances dispatched by the medical clinic just up the road from our house.

"Quinn, come on," I said as I stood up, grabbing my phones and radio and ushering him toward our second floor. I looked calm, but internally I wondered if that was it, if we would be evacuated. I was at odds with my rational self, knowing for safety's sake that an incident like this could mean the end of our time in Nigeria, something I was emotionally unwilling to accept. A wave of anger washed over me. I wasn't done yet. I didn't want to go. Nigeria was home. While I knew that wanting to stay in a country teetering on the edge of chaos was probably not the most reasonable thought that I should have been having at that moment, it was exactly what was on my mind.

"Mom, are we okay?" Quinn asked nervously.

I looked at him and smiled. But the truth was, I had no idea.

PART ONE

LIKE ALICE
DOWN THE RABBIT HOLE

chapter 1

How Does a Cowgirl End Up in Africa?

"What would you say about moving to Africa?" my husband, John, asked casually.

It was early 2009 and we—John, Quinn, and I—were sitting at our dining room table in Germany enjoying a homecooked meal as we did most evenings. His question was definitely not the one I had expected. Maybe "How was your day?" Or "What did you learn in school?" But not what we thought about moving to Africa. There we were, having curry; I had just poured some red wine for John and me and was about to take a sip when he asked the question that brought everything to a halt. I just stared at him.

Quinn, suddenly very intent on the conversation, was the first to react. "Where in Africa?!" he asked almost springing out of his seat. Even at five years old, his mastery of maps and geography was better than that of most adults. He was especially keen on Africa, as John was an Africa specialist for the navy working at the newly established United States Africa Command (commonly referred to as AFRICOM) in Stuttgart, Germany. John, a history and geography nut himself, would spend hours with Quinn, regaling him with stories about the countries he was working with. Quinn soaked up his dad's every word, then would sit down on his own with a map to discover the places for himself.

"Well," John started, "how would you like to move to Cameroon?"

Wow. Cameroon. Cameroon?

That was not the country I had expected him to say, nor did it match the image I had already conjured up in my mind of living in Africa. I will shamefully admit here that the first thing I had actually pictured was me as some version of Karen Blixen in *Out of Africa*, but that thought quickly shattered as Kenya and Cameroon are nothing alike. And to be perfectly honest, Cameroon wasn't even on my list of places to live in Africa as a family. All I knew about Cameroon was its location—what people jokingly referred to as the armpit of Africa—about halfway down the massive continent along its western coast.

"It's a bit of a long shot," John continued, "the job doesn't even exist yet. But it will be a navy job, and since it's not in the easiest of places to live, people won't be jumping at the opportunity, so if we volunteer, we might have a chance of getting it."

I finally took that sip of wine. While John continued to explain a bit more about the yet-to-exist job, I found myself having a "how did I end up here" moment. Moments like this are not uncommon for me, I have had them at all manner of points—ordinary, significant, bizarre—throughout my life. I guess I am just one of those people who is predisposed to childlike wonder, to never losing the sense of awe at this glorious adventure we call life, and also realizing just how little control we have over it. I have often felt that fate is a silent partner in our journey and that most of the time it's simply waiting for us to grasp the opportunities placed in front of us. On that evening, at that moment, while John was still talking, my inner dialogue was something along the lines of this—*Move to Africa? Me? But I'm just a simple country girl. Why would I belong in Africa? Why would they let me move there? I'm JUST a simple country girl.* No matter how many years had gone by, no matter how much water had passed under my proverbial bridge, when push came to shove, I always reverted to type—seeing myself as the simple country girl I had started out as and wondering just how in the heck I got to the place where I was.

Rewind a dozen years from that dining table conversation and you find me sitting in a quiet café having lunch with my friend, Ian. It was a picture-perfect day in California's gold country. The sky was a bright cornflower blue dotted with a few puffy white clouds. We were sitting outside on the restaurant's patio, as that summer day it was nice enough to be out there without dying of heat. The air was sweet, normal for the region that time of year. Brightly colored petunias and creeping morning glories gave the space an added boost of vibrancy. The nearby creek offered a subtle soundtrack in the background. I grew up in this glorious part of the country and it had colored all aspects of my life until then.

"If you were a character in one of my stories, how would you describe yourself?" Ian asked me. He and I were work colleagues. We met at a meeting he was overseeing a few years earlier; I was still a college student giving a briefing about my family's cattle ranch. My briefing prompted him to ask me to work on a project he was pulling together. After I graduated, I ended up working for the same organization he did, but most importantly, we were friends from the very beginning. Part of the reason for that friendship, beyond our work, was that he was a literary-minded soul like me, and writing stories was one of his pastimes. He was in his mid-fifties; I was in my mid-twenties.

We were an unlikely pair, but we were kindred spirits and always enjoyed each other's company.

Caught off guard, I laughed at his question. "Me? One of your characters? I think not." I took a sip of my iced tea.

"Yes, absolutely you," he said in all seriousness. "Now how would you describe yourself?"

His persistence garnered an eye roll from me. I was much better talking about other people or other things and not so good at talking about myself, it made me squirm. "I don't know. I guess you could say that I am just a simple country girl." There. That was my best answer because that's how I saw myself. I was a rancher's daughter from rural northern California. I was born of the land. I had come from stoic, hard-working people. I had grown up riding horses and working cattle. While I had big dreams like any other person, I never seriously saw myself as anything grander than being what I was, where I was.

He looked at me for a moment, his eyes quizzical like he was studying me, which gave me the distinct feeling of being x-rayed, exposed. "No," he finally said in a low voice, as if the answer held weight, "no, that's not you at all. You are so much more than that." He went on to describe to me the Julie he saw—a simple country girl, yes, but one that was strong and resilient and destined for great things, great adventures. I blushed—not the romantic type of blushing because our relationship was never inappropriate, but the type of blushing that happens when you're simply caught out. Ian had a way of making me very acutely aware of my real self, of truths that even I hadn't accepted. So when he told me things—anything from what he had just said to stuff about our work—I wanted to believe him unequivocally.

"Really?" I stumbled, taking another sip of my iced tea to occupy my nervous hands. I felt like I was sitting with a fortune-teller who was about to tell me everything that my life would hold.

"Absolutely, without a doubt," he returned. "What, don't you see this in yourself?"

"Not really." And that was the truth.

"Fair enough. But humor me, let's have a go at this fictional you," he continued, his eyes now bright as he began crafting my story. "First, if you could go anywhere, where would you go?"

"Um," I started, "I don't know." I was still hesitating. Even though I thought of myself as a simple country girl, I was decently well-traveled at that point in my life and had been exposed to the larger world, but not as much as I wished for in my dreams. There were still places that called to me. "Denmark, I suppose, where my family is from," I ventured. "Or perhaps Africa," I brightened. I was beginning to enjoy this game. "I've always loved Africa."

He smiled big, "See, you're not *just* a simple country girl. No, not at all. I see you as more of a simple country girl, or perhaps a farm girl, who finds out that she's a great Viking warrior and ends up going on adventures."

It was my turn to have a big grin on my face. I couldn't help but get caught up in Ian's words. Perhaps I was a bit like his fictional version of me. But then, just as quickly as it appeared, his smile faded, turning into a slightly evil grin, "Enough of that though, I will write more and send it to you later. Instead, tell me about this sailor I've heard of that has captured your heart."

Ah, indeed. Recently I had met a sailor, a friend of a friend, more specifically, a naval officer with whom I had fallen head over heels in love. Such a strange match, a man tied to the seas capturing the heart of a girl tied to the land. "His name is John. He's a submariner," and I went on to tell him all about John, how we had met by chance and had had an old-fashioned letter-writing relationship for a year before we finally admitted that we were in love. Honestly, if Ian were to have written a love interest for me into his story, John would've fit the bill no matter how odd it would have seemed.

"Well, as much as I don't want to like him," Ian laughed, digging into his lunch that had just been placed in front of him, "because I know he'll take you away from here, I will say he's a lucky man." He paused, thinking. "Yes, and I think I'll make him part of your story."

Part of my story—I laugh to myself thinking about that now. Ian's narrative prediction most certainly came true both in the story . . . and in real life.

As unlikely as it was, John Tully, someone who had so little in common with the world I came from—my western cowgirl upbringing—captured my heart. He was a native of Long Island, a graduate of the Naval Academy, and an officer on a submarine, and became the part of me that I never knew was missing. Growing up in a world and a culture where few ever leave, it shocked no one more than me when I married him in 1999 and became a military spouse. The cowgirl and the sailor. And as Ian had predicted, John would take me away. I stumbled headfirst into a world foreign to me—a world of moving, service, and sacrifice. But love blinds you . . . and if it's the right kind of love, it also leads you to the place you were always meant to be.

By the time John asked the question about moving to Africa, we had already watched the life we had imagined living be turned on its head and tossed out the window. When we were first married, he was part of the submarine force. We thought, at the time, that we could balance my career in agriculture—with only a few slight modifications—with the wants and needs of the navy. To our naïve minds, we figured the biggest challenge would be a potential job for him in Japan or Guam, and we would bounce back and forth between the coasts. And for a couple of years, it worked beautifully. So, imagine our shock when John's detailer called with an urgent-fill job opportunity as part of our navy's exchange program with the British Royal Navy. We were young and so intrigued by the opportunity that we said a quick yes. I put my career on hold, and we found ourselves and our then-infant son moving to southern England. We didn't realize at the time how that one "jump in with both feet" response would change everything.

Life in England, and the job that went with it, opened our eyes to a world we had never even considered. We thrived being imbedded within the Royal Navy community and as part of a larger multi-national working group. Living and working alongside people from other countries, exposed to other cultures and perspectives, we found a niche for ourselves. When a lateral transfer opportunity arose from submarines to our navy's newly established foreign area officer program, it was no surprise that we sent in John's application. What *did* surprise us though, after his acceptance, was finding out the region where they had assigned him.

John studied German in college and held a master's in European and Russian studies. Plus, with his years working with the Brits, you can imagine our surprise when they said he would become an Africa specialist. Next to South America, it was the last place we had expected they'd pick for us. But that's the way life is in the military—sometimes you just have to roll with the punches. Frankly, I was thrilled. Africa . . . having loved Africa all my life, all I could think of was, *We're going to Africa!* Which was even funnier when our next set of orders said Stuttgart.

Generally, in the foreign area officer program, the new selectees take a one- to two-year posting as an in-country training opportunity somewhere in their region of responsibility. At the time of our transfer into the program, the army had that type of training track, but the navy did not. The navy was still trying to flesh out the logistics of pulling people out of essential jobs for what some inaccurately saw as a paid vacation traveling the world. Therefore, the navy offered John an abbreviated language course in Washington, D.C. to learn French, then a follow-on job at the very-soon-to-be-established AFRICOM. As confused as I was by the navy's placement decision and training path, I went along without complaint. That's how I was raised—you take responsibility for your choices and ride them out. It would be an adventure, and I knew it meant we would be tied to Africa from then on. I also knew another overseas tour would sound the death knell of my dormant career. But if I couldn't be a cowgirl, if I couldn't work in agriculture, then Africa seemed a fair trade. Fate had decided to reshuffle our cards, so why not see where it took us—and what's not to like about a few years in Germany?

"Well," John was still looking at me from across the dinner table as I slowly sipped my wine, waiting for my answer. "What do you think?"

Quinn was still excitedly chattering about the geographic location of Cameroon, and it was obvious that there was no question in his little mind about moving there. And honestly, there was no question in my mind either—my hesitation was merely that gut reaction you have before taking a leap. That moment when you take one last gulp of air before jumping.

I grinned at John—a big, wide grin—and said, "Let's go to Africa!"

chapter 2

We're Moving to Africa

W̲e were moving to Africa, and it all seemed so monumental.

Because of our decision, I expected that our life would be—if not immediately, then in a very short time—turned upside down. That's what a permanent change of station (PCS), aka military move, does: it turns your life upside down and inside out for months on end. One day you are just living your regular life, then you receive a phone call from the detailer (the person in the navy that controls your fate) telling you they've decided where you're going. The next day begins a whirlwind of paperwork, cardboard boxes, and suitcases that will eventually deposit you at your next duty station. That was what I expected to happen and was mentally prepared for—except it didn't happen. After John told the detailer, "Sure, we'll go," everything went silent.

Have you heard anything? I sent that message to John so many times in the months that followed that I thought he might eventually block my chats with a sly, Julie? Julie who? But the poor guy was such a good sport about it, generally responding with, No, nothing today. I will wait a week or so, then ask again. He never chastised me for my impatience, never once saying something like, "This is my job, not yours," because he knew how much I had sacrificed to follow him and that my life hung in the balance too. I tried my best to not be a thorn in his side, but it was hard. Every time I bugged John about it, I could hear my dad's voice in my head, telling me to slow down, like he used to say when he was teaching me how to trail the cattle. "Don't be in a rush, don't push them so hard," he'd instruct, "they'll line out and get there in the end." Sage advice that worked for more situations than just trailing cattle, but waiting is hard when your life hangs in the balance and bureaucrats are certainly not as likable creatures as cows. It took a lot for me to not write terse emails demanding the powers-that-be to just get on with it.

Silence with no solid confirmation that the job was ours was an unexpected stressor. We couldn't talk about it with anyone outside of those directly working on its creation—which meant that we couldn't say anything to our family or friends. So we had to just sit and wait and be quiet, even when the inevitable questions of where we were moving next began as we approached the third year of our tour in Germany. People knew we were due to leave the following December, and usually, about nine months out, we had an inkling of where that would be.

"Shouldn't you guys know where you'll be going by now?" That was the question most often asked, especially by our family. The white lie we told in response was painful, as we had already been overseas for two consecutive tours, and they were hoping for our return stateside. "Yes, technically we should, but the orders process is really slow right now," we said, hoping the white lie would hold. "We should know something soon." It was so hard to tell them that, knowing that we had bet everything on a job that would take us even farther away from home than before, but deep down, we knew it was the right thing. And we just hoped everyone would understand.

Our official orders arrived over a year later. Finally, we were moving to Cameroon. But let me clarify right here that *talking* about moving to Africa and actually *moving* to Africa are two *very* different things. All those months of sitting and waiting vanished overnight and we had less than five months to jump through all the hoops necessary to leave Germany and get to Cameroon, which was also going to be unlike any PCS we had ever gone through before.

The morning after our orders arrived, I pulled out a bright, goldenrod yellow notebook and sat it on the dining room table next to my coffee cup. A hard copy of the orders on one side, various colored pens and post-it tags on the other.

"Ah," John glanced at it as he was preparing to leave for work. "Is that the new war book, Jules?"

"Yep," I replied, patting the cover. "Time to get this circus on the road."

My move book—or war book as John had come to call it—was where I kept all the information about our moves. I started using one when we moved to England in 2004, when I still had a bad case of new mom brain fog and felt overwhelmed by the sheer volume of details I had to keep straight. I had tried a file folder, but found out that it just wasn't enough, because even though I needed to keep bits and pieces of paper organized, it was also very helpful to write down detailed notes of conversations and to-do lists. And even though it was the 2000s and things like electronic organizers were readily available, a disastrous failure of my Palm Pilot on our move to England prompted me to revert to analog methods for anything of great importance—there was less likelihood of me losing my mind knowing that my old-school notebook couldn't magically erase all of my important information in one fell swoop.

Picking up a black sharpie, I inscribed **Move Book: Germany to Cameroon** on the notebook's cover. At that point, it all became real: Africa, here we come! I opened to the first page and began jotting down questions I knew I needed to find answers to:

- **Can we take our household goods?**
- **What about our Jeep?**
- **What type of medical prep do Quinn and I need to do?**
- **Do we need no-fee or diplomatic passports?**
- **Mail?**
- **Banking?**

The list grew and grew—questions in green ink, tentative answers in pencil, final answers in black ink. I needed to know when we had to check out of housing in Germany and which hotel we would be staying at during the short interim before we flew out. I had to talk to the school about Quinn's withdrawal and about hand-carrying his records to the next school. I needed to cancel our phone and cable. There was so much I needed to do, and I had only eleven weeks to do it in.

"Cameroon? Where exactly is that?" our families asked in bewilderment when we finally broke the news to them. "And why does the navy need to send you guys there?"

In a way, it felt like a betrayal, like we had broken a promise. Until that point, everyone assumed we would move back home after Germany. Now, not only were we not moving home, but we were also going to a place that would make it difficult—if not near impossible—for anyone to visit. Perhaps the worst part of this feeling of betraying them was the sheer excitement that John, Quinn, and I felt about the opportunity. Unfortunately, our joy came at a cost to theirs.

Friends were equally dismayed by the news, even other military friends. Those who were unfamiliar with John's type of work couldn't figure out exactly why we were moving to Cameroon. Responses became a running dialogue of, "Yes, he will still be in the navy . . . yes, it is an accompanied tour, so all three of us will be going . . . the job will be a liaison between our military and that of the host nation . . . yes, it's perfectly safe for us to be there . . . no, we're not crazy." Then as the shock wore off, everyone became more and more curious about what our life would be like. "You'll write to us about it . . . you'll post on Facebook . . . you'll stay in touch, won't you?" they asked, and we promised we would.

Moving to a new place is one thing; moving to a country that is so vastly different from anything you've ever experienced is another. With the move to Cameroon there were many details that left me at a complete loss. That's when John suggested that I have a mentor. His new boss at AFRICOM had been stationed in Cameroon with his family a few years before and his wife agreed to sit down with me and answer any questions I may have. Within a week, I was sitting in her house having coffee, my trusty move book at hand.

"Okay, you've got your questions, but let me start with some questions for you," she said. "What's the most third world country you've been to?"

I was taken aback. I'd had senior military spouses as mentors before, but her approach of cutting to the chase was new and I liked it—it fit in nicely into my personal philosophy of not sugarcoating facts.

"Make no mistake," she said, "even though you're heading to an embassy and all the comforts that can offer, you are moving to an underdeveloped country, and it will affect everything you do."

Like a good student, I opened my notebook and began writing.

"Now, you'll be sending down a consumables shipment along with your household goods," she continued. "Consumables are meant to supplement your quality of life, to make up for what you can't get in town," she explained. "You'll want to ship any non-perishable food items that you can't live without."

"Like?" I asked.

"Well, seasonal items like cranberry sauce and canned pumpkin. And peanut butter, definitely peanut butter."

I made particular note of the peanut butter, as it was the only thing that Quinn had been eating for lunch since he started going to school. *Good grief,* I thought, *how much peanut butter do I need to ship for two years? About one jar every two weeks, which works out to roughly two per month, times twelve . . .*

"You'll also need a good supply of mosquito repellent with DEET in it, because malaria is a very real risk in Cameroon," she continued. "And a lot of Pepto Bismol . . . and I do mean a lot, because you can't get it there and you *will* get sick. It's not a matter of *if,* but *when.*"

"Okay . . ." I responded as I scribbled, trying to keep up, yet still mentally trying to figure out how much peanut butter we would need.

She smiled. "Oh, and there's a saying about living in Sub-Saharan Africa that those of us who've been stationed down there use: You'll never fart with confidence again."

I looked up from my notebook and couldn't help but bark with laughter, "What?!" *Seriously?* I thought, *What exactly are we getting ourselves into?*

"Oh," she added, "and of course you'll need a lot of dress clothes for receptions and dinners, including nice shoes, but I highly recommend ones with chunky heels, at least two or three pairs. Don't worry if people say they're out of style, because they are absolutely necessary there, otherwise you'll sink into the grass as most of the events are outdoor on lawns."

Yes, hers was the kind of mentoring that I could get behind.

Given that we were at AFRICOM headquarters when we began our move to Cameroon, I made the gross assumption that the process would be rather straightforward.

AFRICOM, after all, was our military's joint command for the continent and dealt with those stationed in Africa all the time.

Almost immediately I discovered how very wrong I was.

The man in the shipping office tapped a few keys on his keyboard, then looked back up to me. "Okay, let's see. Where again are you heading?"

"Cameroon," I responded clearly. "Yaoundé."

He started typing then stopped, looking at me again. "Sorry? Where?"

That was only the beginning of what came to seem like a poorly told joke:

Hey, have you heard the one about moving to Cameroon?

Where?

Exactly!

If we were going to San Antonio or Berlin or Seoul it would have been a no-brainer, but apparently no one I talked to working at the headquarters of the US military's mission to Africa had ever heard of someone actually moving to Africa. Deploying there? Certainly! But *moving* there? An entire military family? No way could that be true . . . until I presented them with a copy of our orders.

At that point, after two back-to-back tours in Europe, I knew the ins and outs of a basic overseas military move like the back of my hand but moving to Africa was a different thing entirely. Not only were we moving to a place outside of the regular military sphere, but we were also crossing into the territory of other government agencies. While John's job would still be a military job, he would fall partially under the jurisdiction of an embassy, and therefore the State Department. All of this made the process tiring, but I kept trudging forward, ticking off the boxes on my to-do list as best I could.

"We'll also need to be on anti-malarias," John explained. Having worked in Africa on a regular basis by then, John was an old pro with the medical requirements. "You and Quinn will need to get a blood test to make sure your system can handle the malaria medication, then you can get your prescriptions from the pharmacy. And both of you will also need to get current vaccinations, including yellow fever."

Like one of John's most loyal troops, I marched my way to the health clinic the very next day to inquire about the vaccinations John said we would need.

"Sure, we do that blood test, I'll just need a copy of your orders stating that you're going to a malaria zone," the corpsman told me when I rattled of the list of things we needed done. "And yellow fever vaccinations are given every Friday at the medical readiness office."

Awesome, I thought. I would be able to knock all the medical requirements out easily and be done with that part of move preparations. I went ahead and booked the blood test and Quinn's additional vaccination updates for the next day.

The following Friday, I pulled Quinn out of school and headed to the clinic, where we readied ourselves for another needle.

"I'm sorry, ma'am, but the yellow fever vaccinations are only for active-duty personnel deploying to an at-risk area," a different corpsman told me. "We don't provide it for dependents just traveling to a country."

"Ah, but we are not just dependents traveling to a country," I retorted, confident that I had the upper hand. "We are on the orders, moving to an at-risk country." I presented him with the printout of said orders and smiled my most winning smile. *Take that,* I thought.

But, once again it was as if the military had never heard of sending an actual family to Africa. The three people working in the office that day all took turns reading the orders. "Ma'am, these orders do not specifically state that you and your son need the yellow fever vaccine."

"Yes, but you'll see the orders clearly state that we are accompanying my husband to Cameroon for two years and the embassy guidance says that yellow fever is not only required for the person working there but also any accompanying family members." Could I not make myself any clearer?

"But this is medical readiness, ma'am, for our deploying personnel," one of the corpsmen said.

"Yes, I understand that, but we are essentially deploying to the country with our active-duty sponsor. And I was told to come here for the vaccination by our primary care provider, just on the other side of this wall."

The corpsman shrugged to indicate that my problem wasn't his.

I wanted to scream but knew there was no way I would win this ridiculous debate. "Okay, well, it's still a required vaccination, so tell me, where do we get it?"

"You'll have to go out in town. There is a doctor in Vaihingen who can do it. You can call them for an appointment."

Fetching the address from them, I gave an undeserved, "Thanks," and left.

"Yes, we give yellow fever vaccinations," the receptionist at the German clinic said when I explained what I needed over the phone. "I will schedule you and your child for next Wednesday. See you then."

Once again, I pulled Quinn out of school, still muttering disgruntled thoughts about why our own people couldn't provide the vaccination since they were the ones sending us to the country that required it. But despite that, I was happy just to be able to get it done and tick one more thing off my to-do list. I parked in the lot nearest the clinic, then we wound our way through the sidewalks and upstairs to the office.

"*Guten Morgen,* I have an appointment for vaccinations," I told the receptionist. As we sat in the waiting room, I proceeded to explain the possible side effects of the yellow fever shot to Quinn. "It's been a long time since I've had one," I told him. "I had to get one in 1988 when I went to Hong Kong to visit my best friend who was living there at the time. I remember that it made me feel like I had the flu. If that happens, this afternoon we might just have to snuggle up on the couch and watch movies."

He smiled one of his big, sweet smiles, which then dropped quickly from his face. "Is the actual shot going to hurt?" In Quinn's world, vaccinations were on his list of least favorite things. At that point in the moving process, he had already had a typhoid shot and several vials of blood drawn. He was reaching his capacity for compliance.

"Well, honey," I started, taking my usual tact of the truth is better than a lie, "I really don't know. I would expect that it might. But you'll be okay. And just think, I have to get the same shot at the same time."

Many years before, while vaccinating cattle on the ranch, I remember telling a heifer while giving her a shot, "I know it hurts, but it's for your own good." I had said it as brightly as I could, thinking my sunny bedside manner would make any difference. Funnily enough, the German nurse said the exact same thing to us as she administered our shots, although her heavily accented English made it sound much more ominous.

Rubbing our sore arms, Quinn and I thanked her and headed home. After all the medical evaluations, tests, and shots we had gone through for this move, I finally understood how that heifer must have felt.

But I was making headway. The list of things to do before departing Germany was shrinking. Slowly.

Shortly before Halloween, I met with the commissary manager to discuss our consumables shipment. Fearing that my need to order cases upon cases of supplies would be met with the same confusion I had experienced with other offices, I was happily surprised. "No problem," he said, telling me that our order would be no different than bulk orders they did for deploying units. I could've kissed him. From what he said, it sounded like our consumables shipment would be the first straightforward part of our move.

"Now, I'll show you how to read one of these," the commissary manager started to explain. He was exceedingly polite and patient. "This is the UPC code, you know, the bar code on the back, and . . ."

"No need to explain," I said with a smile, holding up a hand. "I used to work in the beef industry, specifically with grocery chains. I can read a stock list with the best of them."

"Well, then," he said happily relieved, "this will be much easier than expected for everyone."

"I really just need to know if it's possible to break down a case of something if the quantity is more than I need." I really didn't want an entire case of mayonnaise if I could avoid it.

"For some things yes, others no," he said, showing me some examples.

Over the next couple of days, I diligently figured out just how much peanut butter, taco sauce, canned pumpkin, Band-Aids, Gatorade, and Pepto Bismol we would need for two years.

I emailed the eight-page list back to the store manager. When he confirmed, I was set and scheduled our pack out for the second week of December.

My phone rang two days before the arranged date. "Mrs. Tully?"

"Yes?"

"This is the assistant manager at the commissary. My boss wanted me to call and tell you that your shipment arrived this morning and has been set aside. It will be ready to go on Tuesday, you'll just need to be here to supervise the packing."

"No problem, see you then." *Awesome*, I thought, *one more thing done.* The movers were arriving the next day to pack up our household goods, then I would escort them to the commissary the following morning for the consumables shipment. Easy peasy.

The morning of pack-out day arrived with an ominous, yet silent, blow to my spirits—a winter storm came in overnight and the ground outside was covered in several inches of wet, heavy snow. When the moving truck arrived and tried to back up to our sidewalk, it essentially slid into place. I sat, cradling a cup of hot coffee in my hands, trying to stay warm as the packers wrapped and boxed our belongings and hoisted our furniture out of the wide-open living room window. *It could be worse*, I thought, shivering from the icy wind. But, of course, because Murphy—and his damnable Law—is the sadistic patron saint of military spouses, it got worse. Honestly, there isn't a military spouse alive who doesn't fully believe that Murphy follows them around waiting for just the right time to throw a wrench into things. Spouse deploys for six months? Your washer, dryer, refrigerator break the next day. Preferably, all at once. Got orders to your dream posting? The military changes its mind and sends you somewhere else. We live with Murphy's Law hanging over our heads every day.

Murphy must have been sitting on my shoulder rubbing his hands together in glee as he plotted that particular attack and watched my phone buzz to life on the countertop next to me. I didn't recognize the number. "Hello?"

"Um, good morning, Mrs. Tully, this is the assistant manager at the commissary, I talked to you yesterday."

"Yes?" I said hesitantly, a warning bell going off in my head because nothing good ever comes from a call that starts with, "um."

"Well, you see, the manager asked me to call," he began, stumbling over what he had to say. "It seems that the night shift came in last night and mistook your consumables shipment for regular stock," he nervously cleared his throat, "and, well, they used it all to restock the shelves." He continued to tell me how sorry they were. I pressed the palm of my hand to my forehead.

"So, now what? How do we fix this?" I asked, feeling suddenly very tired.

"Well, the manager said that you can come in as early as seven o'clock tomorrow morning. We'll be here, and he'll have someone walk the store with you and help rebuild the order."

I blew a big breath of air out my lips, hoping the poor guy didn't think I was angry at him, because it wasn't his fault, he was just the messenger. "That'll work. I'll be there at seven. Thanks." I hung up, palm still pressed firmly to my forehead, the sound of packing tape being pulled off its roll providing a very loud and nerve-rattling soundtrack in the background. So much for easy peasy.

"John?" I called out to the next room where he had been keeping an eye on the packers. "Do you think you could go in a bit late tomorrow? I need you to watch Quinn, at least until it's time to drop him at school, while I head to the commissary."

"Sure, I can make that work," he called back to me. "But why?"

"I'll explain in a bit," I sighed. "I'm going to make some more coffee."

Somehow, I would have to shop for twelve-hundred pounds of consumables in a two-hour window. Lovely.

At 6:45 the next morning, I walked out of our apartment and into the bracing cold. Wrapped in a scarf and with coffee and war book in hand, I drove over to the commissary and started to rebuild our order. Thanks to a bit of dumb luck, some of the items on my list were still available in the case quantities I had requested, so those were quickly set aside, but the rest required me to walk the aisles. The manager allowed me to borrow one of his stock clerks and the two of us went along, filling three large grocery carts with my weird cornucopia of goods.

Originally, I was supposed to just arrive, pay the computer-generated bill, and then supervise the movers as they packed it all up. But because of the restock debacle, I couldn't just pay the original bill. Instead, we had to take the overflowing carts through a checkout as if it were a normal grocery shop. Customers stared as the stock clerk and I unloaded it all onto the belt. The cashier was obviously wondering how she managed to draw the short straw that day.

Paying the four-figure bill—consumables, while allowed and encouraged, were also purchased at our own expense—put a mighty dent in our bank account that month. The stock clerk and I wheeled the carts back into the warehouse section and waited for the movers to arrive. When the last box was sealed, inventoried, and loaded into the shipping crate, I sighed loudly. *I am so done*, I thought, *this has got to be the end.*

But it wasn't.

chapter 3

Murphy Strikes Again

W ith only three days left until we departed Germany,
I felt like I was rocking it. We were over the worst of
the outbound process and had moved into the hotel. I
had the day planned out perfectly: I was going to drive Quinn to
school, take a few loads of laundry to our old apartment to run
while I did some final cleaning—my last chance before returning the keys the following day—and then I would take our car to
have it detailed so I could drop it off for shipment. Things were
going smoothly, and it was Christmas time. Being a Christmas
fanatic, the whole thing put me in a particularly good mood.
The end to the first leg of our move was finally in sight.

After bundling Quinn up and giving him his backpack, I
grabbed my own, plus a large plastic garbage bag full of dirty
laundry and a paper cup full of steaming hot, black coffee, and
headed out our hotel room door to the elevator. John had sweetly gone down a few minutes earlier with another bag of laundry
and the offer to start the car and scrape ice off the windshield for
me. As Quinn and I departed the elevator and headed toward
the exit to the parking lot, I thought, *I've got this.*

I shouldn't have been so cocky.

Quinn was already across the street, halfway to the car, when I stepped into the crosswalk and directly onto one of the white stripes—stripes that were made with a highly reflective, ice-resistant paint. On that frosty morning, while said stripes were indeed clean, shiny, and free from ice, they were also slick as snot. Before I knew what was happening, my feet went out from under me, and I found myself heading toward the ground—fast. Not thinking clearly, I threw out a hand to brace for impact which came with a loud thump and a sickening crack. I found myself seated in the middle of the crosswalk, one hand high in the air with the cup of coffee still intact, the other hand resting at an odd angle to my side.

"Mom!" Quinn screamed as he turned and saw what happened. "MOMMY!!!"

The pain radiating from my wrist was so sharp I could hardly speak. "Quinn," I said, trying to breathe, inhaling sharply, and mustering all my strength to talk, "run over and get Daddy to help me. I can't move and I need him to help me up." John hadn't seen what happened and couldn't hear us over the sound of the car engine.

"But Mommy!" Quinn was in more shock than I at that moment and didn't move. But given that I was smack in the middle of the road, I needed to get up and quickly. I started shouting for John. After several lung-bursting and pain-inducing efforts, John heard me and ran over.

And that's when I started laughing.

Months of built-up stress and the absurdity of what just happened struck me as the funniest thing ever. Plus, I knew I must have looked a sight—sitting casually in the middle of the road with my backpack, laundry, and coffee cup, as if I was just relaxing for a moment.

"Are you okay?!" John cried in shock. I looked up at him and kept laughing, wondering what else good ol' patron saint Murphy could possibly have in store for me. If I could've managed a sip of coffee, I would have.

John heaved me, ever so gently, to standing. Once upright, I composed myself as best I could and said matter of factly, "I'm okay, but I'm pretty sure my wrist is broken. You need to take the morning off work because I'll need you to take Quinn to school and then get me to the clinic." While my instructions came out succinct and calm, the knife-stabs of pain that were pulsing through my hand and arm were making me nauseous.

"No problem," he said without hesitation. "Let me call work and let them know, then we'll be on our way."

An hour later, for what seemed like the hundredth time in the last two months, I sat in my doctor's office at the base health clinic. I had really come to like my doctor over the three years we had lived there—he was a straight-forward, no-nonsense kind of guy and we got along just fine. However, if an outsider had been observing us when he entered the room that morning, they might have thought otherwise.

"Well, don't you look a mess?" he said, taking in the state of my jeans and previously white jacket, both of which were now covered in mud and bits of pavement. "I thought I had seen the last of you the other day, I even signed off on your records."

"Yeah, well, I just couldn't get enough of you." I grinned through the pain. "No one ever accused me of making a graceful exit."

He laughed, helped me take my jacket off, and then took my wounded arm in his hand. Gingerly he pressed around the wrist, which was already swelling. My pale skin turning unnatural shades of purple, red, and green. "Ow," I took a sharp breath. He stopped, put my arm down, and looked me in the eye.

"As suspected, you most likely broke your wrist, but it's hard to tell the extent of the damage without an X-ray," he said. "When are you scheduled to fly out?"

"Saturday, first thing in the morning."

"Hmm, this is going to be tough," he continued. *Oh joy,* I thought. "You should see a specialist, which means that I need you to go out in town to the hospital. He can take an X-ray and determine if surgery is necessary. If it isn't, then you can come back here, and we will put a temporary cast on you. In a week's time you will need to find a doctor wherever you're at and have them put a hard cast on." He patted me on the shoulder. "I'm sorry, but I would venture a guess and say you'll be spending a couple of months without the use of your hand."

Fabulous. And it was my right hand to boot, my dominant hand, the hand I did everything with, the hand I needed for filling out the paperwork that went along with this move. There was still a lot since we had two more months of transit and training ahead of us. *Come on,* I screamed in my mind, *all I want to do is move to Africa! Why does it have to be so hard?!*

After the local hospital determined that it was only a fracture and surgery was unnecessary, I headed back to the base clinic for my temporary cast. The corpsmen that put it on were obviously not worried about its aesthetics, with it turning out to look more like a club than a cast. When my doctor came back at the end to check on me, he laughed and said, "Well, that ought to be fun to travel with." As he turned to walk out the door, he added, "And I've signed off on your records again, so I don't want to see you anymore." He continued laughing as he went down the hall.

Somehow, despite being on a lot of pain medication and all the unforeseen bumps in the road, we managed to finish everything we needed to do in those final couple of days in Germany.

The morning of our departure was bitterly cold as a snow-storm had blown in overnight. I couldn't have written more drama into that day if I tried. Flights were being cancelled left and right. Because of my useless arm, John ended up having to carry all our bags as we made our way to the taxi and through airport check-in. Our flight out of Frankfurt was the last to take off before the airport closed due to the weather. Then Quinn, bless his heart, came down with a stomach bug, throwing up three times before we reached California twenty-four hours later. When we finally made it to my parents' house for the start of our much-needed R&R, we passed out and slept for hours.

As much as I would like to say that that was the final hump, that we had smooth sailing for the rest of our journey, I can't.

We spent the next two months fluctuating between the joy of visiting with family and the ongoing pain of our final preparations for Cameroon. After two weeks with my family in California, we made our way to New York to spend time with John's family. Quinn was loving life, being spoiled by grandparents, aunts, uncles, and cousins. John and I, however, still spent the majority of our days wading through the remaining requirements for the move. It was never-ending. There always seemed to be one more piece of paperwork that had to be done or redone. The worst for me was that we had to fight to get my arm recast in California, and still needed to negotiate the cast's removal for some time before we left the country. We finally got our insurance to agree that I could go to the air force hospital in Dayton, Ohio, where we would be for an interim training course John had to go to in January.

We also were caught in a never-ending battle over passports. The job in Cameroon required us to have diplomatic passports, which we had applied for while still in Germany. Due to timing, we had arranged for the passports to be held in Washington,

DC. We could pick them up while in town, sign, and then forward them to the Cameroonian embassy for visas. It all should have been perfectly straightforward, however, there was always just one more thing—one more signature, one more delay, one more issue. By the time we returned from John's course in Ohio it was mid-February, less than two weeks from our scheduled departure, and we still didn't have our completed passports and visas in hand. When we left for our final required course—a safety course in West Virginia where we would learn things like how to drive in dangerous conditions and how to shoot a variety of firearms—we were nervous that we'd be rebooking our flights and arriving to the job late. But then after a lot of back and forth with the Cameroonians and a lot of favors cashed in by various people, we received a FedEx package at our hotel with our shiny new diplomatic passports—complete with our official Cameroonian visas. We were good to go.

Leaving West Virginia for a brief overnight at John's parents' house in New York before we headed out to Cameroon, we stopped along the way at a Cracker Barrel for dinner. In the gift shop attached to the restaurant, I spotted a Gumby toy and bought it. It became our family's official mascot, because if there was one thing we'd learned during that move it was if we weren't as flexible as Gumby, we'd never survive.

Five very long months after receiving our orders, we stood in the departure lounge of Heathrow Airport, where we waited for our flight to Nairobi, the second to last leg of our trip to Cameroon. What a sight we must have been: exhausted from everything, including the previous red-eye flight from the United States, bundled up against the cold yet standing in line for a flight to a part of the world that would meet us with heat, me with my arm still in a brace. But we had made the leap. We were almost there.

As we settled into our seats on the Kenya Airways plane, John laughed and snapped a picture of me. "Look at you," he said, turning the phone so I could see. "Look at how happy you are." Despite everything, there I was, completely disheveled from hours of travel yet grinning like the Cheshire Cat, truly happy for the first time in a long time.

I was moving to Africa!

PART TWO

CAMEROON

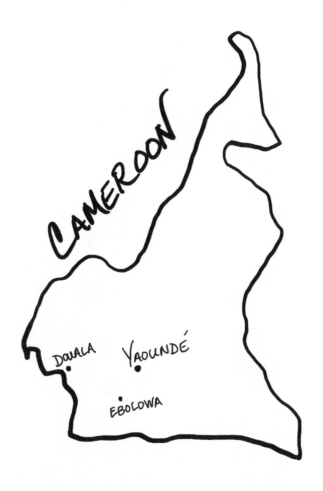

chapter 4

Cowgirl in Cameroon

Three airports, eleven hours of layovers, and twenty hours of flying later, we finally made it to Cameroon on February 22, two days before my thirty-eighth birthday.

As our plane began its final approach for landing, I wondered what exactly that meant because all I could see out the window was dense rainforest. Then as the wheels lowered, I spotted a hole in the vegetation: Yaoundé Nsimalen International Airport. Even after we touched down, it looked so small—our 737 was not the largest plane there but still almost comically big in the setting. As we stepped off the staircase and onto the tarmac, the heat and humidity slapped us in the face, a stark contrast to the bitterly cold East Coast winter we had left behind.

Quinn looked up at me, his cheeks already a bright cherry red, and said, "Mom, this is not like Germany. This is hot." No kidding.

We made our way into the terminal, through the slow crawl of immigration, and out to baggage claim. Like the airport in general, the baggage claim area was small and cramped—people were everywhere, all jostling for a spot near the luggage belt. As we made our way into the throng, an arm shot up above the crowd: John's friend and new coworker, our official welcome party. Shoving through the throng of people, we pushed our way over to him.

"You made it," he said, giving John's hand a good shake. "Welcome to Cameroon!" he then turned to Quinn, giving him an equally hearty handshake and me the adopted European greeting of a kiss on both cheeks—after all, the country's last colonizers were the French. Originally colonized by the Germans in 1884, Cameroon became a protectorate of the French and the British at the end of World War I, by mandate of the League of Nations via the Versailles Treaty. It gained independence in 1960 during the great African decolonization. The French and British sections eventually came together in 1961 to form the country we stood in; however, the French influence was still strong, evidenced by the double kiss greeting. "Let's find your luggage and get out of here," he said. Soon, with both ourselves and our bags loaded into the embassy SUV, we headed toward the country's capital, Yaoundé.

The landscape was what struck me first—lush and incredibly deep, brilliant green trees were everywhere. I was struggling to keep my tired eyes wide open so that I wouldn't miss a thing . . . like the man in the roundabout holding a giant snake that he was selling as meat. Beheaded and over five feet long, the thing was as big around as a fire hose. "Dinner anyone?" John's colleague quipped as we drove by. He had lived in Cameroon and Africa for a while at that point and nothing shocked him. John looked at me and snickered—I hate snakes, like in an Indiana Jones kind of way. What a welcome to our new home.

We continued on. Still on the outskirts of the city, poverty was visible everywhere. Houses that hardly merited that name dotted the hills. Some were very simple concrete rectangles partially open to the elements with flimsy tin roofs; others were best described as shacks, built with bits and pieces of whatever was available. People sat there, selling items like fruit, cell phone top-up cards, and tires from their makeshift porches. Others simply stood around looking as if it was the only job they had.

As we reached the center of Yaoundé, the signs of sprawling poverty gave way to a somewhat more organized modern city, but the architecture was all over the board. Most of the buildings appeared to have been built in the 1960s and 1970s in the African modernist style that was popular during that time. It wasn't a capital city like we were accustomed to—all polished and shiny like London or Paris. Yaoundé had a beauty to it but was grimy and worn at the same time.

Further in, traffic on the road came to a halt. Ahead of us on the left, a crowd of people circled around something on the ground. There was anger in their faces, and they were yelling. Car horns were honking. There was so much noise. At first, I figured it was an accident, but then the crowd parted slightly, and I could see two men on the ground being beaten by others around them. It wasn't a simple fight; they were being bludgeoned with sticks and trash can lids. I stared in astonishment. Both the embassy driver and John's colleague remained rather calm about the whole thing, as if it was nothing unusual at all. "Sorry you had to see this on your first day," the colleague turned to say. "It's vigilante justice. Those men are probably thieves and the people here do not tolerate it." We navigated slowly past the scene, through the potentially volatile bottleneck. I could see the accused men lying there with fear in their eyes. A taxi attempted to "help" the crowd by trying to run them over. There were no police to be seen. Justice was being carried out their way. Thankfully, Quinn was asleep.

Our temporary house was close to the embassy on the other side of town, part of the wealthier neighborhoods near the presidential palace. By the time we arrived, my head was spinning—partially from jetlag, partially from all that I had seen. It was so much to take in. During the year leading up to our move, I had read and watched all I could about Cameroon, but the real thing is always different—and that's exactly how I felt. I had pictures in my mind of what it would be like, but those mental snapshots were now blurred and fuzzy. It was time to start over, to let go of my preconceived notions, and allow the country to speak for itself.

Snakes. Vigilante justice. Beautiful, lush green vegetation. Rampant examples of poverty. Bizarre displays of wealth. So many contradictions, so unlike the places I had lived in before. It made me think of what Leonardo DiCaprio's character said in the movie *Blood Diamond*: "TIA—This is Africa." And I was captivated.

Welcome to Cameroon.

chapter 5

Feels Like Home

I really wasn't sure what to make of the temporary house the embassy provided us with. To begin, it was HUGE—two stories with a finished basement/garage, and as it was just our temporary house, it was only minimally furnished and therefore half-empty, which made it seem even larger. But perhaps more than the size, what puzzled me most was the décor—it looked like it was designed with Liberace in mind. The flooring was white marble. There were white, Roman-style columns in the main living room. The bathrooms had gold and bubblegum pink sinks and toilets—I cringed and giggled every time I walked into one.

And as we had been warned, because it was the tropics, mosquitos were abundant and carried the very real threat of malaria. During the day we did our best to avoid them by either wearing long sleeves and full-length trousers or spraying ourselves down with repellent. But having mosquito nets over our beds at night was something I had to get used to.

When I was little, I begged my parents for a canopy bed. When they finally caved to my repeated requests, I was somewhat disappointed with the version they got me—one where the canopy didn't fully enclose the sleeping area. I felt cheated. However, thirty years later when I finally slept under a mosquito net, I saw the error in my childhood wish. On our first night in Cameroon, Quinn had a bad dream and cried out in his sleep. I tried to bail out of bed to comfort him but forgot about the mosquito net and got tangled up, yanking and pulling to free myself. Once free, I stumbled through the unfamiliar house only to once again get tangled up as I searched for the opening to Quinn's mosquito net. Poor kid, it took me ages to finally give him a hug. My one-time romantic ideal of a bed covered in gauzy fabric had been well and truly dashed.

Also, according to everyone we talked to, the rainy season had come early that year. Cameroon essentially has two seasons: the rainy and the dry. The rainy season generally ran from April to November and dumped an average of 100 inches of rain per year. During the tropical downpours, rivers, creeks, and drainage ditches would swell and overflow. Roads in low-lying areas with poor drainage would either be nearly or completely impassable. And I could verify their claims that that year's rainy season came early because the temporary house had a zinc roof, which echoed as the water came down in torrents outside. In a way, it reminded me a bit of the ranch, where I would listen to the rain hit the tin awning that hung over my bedroom window. Well, until the storm reached monsoon levels and the roar of the rain on the roof became deafening. It would take a while to learn to sleep through that.

We arrived in Cameroon on a Tuesday. Quinn restarted school that Friday—his second first day of first grade. We took that suggestion from an embassy spouse, who also worked at the school. Rather than putting Quinn through an orientation, he would join his class for half a day, come home, and take the weekend to work through his jetlag. She also kindly offered to drive us there, telling me that once we got Quinn settled in, I could hang out for a bit, then she would drive us all home. While I had no idea what she meant by hang out—no school I knew, aside from colleges, had spots to hang out—I gratefully accepted the offer. With nothing else on my calendar, I figured it would at least give me a chance to see something new.

The American School of Yaoundé was perched on top of a hill in the middle of the city, its neat white buildings nestled amongst lush green trees. As with most places catering to expats and the wealthy, it was gated and guarded and was certainly in better shape than the local schools. After depositing Quinn with his new class—a group of nine children of various nationalities all very eager to greet their new classmate—I took a tour of the school. It didn't take long, as there was only one classroom per grade level for the elementary school, plus separate rooms for art, music, and technology. When I exhausted my parental inspection, our friend suggested I go get a coffee at the cafeteria while I waited.

The cafeteria was no basic cafeteria: it was the Parrot Cantina, a place where everyone with access to the school—students, staff, parents—could get a hot meal or a refreshment. I sat down in a wicker chair in the cantina's open-air dining space and placed my bag next to me. I was still exhausted from jetlag, plus the nerves of getting Quinn resettled into school had worn me out. I took a deep breath and closed my eyes.

"*Bonjour madame,* can I bring you something?" I jumped a little, opening my eyes to see a man in a crisp white steward's coat standing in front of me, smiling kindly. "I am sorry."

"Um, no worries," I stuttered, sitting up, regaining my composure. "Sure. Yes, please, I would love a coffee."

"*D'accord,*" he said, then added in an almost conspiratorial way. "Perhaps a croissant to go with the coffee?"

"Sure, why not?" I smiled. Damn the calories, he knew exactly what I needed.

The cantina was definitely not a typical school cafeteria; rather it reminded me of a café on a college campus. It was open all day, even after school for a few hours when it offered beer for adults seeking an afternoon's respite.

Not too bad, I thought, settling in for a couple hours of quiet. It was the first time I had been alone in three months. I pulled out a notebook and pen from my bag and began jotting notes. Something had been sparking inside of me since we arrived, a feeling that I was right where I belonged and I wanted to make sure I wrote down whatever that was.

I had been well into my pregnancy with Quinn when I quit my job. No, let me clarify that, I quit my *career*. At the time, I worked as a marketing executive for the beef industry. For years before that I held other positions in the industry—it was all I knew, my heritage and my career, and I was good at what I did. But the job I had in 2003 required a lot of travel. With John working ridiculous hours on a submarine, heading out on underways and deployments, we knew that something would have to give when the baby arrived. And even though my career was the more lucrative of the two, I let go of my job. The one thing that had made that decision palatable was that, in the back of my mind, I thought it would be a temporary pause. I had planned to return to work when Quinn was old enough to start school.

And then things didn't go as planned, because, again, Murphy's Law.

Making the decision for John to accept the job in England, and then to transfer to the foreign area officer community— both absolutely spot-on decisions—well, those decisions sounded the death knell of my former career. At first, I was fine. I was living overseas and had my hands full with an infant and then toddler and the days passed swiftly. But as Quinn went off to preschool and I had more hours to myself, I began to feel the ache of what I had given up. Sure, I could've gone back to work while we were in Germany but not in a position that suited my training or skill set—working there would've been for a paycheck rather than job satisfaction. I grew restless, which is never a good thing for a military spouse. I needed an out, a plan, anything to keep me from feeling at loose ends. So when John returned from an extended work trip to Burkina Faso and told me how he had seen first-hand how a spouse could play a valuable role in the foreign area officer world, I knew there was an opportunity for me.

Military spouses, while vitally important to the greater military community, rarely play an active role in the service member's actual job. We support. We keep the home fires burning. But we also stay out of their work. However, for a foreign area officer, that's not always the case. When assigned to an embassy, the foreign area officer's military world crashes into the diplomatic world. And in the diplomatic world, an involved spouse is seen as an asset. The spouses of diplomats become diplomats by default in the eyes of the community. They host events and attend receptions, becoming an additional conduit for conversations with contacts. Because of this—what John had seen another military spouse do while he was in Burkina Faso, and with my background in public relations—John knew that I could be a real asset to him. It left me thinking that if only we could get a job on the African continent, I might be able to forge a new path for myself using some of my old skills. Hence my willingness to say yes to Cameroon.

That day, as I sat in the school's cantina waiting for Quinn and listening to the sounds of our new home outside the fence— the taxis honking their horns, shop keepers calling out to passersby, the odd melodic bird singing above it all—I had my first real chance to breathe and, not knowing why exactly, thought, *This is where I belong. There is something about this place. This is the start of something new.* I hadn't really felt that way in England or Germany. While I loved living in both places, they just didn't light the same fire within me that Cameroon did. And I hoped John and Quinn felt that way too.

Later that evening, when John was telling us about his new job, he said he thought it would be both challenging and interesting. He was smiling, happy.

And when John asked Quinn how his first day at the new school went, Quinn almost exploded with excitement. "It was AWESOME!" he bubbled, telling us all about the kids in his class and his teacher, things I had heard on the ride home that afternoon but was happy to listen to again.

I took another deep breath and thanked my lucky stars. We all seemed to be falling in love with our new life. So far, so good.

chapter 6

Lady of the House

I hired house staff.

Having been raised in a culture where doing your own housework was a source of personal pride and a mark of strength, I struggled to convince myself that I needed help around the house. While I was no Marie Kondo, I kept a decent home. However, when you lived in Africa and were considered a "wealthy expat" by the locals, you hired house staff—not so much to help you manage your house, but to help you fit in.

Esme came recommended to us by the same friend who worked at the school. She knew Esme's current employer, another embassy family due to depart post shortly. Esme had worked for American families for many years. She was one of the more sought-after housekeepers in the community. Since I didn't have a clue about the expat community we had just entered, I was surprised to find that hiring house-staff was nearly a competitive sport. And with the news that Esme would soon be in search of a job, the vultures were circling. However, moving in February had its advantages. We had avoided the peak transfer season of summer and placed ourselves in the perfect position to hire someone when everyone else already had their staff. Had we arrived in the summer, Esme would probably have been poached before we even got there by someone looking to upgrade their staff. It was just our dumb luck she happened to need a job when we arrived.

While I had conducted employment interviews before, I had never interviewed someone to work in my house. Let me just say, it felt very awkward, especially asking Esme her thoughts regarding the cleaning of a bathroom and the washing of clothes. But she impressed me—shy but refined in her manner and impeccably dressed. When I complimented her on the gorgeous navy-blue cap sleeve top and perfect white pencil skirt she was wearing, she told me that she had sewn them herself. She was happy to have the chance to highlight skills she had beyond housework. Despite both of us being nervous, we hit it off, and I offered her the job on a trial basis. She would start the following week when we moved into our permanent house. I took a deep breath as she left and closed the door behind her. *Heaven help me,* I thought.

Having lived out of suitcases for three months, bouncing from hotel rooms to relatives' homes back to hotel rooms and then to the temporary house, we were thrilled to finally move into our actual home. And what a home it was.

When you receive an assignment to an embassy where housing is provided, you are asked to fill out a housing questionnaire prior to arrival. The survey asks basic questions about what you are looking for in a home. Given that we spent our tour in Germany in a small apartment with no outdoor space or privacy, John and I jumped at the opportunity to ask for as much the opposite as we could, the number one request being a LARGE YARD. While we knew that there weren't many embassy homes in Yaoundé that fit that bill, we figured it was worth asking. The worst they could do was say no.

And boy did we luck out—in spades.

See, not every type of embassy job exists in every embassy. John's job—overseeing security cooperation between our military and the Cameroonian military—hadn't existed as a stand-alone position prior to our arrival, which meant that in addition to adding the job, the embassy also needed to add another house to the existing housing pool. So essentially, the house that we ended up with was pretty much picked out for us, and after a couple of weeks in the temporary Liberace house, our permanent residence, the Bat House, was a welcome relief.

The house actually had a proper name, *Les Flamboyants*, after the trees of the same name that grew in the garden but it was known to everyone as the Bat House. Not because of the hundreds of very large fruit bats that nested in its trees, but rather disappointingly because it had once been the overseer's house for the now defunct British American Tobacco (BAT) factory.

The Bat House was a lovely throwback to another time. Much like an aloha house in Hawaii, it was a pale buttercream yellow one story with a porch and verandah. It wasn't too large or pretentious. From the moment you entered the gates of the compound, you realized that what made the Bat House truly special wasn't the house at all, but its garden. The house lay in the middle of its lot, which was a mini tropical paradise. Vibrant green grass covered the rolling slopes of the lawn. Large trees provided shade from the often relentless sun. Striking red hibiscus and bromeliads added pops of color. All of it scented the air with a heady mix of sweet florals and musky earth, except we would soon discover on the days when the neighbors burned their garbage.

Quinn was beyond thrilled to discover that we now had our very own banana trees, avocado trees, and coconut palms. There were also a couple of mango trees that bordered our compound and draped a few of their limbs over the wall, promising to drop fruit on our side when ripe. And beyond the lushness, there was a considerable amount of connected cement walkway around the house, perfect for a little boy and his scooter.

I felt like Karen Blixen and wanted to waltz around wistfully saying, "I had a farm in Africa."

When our household goods arrived, John and Quinn were well settled into their routines, so I was left on my own to unpack, set up the house, and figure out what shape my new life would take.

Well, I wasn't entirely on my own. I had to keep reminding myself that I had staff.

Having people around the house, all day, every day, took some getting used to. In addition to Esme—who showed up promptly at eight every morning and stayed until five in the evening—there was also Denis, our gardener, and the security guards. Yes, guards. As robbery and theft were an issue in Yaoundé, embassy homes had 24-hour security—ours came in the form of Robert and Alex, the day and night guards, respectively, both of whom became just as much of a fixture on our compound as Esme and Denis. The four of them were my team and to them I was Madame Julie.

Every day was a new experience for me. Unlike the majority of my life up to that point, there was little familiar at first. The staff was my salvation. I was constantly asking Denis about the plants in the garden or Alex about the security light system or Esme about how I needed to go about shopping for food. My childlike tenacity for figuring out how things worked endeared me to them. However, my ingrained American desire to do things on my own made them laugh out loud. While they were my source of information, I was most certainly their source of amusement.

"Madame," Esme said one morning, *tsking* her tongue at me, "I know you want to go shopping with me in the markets, but one look at you and oh!" She put her hands on her hips for emphasis and *tsked* me again. I knew what she meant: I wasn't a local and there was no way to hide that fact. While I could indeed go shopping in the open-air market, the sellers would do their best to take advantage of me. "One look at you and you would pay twice as much for everything! You can't hide your white," she laughed. "I will do the shopping at the market."

And as much as I didn't want to admit it, I knew she was right. "Fine. But here's the deal—I will send you with a list of what we need, then I will give you a little extra cash. I want you to use the extra to buy me things you think I should try . . . and I want to try *everything*." That put a smile on her face.

Soon our kitchen was full of local treats. Fruits and vegetables that I had never heard of were laid out for me—soursop, bitter leaf, and *safou*—Esme taking care to explain each one and then turning them into an amazing local dish. Safou was what the Cameroonians called a plum but was not like any plum I had ever had, being cooked with salt and tasting more like a buttery citrus mash. She also made things like *ndolé*, Cameroon's official dish—a stew of bitter greens, nuts, and meat which I loved but the boys didn't—and *egusi* pudding and Poulet D.G. Coconut rice, a dish usually reserved for special occasions, made with chicken, fresh coconut, rice, and vegetables, became our family favorite. I often had her make a huge pot of it—enough that it would feed the staff for their lunch and us for our dinner.

Esme introduced us to local snacks like peanuts and *chin chin*, treats that could be found in almost every Cameroonian home, especially when entertaining guests. Sold in old bottles—one of Cameroon's novel forms of recycling—the peanuts were small, like Spanish peanuts, but so much better—skins removed, pan roasted with salt until they had a smoky flavor to them, smooth and bronze in color. They were unlike any peanut I had ever eaten, deep, rich, and reminiscent of a campfire.

But it was chin chin that became my downfall. The first time Esme presented me with some, I thought it looked like animal kibble—fat little rectangular shapes, small enough to fit through the neck of the old Grant's Whiskey bottle in which they were sold.

"This is chin chin," Esme said, shaking some out into her palm, then popping them into her mouth. "It's a treat, like your cookies."

That was an understatement. She shook some into my hand. I lifted them to my nose and inhaled. They smelled of rich caramel and butter. I put one in my mouth and bit down. It was crunchy and tasted like the very best shortbread. They were so moreish. "Esme, these are WONDERFUL," I said, shaking more into my hand. "But you are going to make me fat, bringing treats like this!"

She laughed, clearly pleased with herself and her role as my guide to all things culinarily Cameroonian, a role that suited her well.

Many times, after unpacking yet another box of our stuff, I would take a break and retreat to the room we had turned into our study with a fresh cup of coffee and a small bowl of chin chin. From the loveseat we had in there, I would sit and look out the window onto the wilder part of our garden. It was almost always shaded because of the giant mango and flamboyant trees that spread their branches over the area. I had little else to do; Esme and Denis saw to that, clicking their tongues if I did too much manual labor, reminding me that I was paying them to work, so let them work. It was during those days, sitting there and staring out that window that, I began to wrap my head around our new life.

No longer did we have a traditional military life—we were now on the periphery. Yet, slowly, I could see opportunities opening, things that felt familiar. John's job as the head of security cooperation—the person responsible for cross-national partnerships with Cameroon's military—was no longer one I was entirely excluded from. In fact, if anything, my understanding of his work was a benefit to him, allowing me to be an active participant in the more social responsibilities that went along with it. Similar to the world I grew up in where my parents worked together and played off each other's strengths, this new world I found myself in was beginning to fit like a glove.

Before we knew it, three months had passed since our arrival in Cameroon. The powers-that-be like to tell you that when you move to a hardship post—which was what Cameroon qualified as—you'll experience a multitude of emotions: highs (the excitement of living in a radically different country), lows (again, the whole living in a radically different country thing), and the somewhere in-betweens (realizing that living in said radically different country means many challenges, but you can indeed live there) . . . oh, and that this emotional rollercoaster will last your entire tour.

I was never quite sure where I fell on that emotional rollercoaster because I wanted to believe that I was always in the high area. Of course, that could have been the Pollyanna in me, wanting to think everything was under control even if it wasn't. I saw others at the embassy who were most certainly, and very obviously, at a low point—quiet and withdrawn—and yet there I was smiling like the village idiot, going on about my life. Sure, I had a few quasi-low points where I would've gladly sold my soul to the devil if someone had just built a Starbucks in Yaoundé. Or shot me when I felt like I was dying from food poisoning, but those low points had been temporary. Life was still life. To make it in the world of the military or the foreign service, you had to learn that your home was not always going to be on some beautiful tree-lined street in a cozy suburb of America with every creature comfort at your fingertips. To survive the lifestyle, you had to realize that home and life, no matter where you were or what you were doing, was only what you made of it.

And at that time, my home was Cameroon and after those first months, this was what I knew: I no longer cringed while riding in a car on Cameroon's crazy roads, thinking, *Gee, that taxi/truck/motorcycle is awfully close to hitting us*; the fact that our power went off and on several times a day no longer surprised me, but it did mean that I spent a lot of time resetting tripped breakers; some days there simply was no sugar/cream/skim milk/cheese in Yaoundé and it was just something I had to live with; lightning wasn't close until you watched it strike something on your compound; consistent access to phone/internet/TV was overrated; knowing the internet was so slow that it took an entire day to download an hour-long TV show just made you choose your entertainment more wisely; until I had a banana from the tree in our yard I had never truly tasted one; trusting people to show you why they love their country was the way to learn about a country; and, finally, chin chin was the food of gods.

Up to that point, Cameroon had been an eye-opening adventure. It was colorful, noisy, friendly, and still just a bit strange. It was unlike anywhere in the world I had lived before, and I was in love with it.

chapter 7

New Continent, New Life

There is an unwritten expectation that spouses of foreign
area officers, when accompanying the officer to a tour
at an embassy, will accept the role and responsibility of
a diplomat—albeit, unofficially and unpaid—because as I have
mentioned, in the diplomatic world a spouse is seen as an exten-
sion of their partner. And even though this participation is not
a requirement, it's still an expectation. Some spouses choose to
play along, others do not. When the invitations to representational functions began coming in and I was invited alongside
John, I had no problem with being included. For years I had
watched my mom work alongside my father at agricultural
events. I trailed along with them for a time. I learned the ropes
of polite conversation and observed the distinct advantage that
having someone at your side can add to a situation. The diplomatic circuit was very similar, just at a different level. For me,
falling into that world was a piece of cake.

Except for one thing: the language barrier.

While Cameroon is made up of more than 240 distinct tribes
and an equal number of distinct languages, French and English are recognized as its official languages. However, once we
arrived it became obvious that French was the language most
widely used within the population and especially within the
diplomatic circle. Although I knew *bonjour* and could stumble

through reading the French labels at the grocery store, being able to attend a reception and not just stand there mute when people spoke to me was an altogether different matter.

It quickly became clear that I needed to learn French.

Our embassy provided French language instruction for employees wishing to improve or maintain their proficiency while in-country and, if space was available, spouses could sit in. Trying to prove that an old dog could indeed learn a new trick, I enrolled in the beginning French class. I was essentially learning the same things Quinn learned in his first-grade version of the course—how to introduce myself, simple greetings, and how to conjugate verbs like "to be" and "to have." Three mornings a week, I would grab my notebook, my French-English dictionary, an assortment of pens, and a travel mug full of coffee and head to class.

"*Bonjour*, Madame Tully." My instructor was Ahmad, a Cameroonian who had worked for our embassy for years teaching French. "*Vous avez café . . . encore.*" He found my coffee habit amusing.

"*Oui, c'est necessaire.*" That got a laugh from him. He probably thought that was a joke, but I was serious. At ten o'clock in the morning, trying to learn a new language definitely necessitated coffee.

Every class we would chat our way through the lessons, covering the basics of the language. In the beginning, I had explained to Ahmad that the reason I wanted to learn French was to help me with our diplomatic responsibilities and to better understand his country and its people. Therefore, when possible, he would tailor the lessons to accommodate not only useful conversation tidbits, but also things like how to haggle with market vendors and the nuances of Cameroonian French.

Another morning, another French class. I sat down at the table, took a sip of coffee, and opened my notebook. "Ahmad, I have a lunch to go to this week. Can you help me with things like 'It's so nice to see you again,' and 'This food is fabulous'?"

"*Mais oui, madame,*" he smiled. "We will make you the perfect diplomat. *Nous commencerons avec . . .*"

Returning home after class, I practiced my new phrases on Esme. "*C'est un plaisir pour moi de vous revior,*" I said to her as I walked into the kitchen where she was busy preparing lunch for her and Alex.

She stopped chopping the onion on the cutting board, a huge smile spread across her face. "Oh, madame, listen to you! Soon you'll be one of us," she said proudly. Her praise made me feel pretty good about myself.

"*C'est un plaisir pour moi de vous revoir,*" the words came out of my mouth slower that time, as I wanted to make sure I got the phrase right and not say something offensive or ridiculous to our hostess.

The beautiful, statuesque woman smiled in surprise at my fledgling French, the last time I saw her was before I began my lessons. "*Quelle surprise!*" she said, hugging me and kissing both my cheeks in turn. Little did she know that that short phrase was about the extent of my speaking confidence.

It was a warm, muggy day and John and I, along with three others from the embassy—sans kids, who all happily stayed home with a Cameroonian babysitter that spoiled them rotten, Quinn included in that mix—had been invited to lunch. Our hostess and her husband—one of John's contacts, a high-ranking member of the Cameroonian military—wanted us to join them for a working lunch in reciprocation for a recent dinner. While the initial invitation had said we would meet them at a restaurant, the hostess—the prefect of a nearby city—had changed her mind and wanted to extend a more localized hospitality experience, to show us the Cameroon she was so proud of. Not knowing entirely what to expect, I was truly surprised by the destination—a small village restaurant, part of a budding eco-tourism site stunningly located on the banks of the Nyong River, about an hour and a half outside of Yaoundé.

It was like stepping into the pages of a book, one written about a place so exotic that you could never imagine being there—and yet, there I was. Tables had been set out on a large open verandah and filled with a buffet of traditional Cameroonian dishes. It was a riot of colors and smells. Vibrant verdant green banana leaves cradled food that was fanned out like peacocks trying to impress us with their plumage. Fish, chicken, and porcupine emitted the rich smoky scent of the wood fire they'd been roasted over. Plates overflowed with fried sweet plantains and *bobolo*: a local favorite made of cassava that had been finely grated, formed into fat, finger-like shapes, wrapped tightly in leaves and steamed to softness. There was *pilé pilé*, a mash mixture of red beans and plantain, and big platters of freshly cut sunshine-yellow pineapple. It was a sumptuous feast meant to be enjoyed while gazing out over the lazy, meandering river—I was in heaven.

I tried my best to keep up with the rapid-fire French, but my focus happily reverted to the food when it became too difficult. Every bite tasted like the Africa I had dreamed of as a girl; even the porcupine tasted like a slightly sweeter version of domestically produced pork.

Full of food and wine, the meal ended. Our hostess, rising from the table and waving her arm toward the river's edge, said, "And now we have a treat for you—canoe rides."

Okay, I know there are those who think that there are far more glamorous places to be stationed at in the world—embassies where posh garden teas and exquisite sparkling dinner parties are the norm—but at that precise moment I knew that I would never trade our time in Africa for one of those places. I would opt for grilled porcupine and a canoe ride in the middle of Cameroon any day.

Making our way down the dirt path, a group of hand-carved, dugout canoes awaited us on the bank of the river. I tentatively walked through the mud and grass to the edge of the water, trying to find footing on the few rocks available, and then stepped into my private canoe. I had dressed for lunch at a restaurant—sundress, wrap, a pair of beautifully beaded leather flip flops—and was feeling very self-conscious when the canoe man sat down in his seat behind me. I looked like some posh *memsahib* waiting to be rowed leisurely down the river, bright red toenails and all.

Where we were, the Nyong River flowed wide and smooth through the tropical forest. The day was overcast and grey, which amplified the green of the trees and vines. The water was a murky dark brown, its movement resembling creamy hot chocolate. But the most remarkable thing was the quietness, something rarely found in the bustling confines of Yaoundé. It was glorious. As a teenager, I used to go for walks near our mountain cow camp—my family's piece of heaven in the Sierra Nevada mountains—finding a boulder on top of a hill to sit on. There amongst the firs and pines, I would gaze out toward the higher mountains in the distance. Soaking in the quiet, only interrupted by bird song or a chatty chipmunk, it was free of manmade noise. That was what it felt like that day on the river, the quiet broken only by the light splashing tap of the oar as it entered the water, pushing us along and the occasional call of a bird high in the trees. It was incredible.

We made a slow loop with the canoes and then returned to shore. I glanced at my watch and realized that it was late after-noon—our lunch had turned into an all-day affair. We had told the babysitter we'd be back in a few hours, but now we'd be lucky to make it back to Yaoundé before dark. As we made our profuse thank yous for the day, our hostess said, "I know we've kept you, but would you like to visit my pineapple farm? It's close on the road back to the city."

As much as I wanted us to start home, the words "pineapple" and "farm" caught in my ears. I was willing to add another hour to our return for that.

The farm was, as promised, just off the main route. We pulled off onto the roadside and walked into her small plantation. Having visited pineapple farms with John when he was stationed in Hawaii before we were married, what I saw was not entirely what I expected. Rather than the tall, oblong fruit I was familiar with, these pineapples were small, near-perfect globes, about six inches in diameter. In a mix of French and English, our hostess explained the farm and where she sold the fruit. "The pineapple you ate at lunch was from here," she said as we walked. "Now come, I will send you all home with some."

As our driver loaded the box of pineapples into the back of the SUV, I turned to our hostess and said, slowly again to make sure I got it right, "*Merci. Aujourd'hui était merveilleux.*" Thank you. Today was marvelous.

She hugged me again, "*Merci et à bientôt.*" Thank you and see you soon.

Later, at home, I made a note to ask Ahmad about agricultural terms during my next class and how to describe that incredible pineapple, which had tasted like it was crossed with a coconut and dipped in cream.

To an outside observer, our lunch on the river may have appeared an awful lot like over-the-top schmoozing, however it was anything but. Just as where I grew up and the community in which I was raised, in Africa relationships are key. Before any business is conducted, hospitality has to be extended and human understanding established. For newcomers to the country, like John and myself, a show of culture was vital to bring us into the fold. That was the world I found myself in. The longer we were there, the fuller our social calendar became and the more successfully John was able to do his job. Although we told family and friends back home about some of the programs and partnerships that John was working on, we also told them about the numerous meals and receptions we attended—of course, it was the latter that stuck in their minds. But party or not, it was all part of the job. Therefore, I would be remiss if I didn't talk about the flip side of our social world, the reciprocal events that were hosted on behalf of the United States. These were where we let our own culture shine for the night, giving our host nation and others a taste of America. In all honesty, Americans do representational entertaining very well.

While an embassy has many roles—assistance for citizens living abroad, assistance to others wanting to visit the country, management of cooperative programs with the host nation, and sometimes, in times of crisis, a safe haven—first and foremost, an embassy is the face of its nation. Few things give an embassy more opportunity to say "this is who we are" than its national day celebration.

The scope and shape of an American embassy's Independence Day celebration is dependent on the current ambassador—each have their own way of doing things, their own perspective on how to best represent our nation. For example, a previous US ambassador to Cameroon favored an afternoon reception, but the ambassador during our time opted for a more formal evening event. That first year we were there, the already beautiful embassy grounds were transformed into a sparkling red, white, and blue oasis for the night. Tents were raised and strung with lights—a giant American flag gracing the back of the welcome tent where the official receiving line stood. Servers wearing paper Uncle Sam hats swayed through the crowd carrying platters of mini hamburgers. The marine security guards, in their parade dress uniforms, posted the colors while a Peace Corps volunteer sang our national anthem a cappella. Those of us representing the embassy and our country were a smiling, shining example of American culture and hospitality to the hundreds of guests in attendance.

Yet, while most national day events tended to be at least interesting, they rarely treaded into the realm of fun. But that year, our ambassador's wife, a wonderful woman with a zest for life, decided that while our celebration would remain proper it would also include an element of whimsy. It would hopefully surprise and delight the attendees, reminding them that Americans could not only dress up, but we could also have a good time.

Thus was born our embassy's Fourth of July flash mob. Yes, a flash mob, the kind you've seen on YouTube where dancers seemingly pop up out of nowhere and take over an unsuspecting crowd with a choreographed routine that makes even some of the more audacious Broadway musicals look tame. And before you have to venture a guess—yes, I was part of it. Given that I have no natural dancing talent, you may wonder why. Well, I really had no choice for several reasons: first of all, I liked the ambassador's wife a lot; second of all, my other dear friend was the choreographer; third of all, John threatened to sign me up if I didn't volunteer. So, resigned to my fate, my participation spoke volumes.

The things I do for good ol' Uncle Sam.

As it was planned, our performance would begin with a core group of about twenty, growing in number toward the finale. We prepped and rehearsed for a month and a half. The routine—which lasted six minutes—began with "This Land is Your Land," segued into "Living in America," and finished with a rousing rendition of "Born in the U.S.A." If I could be so bold, I thought the whole thing rocked. It was kitschy but fun. Our group went into the event excited at the thought of bringing an element of surprise, something that would make guests remember their evening with us. Everything had been planned to a T—after the ambassador's speech, when the crowd was free to mingle, our music would cue up, and a few of us would begin dancing where we stood, slowly making space for the others and allowing the guests to move aside to watch the show. It was a great plan . . . except for when it didn't work.

On the actual night, as the ambassador finished his remarks and the beginning strains of "This Land is Your Land" could be heard through the speakers, myself and two others, having prepositioned ourselves in the crowd, began dancing—raising our arms and clapping our hands over our heads. In our pre-event minds, we had been sure that our actions would clear out the non-dancers with no problem, because we figured three American women bopping around amidst a throng of diplomats should do that.

We couldn't have been more wrong.

Instead of moving out of our way, the guests just stood where they were and stared at us. Stealing a nervous glance at each other, the three of us started making more noise, whooping and cheering, making larger movements with our arms. Yet still, nobody moved—that was when we realized that the surprise element of the flash mob had been completely lost on the guests, and worse yet, that they really had no clue what a flash mob was. With our dignity lost, we stopped and walked over to the emcee and had him ask the guests to clear the dance area, then asked the DJ to restart the music so we could begin again. After that embarrassing hiccup, it went great.

Our core group of twenty grew to fifty as the Peace Corps volunteers joined us for the final song. Guests were laughing and smiling, not quite sure what to make of our show or the fact that the ambassador's wife was out there dancing with us. But it was working; our national day would be remembered—especially by the Cameroonian dignitary who made the unfortunate decision to stand near the area where I was dancing.

When the guests had finally stepped back to make room for our performance, some of them ended up right on the edge of the pavement where we were dancing. Because of the growing size of our group, we needed all the available space we could get, which meant I would come right up to the onlookers. So, there I was, in a beautiful dress Esme and I had designed together— long and straight, made out of a beautiful hand-dyed wax print fabric in steel blue and gold, my cowboy boots underneath— dancing like a maniac.

The aforementioned dignitary standing on the edge of our dance floor was directly in front of me, only a couple of feet separating us. He stood stoically in his white *boubou*—a traditional outfit of pants worn under a long tunic and a head cap. When I made eye contact with him, I could tell he was obviously trying to grasp the meaning of our interesting cultural display. Then, unfortunately for him, he had nowhere to go as I was forced to decrease the space between us even more. The crowd was too dense for him to move as I clapped, stomped, spun, and shook my body. He stood there trapped like a deer caught in head-lights, his face remaining a blank slate until it was over. Even now, years later, my cheeks burn at the memory. I wonder if he was as embarrassed as I was.

"Well," John smiled as our dance mob rejoined the rest of the guests. "That seemed to go well."

"Really?" I laughed, gladly accepting the glass of champagne he handed me and downing it in one go. "Do you think so? Did you not see that poor man that was standing in front of me? I am pretty sure I have single-handedly set back US-Cameroonian relations fifty years."

chapter 8

Life is Truly a Journey

O ur first June in Cameroon arrived and, almost overnight, Yaoundé became a ghost town. We had experienced this type of exodus to a lesser extent when we were in Germany, as many military families took the opportunity to go back to the States to visit family for the summer, but the exodus in Yaoundé was on an entirely different level. On the last day of school—and for two to three days after—every departing flight to Europe was fully booked. Parents, children, and teachers were all heading out of town for the break. Many would not return until the day before classes resumed.

As we had only been in-country four months, John couldn't afford to take a vacation, so we decided that Quinn and I would also stick out the summer in Yaoundé. Sure, everyone would be gone, but we still had the embassy pool at our disposal and our large garden to play in. We would find ways to entertain ourselves.

"Mom, what are we going to do today?" Quinn asked over breakfast.

It was an excellent question because I didn't really know the answer myself. Normally, I would have had housework or gardening to keep me busy during the days, but those chores no longer existed for me. So, more days than not, I found myself feeling like Quinn and wondering what the day would hold.

That particular day turned into a glorious one—bright blue sky, dotted with cotton ball clouds, not too hot, not too humid—perfect weather to be outside, which gave me an idea. "Well, Quinn, I tell you what," I said, pushing my chair away from the table. "Why don't we grab your rope, and you can practice your roping skills that Uncle Tim taught you last Christmas."

During our leave between Germany and Cameroon, we had spent Christmas at my family's ranch. My brother, Tim, who adored Quinn from the day he was born, essentially nabbed him upon our arrival and made him his constant shadow. Everyday Quinn played the role of cowboy sidekick to his uncle. He helped feed cattle, rode horses, and to his delight, he began to learn how to rope. Quinn loved every moment of his cowboy training, so I figured, why not keep going? Let's rope!

Quinn barreled off his chair and ran to his room, where the rope that my mom and dad had given him as a toddler hung on the wall. He grabbed it, slid on his shoes, and tore off for the door. "Come on, Mom!" he called after me.

"Now, we'll need something to rope." I said, surveying the front yard and finding a decently long stick that was about twice as big around as my thumb. I stabbed it into the grass so that about two feet of it stuck out. "There, it's not perfect, but it'll give you something to aim at."

By this time, our staff had gathered around. Quinn was their darling and could do no wrong in their eyes. They watched over him with the same ferocity and pride that John and I did. That day they watched with curiosity as I reminded Quinn how to build a loop and the proper way to hold the excess rope.

"Okay," I said as I began to show him how to twirl the loop overhead, using a rotating motion with my wrist. "Don't focus on your hand. Focus on the stick. Your aim will follow your eyes." I relinquished the rope to him. He got comfortable with the loop, gave it a couple of twirls, and threw it. He missed but not by much. His adoring audience clapped and cheered.

We practiced that method a few more times, then I said, "You could also try a houlihan. I know that's the one I prefer." I took the rope from him to demonstrate the overhand throw.

At that point, Alex, the security guard, came closer to me, watching intently.

"Ma'am," he said quietly, "can I try?"

I was surprised but not shocked—we liked to have fun on our compound, so it wasn't a huge leap to think that he just wanted to join in on the amusement. However, when he took the rope in his hands, built a loop, and threw a houlihan that landed right on target, well, then I was shocked. "Alex?" I said, my voice incredulous. "What on earth? How did you know how to do that?"

Alex was a soft-spoken man with a kind face and quiet manner. He grinned and said, "Ma'am, my family has cattle in Bamenda. I grew up taking care of them for my grandmother. I had to trail along behind them to take them to grass. I had to rope them, just like you."

"Alex, you're a cowboy?" Quinn asked, his eyes wide in amazement.

"Yes. Like you," he laughed and patted Quinn on the head. I walked back to the verandah to sit and watch with Esme, leaving Alex to show Quinn the finer points of roping and allowing me to contemplate how truly small the world was.

Even though the city was a ghost town that summer, it didn't mean that all the work stopped. If anything, John's workload was increasing, especially in terms of social commitments, which, in turn, meant that my life—at least after six o'clock in the evening—began to move at a faster pace.

John had been absolutely right when, back in Germany, he said that I would be able to work alongside of him. As opposed to his years with the submarine force and command staffs, now his job was one I could know about. It was a detail that fascinated my public relations trained mind. My understanding of his work was actually a benefit. In the diplomatic world, at least on John's side of the diplomatic world, an actively involved spouse could prove all the difference when establishing relationships with the host nation and other contacts. This was something that became obvious our first summer in Cameroon as the reception and dinner invitations started appearing with my name tagged on next to John's. And the thing we discovered was that John and I worked very well together.

Modern western society tells us that marriage is a balancing act where two people not only learn the art of compromise, but also how to play off each other's strengths. As John and I began making the rounds of the diplomatic circuit, we realized that we were really good at that and took to our new world like ducks to water. Drop us into a reception and we worked the room with ease. He would make introductions, then I would pick up a small tidbit of information and run with it. For example, when I learned that one of his Cameroonian contacts had a large herd of cattle, well, that was a no-brainer. The work was fun and fascinating; it was the most intellectually stimulated I had felt in years.

However, I still had that little stumbling block called French. While John would translate for me when we were out, I wanted to learn enough that I didn't have to rely on him to make sure every little sentence made sense. So, it was good that even though it was summer, my language classes continued.

"I need more cocktail conversation," I said to Ahmad one morning. Quinn was sitting next to me, keen to see how his mom handled the same information he had been learning. Since most of my classmates were away for the summer, I had asked if Quinn could come along, more to provide him a change of scenery than anything else. Ahmad had no problem with it, so Quinn would join us, bringing along a book and a notebook to keep him occupied. Still, he rarely opened them since he was content to pay attention to my battle with the verb tenses that he had already mastered.

"*D'accord*," Ahmad answered. "But let's begin with what you did last night. Tell me *en francais.*"

Quinn grinned as I forced my mind to switch gears and work in French. "*Oui, d'accord.*" Yes, okay. "*Hier soir, j'ai attendre un autre réception.*" Yesterday evening I attended another reception.

"*Vous été très occupé maintenant.*" You are very busy now. "*Dis moi à propos la reception.*" Tell me about the reception.

That was our routine, to walk through what I had done since our last class in order to build confidence through repetition and conversation. In those early days, it was a mental workout. Exhausting and frustrating.

"*J'ai parlé en francias avec un francias à propos vin et* vineyards, but I didn't know the word for vineyard," I rambled, switching back to English as I described my frustration for not knowing the word for vineyard while talking to a Frenchman that evening.

"Okay, okay," Ahmad laughed. "Let us make a list of things you want to know how to say. We will go from there . . . *en francias.*"

Quinn smirked, enjoying his ringside seat of mommy going to school.

chapter 9

Change Happens Fast

During that first summer in Cameroon, just as we felt we were getting the hang of things, we found out John was being considered for the embassy's next senior defense official and defense attaché (SDO/DATT). Traditionally an army position, the job was being transferred to the navy. Despite having been in-country for only a few months, John was already part of the country team and apparently doing his job so well that the powers-that-be thought he would be a good fit. So the opportunity fell into his lap.

For a foreign area officer, an SDO/DATT position was the golden ring you reached for; the chance to be the senior military official representing your country. For John—and me, by default—the opportunity was a combination of hard work and dumb luck. We hadn't taken the Cameroon job looking to jump ranks or climb the ladder, but we accepted the good fortune and went for it, nonetheless. Plus, the position meant a stronger foothold for his career in Africa, something we had wanted since he was selected for the region. Luckily, there was still another year before the current SDO/DATT departed, which gave us the time we needed to become the people we would have to be.

Prospective military attachés are screened for appropriateness and then sent through a training pipeline. In the navy, spouses are also screened and interviewed before the prospective attaché is accepted. Our path circumvented parts of the process because we were already in-country and a known entity. However, we still had to sit through a two-hour-long phone interview and fill out mountains of paperwork—including the overseas suitability screening. This bureaucratic loop made me laugh given that we'd been living overseas for seven years at that point.

Then it came down to learning the ropes.

I had thought we were busy before, but now it was an entirely new ballgame.

Along with increased invitations to events where we met the people we would be working with throughout the rest of our time in the country, we also had to learn what would be expected. That meant learning about the fine art of being the DATT's spouse.

There are basically two approaches in being the spouse of an SDO/DATT. Either you can stay in the background and live a life independent of your spouse's position or you can actively participate along with your spouse. The role I would play was a no-brainer for John and me—with my background in public relations and an innate curiosity about how the world worked, I would continue to be an all-in spouse. But, despite my past experience, there were still rules and guidelines to learn and follow. So, of course, I got out a notebook, made myself a nuisance to those who could guide me, and got to work.

Things I had to learn included the following:

- How to plan receptions, as in who to invite, who not to invite, timing, location, layout, etc.
- How to plan receptions, as in what food to serve, how much food to serve, what drinks to serve, theme or no theme, etc.

- How to plan smaller events like dinners and coffees and the nuances of where to seat people
- How to keep track of expenses and how to fill out expense forms

While such things might seem trivial and basic, they most certainly are not. Attention to detail kept you out of trouble in the world of diplomacy. Offend an honored guest with a thoughtless addition of someone they did not get along with? Serve food that contained pork at a reception attended by those whose religious beliefs prevented them from eating it? Yes, those missteps could quite literally become diplomatic nightmares.

It also meant I had to step up my language game.

"Ahmad, I have a dinner to go to," I explained one morning.

"*En français, madame,*" he corrected me—again.

On days like that, even though I tried my best, I became frustrated with my lack of vocabulary. I felt like a toddler trying to find the words for what I wanted when all I really wanted to do was whine. "Okay," I said, starting over. "*J'ai un dinêr cette semaine. J'ai besoin aide avec mon vocabulaire.*" John and I had been invited to the house of what would become one of his key contacts in Cameroon. The dinner would be a small gathering with less than six people, so any lack of conversational skills on my part would be noticed.

"*Oui? Donc, quel type de phrases voulez-vous apprendre?*" he asked as he took the cap off his dry erase marker and stood by the whiteboard.

"*Bon, maintenant en anglais,*" I started, switching back to English out of necessity. "I need to be able to talk about the food, to ask about the dishes served. I need to be able to make small talk about what village they come from. I need to be able to explain more about where I am from and my life."

I always felt like I was a great source of amusement for Ahmad. The eager student who took in as much as possible yet still hungered for more. As the dinners and events kept coming, I kept working on my language skills. The life I dreamed of in Africa came at the price of educating myself, a process that at the time never seemed to stop. And while I may have been starting to regain my sense of purpose, it took a lot of hard work to get there.

chapter 10

The Darker Side of Life

Our life wasn't always diplomacy and parties in Cameroon. Nor was it always pleasant. There were things we dealt with on a regular basis that we had never had to deal with in the places we previously lived. Some were relatively minor inconveniences, like taking care to avoid being mugged when out in town or being shocked in the shower because the electrical wiring in the house was faulty. Still, others were far darker and brought to light the harsh reality of a country not entirely comfortable with its own growth spurts or civil society. Like when a man was killed right outside our compound.

It happened less than a hundred feet from where I had been sitting, watching TV on a quiet September night. Quinn was already asleep since it was 10 p.m., and he had school the next day. John was away on a business trip in Italy.

Robert, the night guard, rang the doorbell. "Madame," he said, looking at me with concerned eyes. "I'm sorry to bother you, but there is an emergency outside your gate. A man has been killed. I have called the embassy. They are sending people now."

We lived behind a wall that encompassed the entire compound. We had security lights at the gate and inside the garden. We had

24-hour guard patrol. Yet, that didn't entirely stop things from happening. Our street was quiet and relatively dark, bordered on one side by the abandoned tobacco factory whose grounds were overgrown and jungle-like. There were no streetlights—those didn't really exist in most of Yaoundé. If someone wanted to commit a crime, our street was an inviting place—and that night, it cost a man his life.

I blasted off several texts to John, who was asleep and subsequently woken up, given that it was 11 p.m. in Naples. I went outside to talk with the embassy's security officer. The local police and our embassy's security team determined that the man had hired a motorcycle taxi, which although technically prohibited in the city center was not uncommon to find. They figured the driver and an accomplice brought the man down our road, out of sight, then stabbed him. Having heard the struggle, Robert ran up to where our driveway met the road, and spooked the assailants, causing them to flee. The victim lay prone on the street, his flip flops knocked off his feet not too far from him, his umbrella on the ground next to him. A small wad of cash lay in the dirt beside the body, proof that the men didn't get everything they were after.

After that incident, we had increased security around our compound for a time. Additional lights were installed along our fence. We were cautious coming and going, sadly aware that our bubble of security did not keep every evil away. But for me, the hardest part was the knowledge that the man's death would most likely never be solved. In a country where resources for public safety were scarce, a crime like that was a low priority. Even worse, if no one came forth to identify the man, he would simply become just another death. A sobering thought as we continued on with life from our privileged position within the country.

There were also less severe, yet still nerve-wracking, inci-
dences that occurred. And unfortunately for poor Robert, they
always seemed to happen while he was the guard on duty.

Quinn and I had been outside one evening, enjoying the
golden hour and eagerly awaiting John, who was returning from
yet another business trip. The garden was bathed in the most
perfect warm tones of light. Quinn rode his scooter up and down
the driveway and then around the path into the back garden. I
strolled leisurely through the vegetable plot, checking to see if
there was anything ready to pick that Denis might have missed
earlier that day. As the light faded, Robert began turning on the
security lights. The sound of tires crunching along the dirt road
announced John's arrival. Robert swung the massive gates open,
and the embassy car pulled into our compound.

"*Bonsoir, monsieur,*" Robert said to John as he helped unload
the luggage out of the back.

"*Bonsoir,* Robert," John replied, but before he could say anymore, Quinn started in with questions about his trip, practically
dragging his father into the house.

I turned to Robert as he closed the gates once the car left.
"*Merci, Robert, et bon nuit.*" Then I entered the house and locked
up behind me.

Not thirty minutes later, the doorbell rang. Robert stood
there in the light of the verandah, motioning for us to come out.
"Sorry to disturb," he said. "I want to show you something."

Now completely dark, John and I walked along the path toward the guard shack where Robert had stopped and looked
down, directing our attention to the ground next to his feet.
There, in the dim light, was a dark, thin shape. Before Robert
said anything, I knew what it was. Flashes of the ranch popped
into my head, visions of similar shapes at various times in my
youth. The threat of danger sparked in my brain. It was a snake.

"I killed this mamba out where Quinn was playing," he said, then took his walking stick and started to turn it over. Almost decapitated, its head only connected to the body by a sliver of skin, it wiggled a little bit when he touched it from the nerves that hadn't yet died. All three of us jumped a little—an irrational yet involuntary impulse. "It is only a young one; probably came down the hill from the old factory," Robert said. "That is why you must keep the grass cut and the garden clean."

No kidding, I thought, staring down at one of the deadliest snakes on the planet that had, until moments before, been slithering through our lawn.

The next morning, as soon as Quinn got on the bus to school, I asked Denis to mow the lawn and clean up any excess debris, then I told Esme to make sure the doors to the house were always shut tight. From that point on, come the golden hour, I kept Quinn away from areas where any unwanted guests might slither about.

chapter 11

Christmas Actually

G rowing up in northern California at the edge of the Sierra Nevada mountains, I was what I like to call seasonally spoiled. As in climatically, we enjoyed four very distinct seasons. However, my favorite has always been winter.

When the days grew shorter and colder, I grew happier. My family members may argue that winter is a very hectic time on the ranch between peak calving season, muddy fields and cold, fog-shrouded mornings. But I always looked forward to the baby calves bouncing around the hillsides, the hearty meals my mom would make, and the crackling wood fire that burned almost non-stop that time of year. And given that seasonal preference, it should come as no surprise that Christmas is my favorite holiday.

As a child in the 1970s and 1980s, I soaked up the deluge of Christmas commercials that flooded the television immediately following Thanksgiving. I was entranced by the picture-perfect snow scenes, the kindly red-cheeked Santas, the sentimental music. Plus, my hometown, with a Main Street that looked as if it came straight out of a Hallmark movie, went all out with garland and lights during the holidays. My romantically inclined mind soaked it up every year. Even when we lived in Connecticut, England, and Germany, I was still surrounded by perfectly imagined holiday scenes of our western hemisphere culture. So you can imagine the culture shock I went through our first Christmas in equatorial Africa.

When the calendar slid past Thanksgiving 2011 and the days showed little climatic difference, my poor brain struggled to cope. I had to convince myself that Christmas was approaching and embrace what the season had to offer in Cameroon.

Like their western counterparts, the stores and markets in Yaoundé decorated for Christmas at the end of November. Inflatable Santas and red and white striped North Poles appeared in a country where it never froze or snowed. The supermarkets, especially those that catered to expats, added aisles of toys not normally stocked. If I closed my eyes and imagined really hard, it was almost like home.

Okay, not really.

Well, maybe a little.

Even though it was ninety degrees outside, and the air was filled with the choking dust of the dry season, there was still a distinct feeling of Christmastime—mostly provided by the absolutely miserable traffic conditions that descended upon the capital during the weeks surrounding the holiday. The streets of Yaoundé became a nightmare as people started their shopping and prepared for festivities. Trips that normally took five to ten minutes suddenly became three to four times as long. It reminded me of when I was a kid, my family would drive to the mall in Sacramento for our yearly Christmas shopping spree, only to arrive at a nearly full lot and spend forever trying to find a place to park.

But the thing about the traffic in Yaoundé was that the worse it got, the more creative its already abysmal drivers became. When things slowed down to a near stop you knew you were in for a treat. The small motorcycles preferred by the locals would weave crazily in and around traffic, barely clearing most cars and sometimes banging the leg of their passenger into a bumper or two. If no blood was lost, no harm was done. While obnoxiously aggressive on a normal day, taxis practically ran people down to get to their next fare during December. Two-lane roads quickly expanded to three or four or five and came to a halt. Sidewalks were transformed into an additional lane—and yes, I was guilty of driving on the sidewalks occasionally, because, well, when in Rome. Christmas in Cameroon was the only time I ever considered hiring a driver.

Nevertheless, it was Christmas and Cameroon shared its version of the spirit with us. And if it weren't for that god-forsaken traffic I would have driven too quickly and missed things like the somewhat artistically strung lights in the roundabouts and on buildings. I wouldn't have seen the rickety wooden table at the edge of the street where a woman was providing gift-wrapping service for a small fee. And I certainly would have missed the man who stood on the roadside selling partially decorated artificial trees that made me think of the ones in *A Charlie Brown Christmas*. All of those small details put a smile on my face, because despite the heat, dust, and traffic, there was still a feeling of Christmas.

chapter 12

Mom and Son Adventures

"Mom, that van is going to slide into us," Quinn said, a note of concern in his voice.

And as much as I hated to admit it, it looked like he was right.

The two of us were sitting in the back of an embassy SUV, the second of a two-vehicle caravan. The fifteen-passenger van in front had just started up a small hill but then began fishtailing backward toward us.

"Yes. Yes, it is," I responded, doing my best to put on a calm face for him. *Well, this ought to be interesting.* The van's tires were caked with the red clay mud that, when dry, made a decent road but at that moment was more like a giant slip-n-slide. We were miles outside of the nearest town and we had no cell service, so having an accident would be a nightmare, and getting stuck would take on a very literal meaning. I wondered how that information would come across in a phone call to John. At that moment, he would be blissfully unaware of our predicament and asleep in a hotel room bed, thousands of miles away in Washington DC.

As a military spouse, you get used to spending a lot of time on your own—including playing the role of parent supreme if you have children—while your service member is away for (check all that apply): duty, deployment, temporary duty assignment, etcetera, etcetera. The things that keep you apart from the person you married become part of your life, whether you want them to or not. However, the service member generally departs for remote locations, leaving the spouse and family safely tucked in back home, which was not the case for us when John departed Cameroon that April to attend attaché training. Since Quinn was well into his second-grade year, we knew that yanking him out of school so that I could go to attaché spouse's training wasn't fair. The poor kid had gone through a three-month transit the year before, carving his entry into elementary school in half. We weren't about to do that two years in a row, so Quinn and I stayed behind in Yaoundé. We had our house, our home, our life, and our friends; we were comfortable. Yet, it wasn't without risk. We lived in a place where seemingly simple emergencies—broken bones and anything more than a minor illness—would be cause for evacuation. And there was always an undercurrent of uncertainty in that part of the world, a region where the political climate could go from stable to unstable in the blink of an eye. This time John would be back in the States. He was in the warm bosom of American familiarity. He had reliable power, and an abundance of choice for his morning coffee and played the role I had during his deployments to far-flung locales. Meanwhile, Quinn and I would be in the heart of Africa, in a country that could potentially turn on us in a heartbeat. Yes, we had flipped our roles.

"Promise me that you won't just sit at home," John had pleaded while he packed. He was worried that our lives would shrink into the confines of our compound.

"I promise," I said to him for the umpteenth time. "We are fine. We are happy here. This is home."

"I know." He was never good at leaving, no matter where we were stationed. John, a true family man, always chose to spend any free time at home with us rather than pursuing independent activities. However, when he did travel, he took full advantage of where he was at . . . and he expected us to do the same in his absence.

"We have plenty to keep us busy," I reassured him. "And," I started before he could say it, "we will be safe. You don't have to worry, I know what I am doing, plus we have plenty of people here that will be watching over us." That was the hardest part, convincing him that we'd be okay. He had never been the one to sit at home, living with the worries of an active imagination and thinking about all the things that could go wrong.

And we kept our promise. For Quinn, school had occupied its normal facets of life, and outside of school there were playdates and birthday parties galore. I kept up with my French classes and had taken a few odd jobs around the embassy. Our proverbial dance cards were full.

However, I did have a strict rule where I would not compromise—I didn't do things without Quinn. Aside from work events, if an opportunity presented itself for me to travel or experience something in the country, I made it known that I would only go if Quinn could come along too. That was the way it had always been. Over the years, Quinn and I had spent months and months on our own in foreign countries, far away from our families and their support. Knowing that it was often just him and me, I had become extremely sensitive about abandoning him to provide myself with an enjoyable outing. Quinn hadn't asked to live a life by himself, nor did he want to, so as far as outings and entertainment were concerned, if we couldn't do it together, we wouldn't do it at all. I had made a promise to John before Quinn was ever born that due to the nature of John's career and our decision to maintain his career over my own, I would be the constant in our child's life, the one who was always there. And that wasn't about to change now.

"Madame Tully," Ahmad began, "I am organizing a trip to the south in cooperation with the Peace Corps. We will be visiting some of their projects in the Ebolowa region and using the opportunity to practice our French skills. Can I assume you will join us?"

I really wanted to go on the trip, to be able to see a part of Cameroon that I hadn't had the opportunity to visit yet, but I hesitated, "Are kids allowed to go?"

"No," he replied. "Unfortunately, not."

"Then I have to decline," I told him. No Quinn, no me. And I left it at that, no hard feelings.

But at the next class, Ahmad started by saying, "Quinn can come along. I have talked to the other participants and while they have no desire to bring their own children, they have no problem with Quinn going."

I was thrilled. Three days visiting small villages and seeing the south. Finally, we were going to do exactly what John had wanted—we were going on an adventure.

The van continued its slow, fishtailing descent toward us.

During Cameroon's rainy season—April to November— storms bring monsoon-level rains to the country. A single storm could drop inches of water in no time at all. Strong rains the day before our trip had turned the normally hard dirt road we were on into a ribbon of thick, oozy mud, and while our SUV had four-wheel drive, the bulky, fully loaded fifteen-passenger van did not. Our driver threw our SUV into reverse and backed us up far enough to be out of the way of the struggling van. Finally slithering to a stop at the base of the hill, we watched as the van's doors opened. The passengers got out—gingerly stepping into the mud in their street shoes, some slipping and sliding as they made their way onto the grassy verge of the road.

Now a thousand pounds lighter, the driver of the van gunned its engine and we watched it bounce, slip, slide, and climb its way to the top of the hill—and then watched as the passengers walked the same path along the verge. Being fully loaded ourselves, we couldn't offer them a ride. I silently congratulated myself on choosing seats in the SUV, as we made our way up the same mud slope with the grace of a mountain goat.

Being a cultural tour, at each stop, we were educated, entertained, and fed. We would roll into a location with our large American vehicles and be greeted with cheers, dancing, and, sometimes, bouquets of flowers, as if we were the ambassador— which none of us were. Depending on the place, we would be briefed about how our American partnerships had benefitted that particular group or community—new water storage systems, rebuilt schools, agricultural innovations—and then we would be presented with the obligatory feast. Stop after stop, our group smiled and praised the culinary delights laid out for us. We did our best to make a good show of eating despite being stuffed already from previous stops. We ate fire-roasted chicken and pork and snake, mashed plantains and bobolo and pilé pilé. There was an abundance of freshly squeezed juices, Fanta, Sprite, and palm wine.

That was my first encounter with palm wine. Most of the Cameroonians that John and I spent time with preferred expensive imported wines and whiskies. In contrast, palm wine was considered the drink of the village. I can best describe it as their version of moonshine. To me, it smelled like a vinegary form of paint thinner, the fumes enough to tingle the inside of my nose.

At the first official stop of our trip, our group was led into the main village house, after official greetings were rendered. It was crowded but spotlessly clean, and the dirt floors swept smooth. The combination of the cement walls and lack of breeze through the glassless windows made the air heavy, the smell a deep combination of earth, hot human bodies, and roasted meat. After Quinn and I filled our plates with food and I grabbed a Fanta for Quinn, a small jam jar of palm wine was pressed into my hand by one of the men of the village. Despite the fact that it was very early in the day, only 10 o'clock, I could not object.

I smiled and said, *"Merci."*

However, and to my misfortune, the presenter of the palm wine had neglected to tell me that I needed to add sugar cubes—which had been on the table beside the pitcher of wine—before consuming. After taking a bite of pilé pilé, I raised the jar to my lips and took a sip. Not only did it smell like paint thinner, but it tasted like it too. The liquid burned like fire in my throat, sour and strong, and I did my best to not cough. I gave a brief moment's thought about what it was doing to my internal organs. Our hosts, watching me as I sipped, betrayed no trace of humor at my predicament. Somehow managing to not sputter or spit it out, I put on my best smile and raised the glass to them in salute. They nodded, pleased with my effort, then went on talking to the rest of our group. When their eyes were finally off me, I snuck a sip of Quinn's Fanta and shoved another bite of pilé pilé into my mouth, allowing the mixture of mashed plantains and beans to soothe and cleanse my napalmed palate.

In between the presentations and the feasting, there was dancing. A lot of dancing. Dancing is integral to Cameroonian culture. You tell stories through dancing; you celebrate through dancing—dancing is a part of life. Sometimes during these displays, our group was simply onlookers. Sometimes we were participants. And almost every time, Quinn was pulled into the fray, much to his introverted dismay.

As the only child on the trip and the only American child some of our hosts had ever seen outside of television or print media, Quinn was a novelty they simply could not resist. He tried his best to hang back and stand behind me, but then he would discover he was too short to see what was going on, so he'd move forward. Sooner or later, an older woman or an exuberant young man would spot him and head his way. A beckoning hand extended, Quinn would flash a look of fear, pleading to me with his eyes, but there was nothing to be done except shrug slightly and give him a gentle nudge forward—refusing would have been insulting to our hosts.

Unfortunately for Quinn, he comes from parents who have little natural dancing ability—recall the earlier recount of the flash mob dance—therefore he would stand almost motionless when first pulled into the throng of gyrating bodies. But Quinn's hesitancy did not deter the villagers. They would take him by both hands and begin to sway, then they would clap as Quinn started his own version of the dance, stepping side to side, sometimes jutting a hip. As they cheered and sang, he'd shed a bit of his inhibition, eventually losing himself in the fun.

After each stop, when we climbed into our seats in the SUV and headed off to another place, Quinn would look at me and ask, "Do you think I'll have to dance again?"

"Most likely," I'd say. "But look at it this way, you are so different and unique to them. It's as if they are meeting our ambassador. You're on a goodwill mission for the United States!"

His eye roll said it all—he would continue with the dog and pony show, but he would remind me of his sacrifice on behalf of diplomacy later.

As we headed home at the end of the weekend, Quinn was full of chatter about all we had seen and done. He had thoroughly enjoyed himself. But, of course, when recounting our trip to John on the phone, Quinn's first highlight to share wasn't the food or the cool sights we saw, or even his dancing. No, rather, he began with ". . . and then the van was sliding down the hill toward us . . ."

chapter 13

Becoming Mrs. DATT

We had just arrived on the flight from Brussels, Quinn and I returning after summer break spent on the ranch, John returning from his attaché training. The embassy's airport expeditor met us as we approached immigration.

"Welcome home, sir, and congratulations," he said, bowing his head slightly.

John was embarrassed by the star treatment. He knew that returning to post as the SDO/DATT would change the way people treated him and had prepared for it—he just hadn't expected it to happen so soon. Smiling, he thanked the expeditor, then did his best to usher us toward our luggage and the waiting SUV.

Two days later, we moved into a new house.

With the SDO/DATT job came a house. The DATT residence was large and rather ostentatious, literally just down the hill from our beloved Bat House. More than 4,000 square feet, it spread over two stories and included a swimming pool. But the size and appearance served a purpose—it was designed for entertaining and entertain we would. A defense attaché is the military's version of a senior diplomat. Now, not only would John have his day-to-day work at the office and any necessary travel, but our after-hours life would be filled with representational entertaining as part of the diplomatic corps. Even though we had been involved in the diplomatic circuit during our first year in Yaoundé, we did not do entertaining ourselves. But John's new position took everything to a different level. There were even more receptions to attend along with the added requirement of hosting dinners, cocktail parties, etc.—all part of the job. The month after our return was a blur as we literally unpacked ourselves into the house and the role and tried to find our new normal.

And before I knew it, I found myself staring at a large tent in our driveway. Wide white and blue stripes, strung artfully with multicolored lights, it was beautiful and surreal at the same time. *Where's the rest of the circus?* I wondered.

Our official entertaining was about to begin; it was time for our first event.

John and I had only finished unpacking and decorating the representational area the night before. Our personal living space upstairs was a different story, still full of boxes. We would get to it later—but the official space was ready. We opted to showcase an eclectic mix of our lives—John with the navy, me with my ranching heritage. On two of the walls, we had hung paintings of submarines and famous warships. High above those, hanging from the second-floor railing, were flags—the naval jack with its Don't Tread On Me snake and a replica of Oliver Hazard Perry's Don't Give Up The Ship battle flag. On the opposite side of the room was my love letter to the world I came from: framed photos of my family's ranch hung alongside my own retired chinks, spurs, and wild rag, and next to those, one of my family's branding irons and a piece of old barn wood where the MN brand had been burned into it. We were pleased with how it turned out, which was lucky given that we had not moved to Cameroon with the expectation of having to put our house on show. We had sent most of our decorations and memorabilia into storage. We made do with the few items we had brought with us and a bulk of Ikea picture frames.

I had spent the afternoon before the event as I had much of the previous two weeks—in the kitchen with Esme. We had made the decision to keep Esme as our housekeeper when we moved to the DATT house, partially because we couldn't imagine life without her at that point and partly because she was a very quick study when it came to food. Having attended a few cooking classes prior to working for us, she could easily mimic anything I showed her. For example, devising the menu for that evening's event. We settled on finger food versions of American classics, like handheld pot pies, cheesy breadsticks with tomato dip, and apple pie bites. I would demonstrate how to make each item, then, before I knew it, she had cranked out dozens more exact replicas. The two of us were a force to be reckoned with when it came to catering.

As we were finishing the last batch of chocolate chip cookies, the always unreliable city power went out for what seemed like the hundredth time that day, causing our big diesel generator to roar to life once more. I walked outside to inspect the situation. I silently prayed that power would return before our guests arrived so they wouldn't be overcome by the generator's horrid smelling exhaust fumes and deafening noise.

Along with Esme, we had Paul, the newest member of our household staff. He had been the SDO/DATT's gardener/handyman/pool cleaner/house cleaner/bartender for the past twenty years. Because Paul was such a rockstar at his job with the previous DATTs, we knew we had to keep him, which also meant that, sadly, we had to let Denis go, although it wasn't a huge problem for him to find work within the community. But Paul, from the start, was amazing and immediately meshed with us. He had been busy stocking the bar with wines, beer, sodas, and water when I came back in from checking the generator, about which I was still grumbling. He just shook his head and laughed at our electrical predicament.

I took one last look around to make sure everything was in place and that I hadn't made any culinary faux pas. Heaven forbid I served the wrong thing to the wrong people because that would literally be a diplomatic nightmare. And, happy with what I saw, I left it all to be.

Esme announced that the local water supply had come back on. Much like the local power supply, running water was always an iffy thing. We had been without city water for three days, relying solely on the embassy's well and water truck to refill our large storage tank. We also had a sizable stash of bottled water, just in case. Water insecurity was just another part of life in Cameroon. While we had—rather embarrassingly—the safety net of the embassy for our backup supply, that wasn't the case for the locals. For them, if there was no city water then they just went without. Yes, I was pleased that the water was on again, but I also cursed the powers that be for allowing such issues to occur in the first place.

By that time, it was ninety minutes before the guests were due to arrive. Esme and Paul were changing, turning themselves out sharply in their white uniforms. I was about to go upstairs to get ready when I realized the compound had gone quiet. City power had come back on, and the generator had thankfully shut down. So aside from the humming of the air conditioner units, it was blissfully silent in the house. I made another plea to whatever gods were listening to allow the electricity to stay on until the event was over, then headed upstairs.

I still needed to get a shower and get dressed but caught sight of my hands and realized I hadn't cut or painted my nails like

I'd wanted to. Instead, they were horribly mangled after all the unpacking. I quickly grabbed my clippers and polish and sat down in our private upstairs living room where Quinn watched a show. It was the first time I had sat all day, so I found it hilarious and fitting that this was the moment when John arrived home—spotting me seemingly lounged in our comfortable chair, relaxing, and polishing my nails . . . if only I had had bonbons to eat.

After a quick shower, I styled my hair, slipped on my cocktail dress, and made sure that Quinn was ready for bed. There were still twenty-five minutes left before our appointed start time, and I thought, *Gee, maybe I can sit with Quinn for a bit before people get here,* but of course, the doorbell rang. John went downstairs to answer it, figuring it was just our guard wishing to ask a question, but no. "Honey," he called to me, "can you come down?" The first guest had arrived—unfashionably early for Cameroon. I let out a long sigh, kissed Quinn, and walked downstairs to begin the show.

While I may have agreed to become the dutiful DATT's spouse and had told John's bosses that I would be fine with high-level entertaining, nothing truly prepared me for hosting my first full-blown diplomatic event. The evening was a blur. Cheek kisses, handshakes, and hugs. The who's who of Yaoundé's military crowd were there, as well as other key diplomats and colleagues. I went from one conversation to the next, bouncing from English to French to English as I worked my way around the room. I caught bits and pieces of songs from the curated playlist that I had put together; it sounded wonderful over the hum of the voices. The whole evening was controlled chaos but beautiful.

Three hours after it began, the event was over. Esme and Paul had gone home. John and I were exhausted. My head hurt from the constant noise and the mental strain of switching languages all night. John's feet were tired from wearing his less than comfortable white uniform shoes. And both of us were starving. You rarely get to eat at your own events. So we grabbed a plate of leftovers and headed upstairs, crashing on the couch, me still in my dress but sans shoes, and settled in to watch mindless television. That was the reality of being "glamorous" diplomats. We looked at each other and laughed. Such was our life now, a far cry from where we both began.

As the months passed, if we weren't hosting an event, we were attending one, and I had become a well-known face on the diplomatic circuit. To not suffer from boredom or appear confused, I read up on John's work, studied the background, and familiarized myself with the key players. Being able to at least look like I knew what people were talking about, let alone ask informed questions, made all the difference in the world. My approach set me apart in a country where some men steadfastly adhered to outmoded chauvinistic ideas about women and their place in society. It also earned the respect of many of John's more forward-thinking contacts.

While I walked out of the embassy's main entrance one morning, I was saying goodbye to the embassy guards when I spotted the head of Cameroon's military cooperation office approaching the door. All of the guards visibly straightened. This colonel was a man they recognized and respected.

Spotting me, he smiled, "Madame Tully!"

"*Mon colonel*," I replied, extending my hand in greeting. I liked him. We had spent many an evening chatting, and he was a surprisingly good student of American history. Most importantly, though, he forgave my linguistic mistakes and happily helped me with my French.

Taking my hand in both of his, he leaned forward, touching his forehead to mine, a local greeting that showed great respect and was usually reserved for men. *"Mon ami, c'est un plaisir,"* he said, as he stood back up.

He explained that he was on his way in to see John. We made small talk for a few minutes until I bid him farewell and allowed him to continue on to his meeting. Once he was out of sight, the guards, having watched our exchange, smiled and laughed. "Oh," they said. "Look at you, Madame! You are important."

I blushed, waving my hand in dismissal. "No, not me; I am still just Julie." That got an even bigger laugh, and they clapped as I walked toward the parking lot.

Although I'd be lying if I didn't say that it gave me a certain sense of pride being accepted by the Cameroonians like that. When you are a stranger in a strange land, that type of acceptance is as close to belonging as you can get.

chapter 14

It's Not All Glitz and Glamour

Our tour in Cameroon was flying by, and we had hit the point where it was time to decide what was next. While some of our previous duty stations had felt right, Cameroon was the first where we felt like we truly belonged, like we were home. And although it was considered a hardship tour, it wasn't as bad as the term made it sound. So many of our friends had told us flat-out that we were crazy to go, that there was no way they would have done it, but we loved Cameroon. However, all good things must come to an end, and it was time to look toward our future.

Much like the evening in Germany four years before, we were enjoying our dinner when John broached the subject of his next job. Pausing between bites, he looked at Quinn and me and said, "The detailer sent me an email today, asking me where we wanted to go next."

Again, I was sitting there with a glass of wine, just like I had been the last time, but recalling that scene, I took a drink before asking what the email had said. As I opened my mouth to speak, Quinn loudly interjected, "I don't want to leave Cameroon!" He was so happy in Yaoundé, so content in his life even with the chaos that John's position brought, and he didn't want to give that up. My heart broke for him.

In general, our navy doesn't like to leave people outside of the United States too long; that's just not the way they operate and as Cameroon was our third overseas tour in a row, I imagined that the locations on that list of possibilities were all stateside. "What are our options?" I asked, knowing I probably wouldn't like the answer.

"Well, there are two," John started.

Two? Two?! What on earth was he talking about? Usually, the detailers gave you a list of half a dozen jobs or so that we could rank in order of preference. But two? That frightened me.

John sensed my confusion and quickly continued, "He said we can either go to Millington, Tennessee . . ." Unfortunately, he let his sentence trail off for a moment, which was one moment too long for me. I may have maintained the patience of a saint most of the time, but not when we were discussing something that important.

"Or?" I prodded him.

"Nigeria," he said.

"*Man . . .*" I whispered.

"I WANT TO GO TO NIGERIA!" Quinn shouted, interrupting me and startling John. "I don't want to move to Tennessee! I want to stay in Africa!"

You see, Nigeria had been a specter for a long time.

In 2008, not even a year after we had arrived in Stuttgart, John heard about a position in Nigeria and looked into it as a way of getting us onto the African continent. In our minds, getting onto the continent was the crux of his becoming a real Africa specialist. However, at that time, the navy thought it best to leave us in Germany. Fast forward to 2012, while John was at attaché school—the rumor started that the navy would be taking over the SDO/DATT position in Djibouti. Knowing that we would soon be looking at follow-on jobs from Cameroon, John asked if the Djibouti job would be a possibility. Always keen to keep their cards close to their chests, the navy detailing system told him it was only an idea at that point. He would more than likely be offered a job in Nigeria instead. So that had been the game—wanting Nigeria but then being told no. And then teased with Djibouti, only to be told that Nigeria was far more likely. Honestly, we didn't know what to think or where to hedge our bets with the latest offer.

During the time that we had been in Germany and Cameroon, Nigeria had had some issues—specifically regarding security. Not having a lot of experience on the continent, Nigeria hadn't seemed like a place I would want to live, let alone take our son to. However, I had not yet come to realize how at home I would feel in Africa. I had initially said no to Nigeria, hoping against hope that the job in Djibouti would magically come through. Although, as time passed and I had a more informed view of what our life would be like in Nigeria, I came to the conclusion that it might work just fine. So, when John asked us whether we wanted to move to Nigeria or Tennessee, the only thing I knew was that, just like Quinn, I wanted to stay in Africa. So, Nigeria it would have to be.

"I agree with Quinn," I said. "I would rather move to Nigeria. You're an Africa FAO, so we should stay on the continent if we can."

"Yeah!" Quinn was putting his all into his vote, stopping himself just short of banging a fist on the table.

"Besides," I continued, "I'm not ready to move back to the States yet."

I was pretty sure John thought that his little family had finally taken that fateful step over the ledge to insanity. But I also

knew that he didn't want the job in Tennessee either. Millington, Tennessee is the administrative home of the navy—yes, a
very long way from the sea, but it was even farther from Africa.
While that job of community manager for the navy's foreign
area officer program would have been a good career move, John
didn't feel the time was right for him to physically step away
from the continent. He was meant to know Africa like the back
of his hand, and the job in Tennessee wasn't going to provide
that knowledge. Nigeria would be different, he would be the
liaison to the Economic Community of West African States
(ECOWAS), which was not the same as the SDO/DATT position he currently filled. Nonetheless it was a job that would
provide the breadth of experience throughout West Africa he
would need as he continued in his career.

"Really? Both of you?" John asked. "You're sure you want
to live in Nigeria? It will be a lot different than here. And Tennessee would definitely be easier." He was right, Nigeria would
mean a more restricted life. Kidnappings and the increased
presence of terrorists had changed the country's atmosphere
and, in turn, the lives of diplomats and other internationals that
lived there. But somehow, those restrictions didn't seem as scary
as they once had. Plus, we had adapted to the rhythms of life in
Sub-Saharan Africa—the United States, on the other hand, was
a different story after nearly a decade away.

"No," I corrected him. "Tennessee wouldn't be easier. It
would be harder. We have been away from the States for so long,
a place like Millington would be more of a culture shock for us
than Abuja."

"Exactly!" Quinn was keen to keep his say in the matter going.

"Okay, okay," John smiled. "I will email the detailer tomorrow. Just know, there's a pretty good chance that it will be a done

deal when I do that. Abuja's a bit of a hard-to-fill position. Most sane people don't want to move there."

"We're not most sane people," I smiled back. But the grin on Quinn's face was bigger than both of our smiles combined.

Our orders to Nigeria were cut in December 2012, and I started another one of my war books as soon as they arrived. In bold, black letters I wrote CAMEROON TO NIGERIA, then began the process of writing out the questions that would have to be answered, the random thoughts I had, and all things that needed to be done.

At the same time, I started a list of what I would miss about Cameroon in my journal:

- PEANUTS
- MANGOES
- AVOCADOES
- NDOLE'

Even though I knew I would still be able to find similar things in Nigeria, I felt a sadness knowing that I would be leaving certain things behind in Cameroon. Unlike living in England, Germany, and different locations in the States, I knew that leaving Cameroon would be final, that I'd probably never get to go back. And, of course, there was much more I would miss beyond the food. I would miss the simple beauty of the tropical climate in which we lived, where flowers like Birds of Paradise and poinsettias bloomed constantly. I would miss the sounds, especially the thumping Afro-Pop that blared from the open windows of taxis. And I would miss the people. I couldn't even begin to think about that. Never before had I experienced such a feeling of loss, and frankly, I didn't like it.

With time flying by, I also made a list of the things— a Mrs. DATT bucket list—that I still hoped to experience in Cameroon.

At the top of that list was attending the Cameroonian National Day reception at Unity Palace.

As John hadn't become SDO/DATT until after their national day in 2012, the 2013 invitation would be our first and only chance to attend the country's diplomatic event of the year. Going to that reception at the presidential palace was the equivalent of being invited to the White House for the Fourth of July.

"Oliver will pick us up at 5 p.m.," John told me over the phone. He was on his way home from the official national day parade. It was already 3 p.m., and he needed to get a shower and change before we headed out again. Even though we lived less than fifteen minutes away from the palace, Oliver, John's driver, recommended we leave at least ninety minutes early because of the traffic we'd hit getting there.

He hadn't exaggerated.

The line of parked cars began just after we turned onto the palace road. It was still almost a mile to the drop-off point, but people walked toward it in the humid, sticky heat of the evening—men in suits, women in dresses and heels.

Noticing my concerned look in the rearview mirror, Oliver said, "Don't worry, madame, you don't have to walk that far. You have a special ticket. I will be dropping you right at the door."

My feet, in a pair of very delicate, strappy heels, thanked him.

However, what I didn't expect was that "dropping us at the door" actually meant dropping us at the start of a red carpet laid out on top of the sidewalk leading to the palace doors. VIP guests—and yes, that included us—entered the reception via the red carpet under the bright lights of the nation's television cameras and shouts of eager reporters. Never had I felt more like a fish out of water as I did when we approached the entrance. I could only imagine that was what it felt like to arrive at the Oscars. *Why, yes, this dress was designed by J. Crew,* I snickered to myself. *And my husband is wearing a classic white choker jacket from U.S. Navy,* my imaginary red carpet interview playing as an internal monologue as we walked.

Passing through the main doors, we were announced to those already gathered, just like you see in the movies. I did my best to smile, trying to find a happy medium between demure and psycho. And while it may have appeared to others like I had my arm casually draped through John's, in actuality, it was more of a death grip.

We were immediately ushered to a dramatic balcony with an open staircase that branched off both sides, leading down to a large ballroom where the VIP guests gathered. In all, over 10,000 people were invited. Those not on the VIP list were kept outside under large tents.

Still an hour ahead of start time, the place was already full, and yet people kept pouring in. We were packed like sardines. It was stiflingly hot. I did my best to stay cool since I had a history of fainting when overheated. I grabbed the hand fan I had tucked into my evening bag and waved air on John and me. Every time another guest was announced, pressing their way into the throng, I cringed.

It also didn't help that we were starving. Unlike other events where the hors d'ouevres began flowing shortly after guests arrived, the palace had decided that no food or drink would be served until after the president and first lady had made their grand entrance. So, it was literally wall-to-wall people and there was no food in sight. I wondered what would be the root cause of my passing out—heat exhaustion or hunger.

I had just turned to face John so that I didn't have to press my chest into a stranger when someone pinched my bottom.

Not an accidental brush or inadvertent touch, an actual groping. Had I been wearing my boots, I would've "accidentally" stomped on their foot.

I was a fraction of a second from whipping around and confronting whoever it was that grabbed me when John, who didn't yet know what had happened, said to me, "That's one of my contacts from the Ministry of Defense."

Still reeling, I stopped and said, "What?"

"Right behind you, that's one of my contacts." He nodded and said to the contact, "*Bon soir.*" Then he introduced me. "*Ca c'est ma femme,* Julie."

Realizing the man he was talking to and the person who pinched me were one and the same, I was shocked to turn around and see a short man whose head barely reached my shoulders. "*Bon soir, monsieur,*" I said, through gritted teeth and resisting the urge to slap his face. He curtly returned our greeting then quickly squeezed through crowd off toward someone else.

"John, he *pinched* me!" I leaned in and whispered once he was out of earshot.

"What?!"

"You heard me," I hissed. "He *pinched my ass.*" In the absurdity of it all, I didn't know if I wanted to scream or laugh.

John was clearly mortified. "I am so sorry," he said, putting a hand on my arm. Honestly, there wasn't anything either of us could do that wouldn't have caused a scene. "Well, I guess it's a good thing you didn't throw a punch before I introduced you." I let a growl rumble behind my diplomatic smile.

And then, as if the heavens knew I was on the brink of losing it, the bartenders took pity and began serving champagne.

After what had just happened, I gladly grabbed a glass off the passing tray and downed it, mumbling to John yet again about the things I did for Uncle Sam.

Finally, an hour and a half late, Paul and Chantal Biya made their grand entrance. We spotted them briefly before they descended the stairs, then lost sight as they worked their way through the guests far from where we were. I only knew they were there by tracking Mrs. Biya's hair which towered above the crowd. Her trademark bright copper wig looked like a lion's mane and added at least half a foot to her height. Sadly, watching her hair pass through the people was as close as we got before they moved outside to greet the guests under the tents. And that was it—the official part of the event was over. Hot, tired, and hungry, John called Oliver and asked him to come pick us up.

Expecting to slip quietly out the door and into the car, we bowed our heads and began to retrace our entrance on the red carpet.

FLASH!

We were temporarily blinded. I only knew it was a camera in our face by the sound of its clicking. *Awesome,* I thought, *I must look fabulous by now, after sweating for hours.* We didn't stop; we just kept making our way out to where Oliver waited.

Two days later, as John and I walked into the main entrance of the embassy, one of the guards came up to John with a folder. "Sir, this was dropped off for you this morning."

Inside was an 8x10 photo—the one snapped of us as we departed the palace, and boy, was it a doozy. My hair was flat and lifeless, my face flushed from the heat. John had put his white combination cap on so quickly that he hadn't realized that it was actually sitting at a laughably jaunty angle. We were caught mid-step on an uneven part of the grass, giving us the appearance of a pair of drunks stumbling home from a wild night out.

"It's a great photo," the guard said in all seriousness.

"*Um*, thanks," John said.

We waited until we were behind John's office door before we busted out laughing. Some bucket list event that turned out to be.

chapter 15

The Gems You Find

"*Bonsoir, mon ami!*"

"*Bonsoir,* Jean Paul!" I beamed, kissing the delightful man on both cheeks.

Oh, how I loved seeing Jean Paul. He was my favorite. But, oh, how I hated that night. It was John's farewell reception, and I knew it would probably be the last time I would get to see my friend. But to tell the story forward, I must begin backward when I first met Jean Paul, the year before.

It had been the evening of our first event, the one with the tent in our driveway when the job was new, and life felt like a circus. As we had lived in Cameroon for a while at that point, I already knew most of the attendees and recognized them as they walked in the door, which made it much easier to say my hellos and then direct them toward either another appropriate conversation partner or the bar. But then, in walked someone unfamiliar.

John guided me over to our new guest and said, "Jean Paul, *permettez-moi de vous presenter ma femme,* Julie."

"*Enchanté, madame,*" he said, taking my hand and bowing slightly. "*Merci pour l'invitation.*"

"Jean Paul *est mon nouveau collègue de la Répulique Centreafricaine,*" John continued, then catching sight of another arrival, he excused himself to go play host, and left me with my new acquaintance.

I smiled at Jean Paul. I found myself hoping that he at least spoke some English, as his Central Africa Republic French was heavily accented, but unfortunately, he did not speak English at all. Mustering all of my brain power, I continued on in French, doing my best to make small talk.

Jean Paul was a very pleasant, older man with deep-set wrinkles that became even more pronounced when he smiled, which he did often. His hair was graying, and his eyes gave the appearance of someone whose age went far deeper than a number. He was jovial and downright sweet.

Once I had exhausted my cache of French cocktail conversation, I hoped that Jean Paul would realize that and accept my subtle nudge toward the bar, but he didn't. Despite the fact that he spoke no English, he wanted to continue talking to me, so we did, even though at multiple points neither one of us could comprehend what the other was saying. But his easy presence made me like him, and I found myself not caring if all we did was smile in uncomprehending companionship. When John finally returned to my side with another guest, I was able to excuse myself and make the rounds, but not before Jean Paul enthusiastically expressed his delight in my kindness. That first meeting with him left a strong impression on me.

In the months that followed, John and I thought more and more about Jean Paul and his homeland. Things were changing rapidly in the Central African Republic—its political stability was crumbling. At the end of December 2012, both John and I were involved with the evacuation of our embassy in Bangui, processing official Americans through Yaoundé. After that, things became grimmer every day, and then in the early part of 2013, the president of the Central African Republic and most of his government fled to neighboring Cameroon. Yet, throughout it all, despite the grave misfortunes of his country and its people, we would still see Jean Paul at all the diplomatic events. He was ever-smiling and polite, fulfilling his duties, yet looking progressively older with each passing day.

In the spring of 2013, John had invited Jean Paul to a lunch at our house. On such occasions, when we were just hosting one or two people, I would send Esme out for a long break and then take care of the cooking and serving myself. For Jean Paul's lunch in particular, John and I found ourselves being quite sensitive to what he must have been going through at the time. We wanted to make sure that it was just a simple, relaxing meal, something to take his mind off the troubles surrounding him.

When Jean Paul arrived at our house, I went out with John to greet him. He stood there, smiling as always, that wonderful smile and wearing the only suit I had ever seen him in aside from his uniform. It was a brown pinstripe that was obviously inexpensive yet spotlessly clean and impeccably pressed, and a pair of white leather dress shoes. I couldn't help but think of his relative poverty and wondered, given the fall of his government, what his financial situation might have been—a thought that caught in my throat as he handed me a beautiful, large watermelon. He would not accept a lunch from us without at least showing his appreciation. It reminded me of when I was growing up and we would visit other ranchers or farmers, always taking a gift with us, like a big bag of walnuts from our trees or extra vegetables from the garden. Simple gifts, but always appreciated, just like I appreciated Jean Paul's watermelon. I kissed his cheeks and told him that his gift was perfect, which it was.

While I am no Julia Child, I am a fairly decent cook and therefore put my full effort into that day's lunch: a chicken cutlet with cranberry coulis and imperial black rice, followed by homemade mango sorbet and buttery shortbread. For my effort, Jean Paul rewarded me with praise. After each course, I received a huge smile accompanied by a *"C'était très manifique!"* His only criticism was that there wasn't more of everything. He was a gem.

You can understand why I found myself looking forward to seeing Jean Paul at every event.

But now, at our final event as attaché, I was faced with the fact that our time together was almost over and it was heartbreaking.

Chatting with Jean Paul and our embassy's deputy chief of mission, Quinn came by for a quick greeting and then continued through the crowd. Since it was our last hurrah, Quinn had been allowed to join the party, and he was being quite the little gentleman. Jean Paul got a kick out of him.

"How many children do you have?" he asked me. Oddly, it was the first time we'd had this conversation.

"Oh, just the one," I replied.

"And you," he turned to our deputy. "How many do you have?"

"None, sir."

Jean Paul was visibly surprised. "Really?" He studied us both for a moment. "Your country, you have so few children in your families."

"True," I said. "But trust me, that boy of mine keeps me busy."

He gave a hearty laugh, then said, "Me, I have twelve." I should note that the entire conversation was still in French. However, it was at that point that his thick accent got the best of us—even our deputy chief of mission, who spoke fluent French—because both of us thought he said *deux* (two) which can be similar in sound to *douze* (twelve).

"Two," our deputy replied. "That's a good number."

That garnered another loud, hearty laugh. "No," Jean Paul corrected. "Not two . . . twelve. I have twelve sons," he said. Then added proudly, "Plus, thirteen daughters."

"Twenty-five," I mouthed barely above a whisper, in shock.

Our deputy chief of mission stopped cold. "Wait. You have twenty-five children?"

"Why, yes, I do," Jean Paul said as if it were the most common of things to have a couple dozen children. He told us about them all, clearly a proud father. When he eventually walked away to talk to someone else, the deputy and I fell into a fit of laughter. Jean Paul never failed to surprise me. Perhaps those sweet old eyes had more of a twinkle in them than I previously thought. Maybe I should have asked him how many wives he had—more than one I would guess—but I had been so shocked by the number twenty-five that I couldn't ask the question.

What a guy. I would never forget him.

The last of our guests left at 10:30 p.m. that night. I sat on the couch in the representational living room, legs stretched out with my cowboy boots propped up on the coffee table. I was having a glass of champagne and tallying the bar numbers in my notebook as Paul counted out the empty bottles. Quinn was still spinning with adrenaline—opposed to our fatigue—so we told him he could watch a movie in bed. He popped in a copy of *The Avengers* while we staggered to our room.

The next morning our alarm went off at 5:45. I begged John to get up first so that I could have fifteen more minutes of sleep. When he finally dragged himself awake at six, I smiled because of my bonus Zs. Waking Quinn up for school at 6:30 was a different story—he was regretting his late-night movie viewing.

Both of my boys were out the door by 7:20 a.m. Closing the door behind them, I headed into the kitchen for some much-needed coffee, a quick breakfast, and a little quiet time to collect my thoughts. We were hosting a lunch for thirty that day, so I had asked Esme to stop for supplies on the way in; she wouldn't arrive until almost nine. I had the house to myself, or so I thought.

A few minutes after eight, the doorbell rang. It was the warehouse staff from the embassy there to do an inventory of our embassy furniture prior to our move, which had completely slipped my mind. I apologized profusely, telling them they could conduct the inventory on their own and to yell if they had any questions; then I returned to the kitchen and began prepping the food for lunch.

Paul arrived promptly at ten and immediately set about rearranging the furniture from the previous night's layout to the one we needed for that day. Esme had arrived and was in the kitchen cleaning the last of the plates and glasses from the night before, so I took that opportunity to run upstairs and get my shower.

John called at 11:15 a.m. to confirm that the group would be on time for lunch, so Esme and I began plating the food and placing it on the table. Paul filled the ice bucket and got ready to man the bar.

At 11:30 a.m., I smoothed my blouse and linen trousers, pulled my freshly painted lips into a smile, and opened the door, playing Hostess with the Mostest to our guests as they arrived—a mix of visiting American military personnel and Cameroonian military representatives. While my French could have been better that day, it was certainly good enough to get through the lunch.

When John and the last guests drove away, I thanked Esme and Paul profusely for their work, grabbed my purse and keys, and took off out the door to Quinn's school. It was his end of the year ceremony—yet another event that John couldn't attend, a fact both he and Quinn were a bit depressed about. I was an acceptable substitute, but it's not the same when you're only one half of the parental unit.

While driving to school on the other side of town, I passed a man walking on the sidewalk wearing nothing but a loincloth with a piece of duct tape covering his mouth. It surprised me less than it should have. After two and a half years, Cameroon and all of its quirks had become commonplace.

Awards received, and farewells said, Quinn and I got home at four o'clock. He grabbed a snack and settled in to watch *Doctor Who* while I took a much-needed nap on the chair next to him, a set of chilled cucumber-infused eye pads placed over my closed lids.

John arrived home just before six as I was reapplying my makeup and stepping into a cocktail gown. We were leaving for the Russian National Day reception in half an hour. My eyes were still puffy despite those silly eye pads. I certainly did not look as refreshed as they had claimed I would—but I suppose there was only so much you could do to erase the signs of no sleep.

An hour into the Russian event and my feet were killing me. I had purposely worn my most comfortable evening shoes but the flagstone patio at their embassy was unforgiving. Somehow, despite the pain, I maintained the smile on my face, although a few minutes later, John took pity and called Oliver to come and pick us up. We were both exhausted—it was our sixth event in six days—and once again, we were starving. I had been so excited at the thought of decent caviar that night—assuming that they would serve the best version of their country's delicacy—but frankly, the caviar had been better at the British High Commission the week before. At the same time, the irony of my privileged position was not lost on me. I was disappointed by the quality of the caviar. Yet just outside the embassy's walls, there were people struggling to survive, living on less than a dollar a day—that knowledge haunted me constantly as we performed our duties.

We still had one more stop to make, visiting with the American military personnel that had been at our house earlier that day. They were having dinner just down the road from where we were.

As we were climbing into the car, my phone buzzed. A text from a new friend I had met at the aforementioned British event. She was the owner of an Indian restaurant John frequented on business trips in Douala. When we met, I told her how much I regretted that I had never been able to try her food. The text on my phone said that she was in Yaoundé and that if I wanted, I could stop by the Hilton and pick up a sample of food she had brought for me. I smiled at John and showed him the text. He informed Oliver that we would now make a quick stop to see the Americans before continuing downtown to pick up our Indian treat.

To our amazement, what my new friend called a "sample" of food was no sample at all but a full-blown meal, complete with samosas, two types of curry, and naan. Chatting for a few minutes and profusely thanking her for her thoughtfulness and generosity, we finally made our way home.

Back in our living room at 11:30 p.m., wiping our plates with pieces of the naan to get every last bite, John and I began slipping into a food coma. It was the first solid food I had had since breakfast. Finishing up an episode of *The Americans*, we looked at each other and laughed. The irony of watching a show about Russian deep-cover spies right after being guests of the local Russian diplomatic corps for the evening was just too much—we were stuck in a fit of giggles for several minutes. Down the hall, we also heard Quinn laughing. He was tucked into his bed, enjoying another late-night movie marathon. Sure, he should've been asleep, but we didn't care—he only had two days of school left.

Falling into bed at midnight, we knew we wouldn't get enough sleep. The next day was our embassy's Fourth of July event; it would be yet another long night. But we had to power through, it was less than two weeks before we would be leaving Cameroon for good.

chapter 16

One Last Hurrah

"Those look good with that dress." John was referring to the cowboy boots I had just pulled on, the ones that had been my birthday present from him and Quinn that year—buttery brown leather with tan stitching. He was right; they certainly complimented the long brown maxi I had chosen for the evening. I was every inch an elegant, glamorous cowgirl.

"Thanks," I said with a smile and a twirl. "Want to know the best part? They are so comfortable!" After the pain I put my feet through the night before at the Russian event, I was thrilled to be wearing something less torturous.

"Shall we go," he said, offering me his arm, looking every bit like an officer and a gentleman in his crisp choker whites.

"Absolutely," I smiled. "Our last hurrah."

The cowboy boots had been a direct request from our ambassador, which he asked of me as we walked through final plans for that year's Fourth of July reception. It was the third and last for us in Cameroon but held special significance because it was the only time John would attend as the SDO/DATT. We were giddy with excitement—it was the culmination of our time in the country, our swan song. We would start the evening as part of the receiving line—the ambassador and his wife, the deputy chief of mission and us—officially greeting the guests on behalf of the United States of America. My boots had been requested because the ambassador wanted no guest to doubt where they were. For the receiving line, we would be standing in front of a 20-foot by 30-foot American flag, which combined with John's uniform and my cowboy boots, there would be no confusion. As the night began and friends and colleagues made their way through the receiving line, we did our duty, shaking hands, and kissing cheeks. John was complimented on the dashing form he cut in his uniform. I was applauded for my choice of footwear. We were sparkling.

And then our friend, the Cameroonian colonel, the one in charge of military cooperation, came through. He started down the line, shaking hands and wishing us a *"Bonne fête."* He grasped John's hand in a firm grip, *"Mon colonel."* Then turned to me, the last in line, took my hand, and leaned forward, touching his forehead to mine, the same way he had done that day in front of the guards. *"Mon ami, mon amiral,"* he said. I had to fight back tears. I would miss him. I would miss Cameroon.

The embassy grounds were so beautiful that night, lush and green. The air was fresh from recent rains but rich with the scent of the grass and trees. Lights strung above the lawns cast a warm, golden light over everything. John and I wove our way through the crowd, never covering too much distance at any one time because people would stop us to chat or take the opportunity to bid us goodbye. We smiled and smiled—the expression never fading from our faces—our cheeks hurt, but we didn't dare not show the happiness we had felt for having had such an opportunity.

"Where are you heading next? Nigeria? Ah, see, you've become one of us, you are African now!" That statement was made over and over throughout the night.

When we finally got the opportunity to pause for a moment at an empty cocktail table, we relaxed our bodies and took a breath. We were sipping water when we saw John's assistant approaching with a tall, older Cameroonian man at her side.

"Sir," she said. "This gentleman would like to meet you. He was an Olympian for Cameroon and wants to meet as many Americans as possible tonight, but especially those in the wonderful uniforms, as he put it."

Upon closer inspection, the man was older than I thought, with deep lines in his chiseled face. He was tall, dwarfing me despite the heels on my boots. He wore a suit and tie and had a miniature medal pinned to his jacket lapel.

"*Bonsoir, bonsoir,*" he said to us, shaking John's hand heartily. He said that he had been an Olympic athlete in his youth, a great honor for him. He told us that he had always wanted to go to America; he loved America, only had never had the chance. But that night, as an invited guest of our embassy—his first invitation from us ever—well, he was just thrilled to be there. He kept complimenting John on his uniform and me for accompanying my husband to Cameroon for the job. He was just so genuinely happy. We let him talk as long as he wanted. Then after taking a picture with us, he thanked us and left.

"That was the highlight of my night," John said.

"Mine, too," I replied. That man was just one reason we had loved our time in Cameroon. Another beautiful moment where humanity shone brightly. A fitting end to our time there.

chapter 17

Adieu, Cameroon

"Goal!" Quinn nearly shouted. We had to remind him to keep his voice down, not wanting to disturb the other guests at the restaurant.

The evening was warm but not too muggy. We decided to have dinner at La Salsa, an old converted house that was our favorite restaurant in Yaoundé. Its verandah was our favorite place to sit because Quinn could see the television that hung over the bar from there. It was always tuned to a soccer match, much to the delight of his little heart. And I could look out over the garden, lit with lights, giving one the feeling that you were deep in the jungle and far away from the bustle of the city.

The waiter had just sat down a plate of mashed avocados drizzled with olive oil and sprinkled with salt and pepper. We each took a piece of baguette from the basket on the table and dipped it in.

"I'll miss this place," I said to John. "I hope we find a place we love as much in Abuja."

"Don't worry," he said. "I am sure we will find something."

I had purposely told Esme and Paul that their last day of work would be the day before we left. There was just no way I could have said goodbye to them and flown out the same day. It had been the right choice because as they changed into their street clothes to go home and came through the living room to say goodbye, I couldn't cope. John shook their hands. Quinn hugged them. But for me, I hugged them, and then I cried. Esme said, "You are my sister." A comment that made me happy and destroyed me at the same time because I knew that I would most likely never see either one of them in person again. These people who had been so good to us, worked so hard and gave so much of themselves—they were part of our family, and we were leaving them behind. It stung.

The following day, our last, I waited until just before we were scheduled to leave to go say goodbye to Alex, our gentle guard. He had watched over us from the beginning, always with a smiling face, even when times were tough. I had put together a box of food from our pantry that we had not been able to finish and threw in some clothes for his new baby boy. On top I placed an envelope, a little bonus to say thanks. Since he was an employee of the embassy, we didn't pay him directly, but I couldn't stop myself from giving him something, because to us he had earned every penny. Alex took the box without looking at the contents, thanked me, shook my hand, and then I walked away.

Moments later, the doorbell rang. There was Alex with tears in his eyes.

"Madame," he choked on the words, "thank you. Thank you so much." It wasn't that much, just a token of our appreciation.

"No, we thank you, Alex."

He stood up straighter and smiled that familiar smile, "God will always watch over you." Then he walked back down to the guard house. I cried and cried.

Just after 6 p.m., one of the guys from John's office arrived. He had offered to drive us to the airport, having insisted, saying it just wasn't right for us to take motorpool on our last trip.

I was a knotted ball of stress and emotion as we loaded the luggage into the back of the SUV, but when I opened the door to get in, I let out a bark of laughter. In the cup holder was an ice-cold, canned mojito—next to it was a sippy cup of bourbon for John and a juice drink for Quinn. "This is just the best!" I laughed again, finally feeling the weight that I had been carrying on my shoulders start to slide away as I took a sip.

"Hey, it's the least I could do," he said. "You were an awesome Mrs. DATT. I had to send you off in style."

It was the weirdest feeling, stepping onto that plane and knowing I would probably never return to Cameroon. It hurt—and not just for me, for all of us.

Endeavoring to keep the mood light, John said, "We just need to get out of here before they stop me for something."

We laughed. Then the plane, loaded and ready, pulled away from the jetway and began to taxi out to the runway.

And then it stopped. We held our breath.

"Ladies and gentlemen, this is your captain speaking," the pilot started. "We apologize, but we need to return to the terminal. We have an issue and will be met at the gate by the immigration police."

I looked at John—whose face was full of shock—and fell into a fit of giggles. Of course, we knew it wasn't about us, but the timing couldn't have been better.

After a quick return to the jetway and an even quicker exit of the offenders, we were once again taxing down the runway. We lifted off over the rainforest and said goodbye to Cameroon.

Somewhere over the Atlantic, I finally took out my notebook and began to write down my thoughts on leaving Cameroon. It was the middle of the night, John and Quinn were sound asleep, but my mind wouldn't shut down. I wrote and wrote.

It had been a couple of very long, very emotional days, and I realized that leaving Cameroon reminded me of when I left California. John and I had been married a year and a half, living in Silicon Valley while I worked in the Bay Area. He went to school in Monterey and then received orders to Connecticut. That was my first true taste of military life and moving—saying goodbye to my family, driving away from the ranch, knowing that I wasn't just leaving on a trip, that I was moving away, leaving California. It ripped my heart out. That's what it felt like leaving Cameroon.

But I had to remind myself, that as sad as I was, we weren't saying goodbye to Africa.

It was time to look forward to Nigeria.

PART THREE

NIGERIA

chapter 18

You are Welcome

"You move your bag!" The woman's rich, sing-song voice, melodic and commanding, carried her words throughout the plane's cabin.

We had just settled ourselves into our seats for the flight from Paris to Abuja. It had been six weeks since we departed Cameroon, having visited the States and our families in the interim. We had also fit in things like dental appointments and shopping for and shipping another couple thousand pounds of consumables. This was the ninth and final flight for our move to Nigeria, and the woman's sudden outburst jolted us—and everyone else on the plane—to attention.

"You move your bag!" she cried out again. We were just moments away from closing the door and pushing back from the gate, but that wasn't going to happen unless she sat down. Craning our necks to see, there she was yelling at another female passenger who it appeared had placed her bag in the wrong overhead bin—the wrong one being the bin directly above the offended woman's seat. The accused woman's face was a mask of indifference. She showed no intention of moving her belongings and simply stood there, her lips pursed in a smirk while the offended woman hurled more verbal abuse at her. "You move your bag! You move it back there! You are dead to me!" The rant continued on and on.

While the flight attendants gathered around the women, it was clear they had no intention of inserting themselves. In their chic French uniforms, scarves knotted just so, they practically rolled their eyes at the situation as if it was something they had seen too many times before. Other passengers in the immediate area began to make hissing sounds, a Nigerian display of displeasure. The women continued their grudge match.

Then in an instant, with no apparent resolution or explanation, the offended woman gave up. Even more odd, both women were now smiling at each other, and the passengers who had been hissing were laughing. It was so absurd, I found myself laughing out loud. Oh, how I'd missed the capricious nature of West Africans while we were on leave. Fury one moment, laughter the next.

With that minor drama over, the flight attendants finished preparations, closed the doors, and we were on our way to Nigeria.

Despite the fact that it was fewer than 500 miles from Yaoundé as the crow flies, I could almost immediately tell that Abuja was different. From the moment we arrived at the more modern airport—much less humidity and distinct lack of hustlers trying to "help" us with our luggage—there was no question that we were in a very different country.

Abuja, Nigeria, lies within the band of savanna and shrubland that separates the tropical rainforests of Sub-Saharan Africa from the arid Sahel. Out the window of the SUV, my first glimpses of Abuja's outskirts were vast stretches of flat land with no villages or people to be seen. Knowing that the airport wasn't too far from the city, I waited and watched for anything that would announce we had arrived in the nation's capital.

Slowly it formed—a small cluster of low-slung houses here, an industrial building there. Then, as if it had been waiting for us to be close enough to the center to fully appreciate it, we passed by the city gate. It was starkly white and soaring into the hazy sky, proclaiming the nation's universal greeting, "You Are Welcome," a large Nigerian flag stretched above it in its bold green and white. However, even with the national stadium to one side of us and a few large buildings to the other, I still had a hard time believing that this was the capital of the great behemoth of Africa.

Abuja had been a planned capital, built to replace the overcrowded Lagos in 1991. It had been picked for its centrality in the heart of the country, meant to place Nigeria's seat of government in a more neutral location. But unlike more established cities, Abuja exuded the feel of a city that had not grown into itself organically. As we skirted along its main streets, I saw its big, newish buildings and ambitious road systems, but to my eyes—however jet-lagged they may have been—it looked unfinished and thrown together. Over twenty years after it was born, the city appeared to be stuck in an awkward teenage phase. In a country known for its audaciousness and vibrancy, this was a disappointing first impression. However, I did smile when John pointed out a small herd of bedraggled cattle freely wandering and munching weeds along the side of the road.

That evening, settled in our temporary digs at the Transcorp Hilton, I gazed out over the cityscape, highlighted by the setting sun. I knew that I shouldn't compare it so harshly to what little I knew of West Africa at that point. I needed to let Abuja speak for itself—which it did as we ate dinner at the restaurant next to the pool. Biting into a stick of beef suya, the spices, which were beautifully exotic at first, lit my mouth on fire. It was as if both Abuja and Nigeria were getting even with my capriciousness, saying, "Don't judge a book by its cover; we have a lot to show you."

John laughed as I tried to temper the heat in my mouth with a big gulp of gin and tonic. "Nigeria will certainly be a different life for us."

I knew what he meant. In Nigeria, John was stepping into the role of military liaison to the Economic Community of West African States (ECOWAS). This job would technically make him both part of our embassy and part of the ECOWAS mission, eventually spending more than half of his time traveling amongst the union's fifteen member states. What it meant for us personally was that even though we would still be part of the diplomatic corps and involved in diplomatic activities, the position did not require us to entertain in-home. Our daily life in Abuja would be one lived a bit more out of the spotlight, a bit more normal.

After a few days at the hotel, we were given the green light to move into our new home in a small, multi-family embassy housing compound in the Maitama district of Abuja. We moved in just in time for John to start work and Quinn to start the fourth grade. Our mornings resembled the suburban dream, with me waving John off to work and then watching Quinn head out on the school bus—except that we lived within a walled compound, complete with razor wire. The school bus included an AK-47 armed guard to deter kidnappers and a police chase car to even further deter kidnappers. Otherwise, it could have been any middle-class life anywhere in the world.

I spent my first days unpacking the 200-plus boxes that held our belongings and playing the "now where will I put this" game. John and Quinn helped when they could and did bonus things like search out a pizza parlor and wine shop so that we could have our traditional Friday night pizza. At the same time, I tried to locate our kitchen items, some of which I eventually found in boxes that had been labeled by the movers as *jouets* (toys) or *salle de bains* (bathroom).

chapter 19

Charlie and Stella

Our lack of in-home entertaining responsibilities in Nigeria meant that we didn't really need to employ full-time staff to keep the place reception ready. I settled for hiring a part-time housekeeper and part-time gardener, which was more than necessary. However, just like in Cameroon, we still needed to be seen supporting locals, whether we needed the help or not. In order to not get under their feet, I spent a good portion of my time either in my office writing or at the compound's gym watching *The Great British Bake-Off* while pounding out miles on the treadmill.

But I couldn't fully justify not lifting a finger for housework, so I took sole responsibility for our laundry— a near-constant task thanks to Abuja's sweat-inducing temperatures and the fine layer of dust that seeped through cracks and overtook surfaces on any day it didn't rain. Our washer and dryer were located inconveniently in the garage, which was accessed by heading out the front door and down the breezeway connected to the garage's side entrance. It wasn't the easiest setup, but at the very least it meant the large appliances the embassy provided didn't take up room inside a house that clearly wasn't designed for our mega-sized American tendencies.

That being said, there was one, or rather two, obstacles that made access to the laundry room even more of a challenge—

their names were Charlie and Stella, a pair of giant African spurred tortoises that lived on our compound.

We had been told about the tortoises the day we moved in but had only seen them in passing and far from our house. Large and slow, they were exactly what one pictured when thinking of a tortoise. No one knew where they had come from—whether they were someone's pets abandoned during a move or simply someone's pets' abandoned offspring—but they had become the unofficial, seemingly innocuous, mascots of the compound.

However, you can imagine my surprise when I walked out our door, full laundry basket tucked under one arm, coming face to face, or rather foot to face with Charlie. Or was it Stella? I had a hard time telling them apart.

"Oh my god!" I gasped in shock the first time it happened, almost dropping the laundry. There, unmoving and parked dead center in front of the garage door, was one of the giant, shelled pair. "Charlie! Or Stella! Whichever you are, what on earth?!" I yelled as if they could understand me.

The thing was, moving a tortoise that size was not accomplished with just a brush of the foot or a gentle nudge with the door. No, if those beasts were content where they were, it was hard to get them to move. I sat the basket down and assessed my options: I could enter the garage through the main garage door, but it was broken and would probably end badly; I could just wait to do laundry until after my tortoise friend decided to leave, which really wasn't an option if I wanted clean clothes for Quinn to wear to school the next day; or I could move the tortoise myself.

Option three it was.

Tortoises will bite if you put your fingers in front of their mouth, as explained to us by parents of compound kids who had done so. I stared at Charlie or Stella for a moment. Then, not wanting to lose any digits, I very carefully kept my hands by its side to avoid giving it the temptation to snack on a pinky. I tried to lift and turn it, but *OH MY GOD*, I did not expect it to be so heavy! It was like trying to lift a small boulder. I knew if I wasn't careful, I would throw out my back. *Lift with your legs!* I yelled in my head.

"Oh, come on," I grunted, changing my grasp slightly, managing to rotate the beast 180 degrees so that at least it was facing the way out. "Come on!" I grunted again with a combined lifting and shoving motion that moved Charlie or Stella about two feet forward, giving me just enough clearance to open the door. Figuring they couldn't turn back around that fast, I quickly dashed into the garage, threw the laundry into the machine, and then ran back out and closed the door. The last thing I needed was a tortoise in the garage. And yes, I realize dashing was probably unnecessary; a moderate trot would've sufficed.

Over time I would learn that you could coax them along by offering carrots, their favorite treat, but even that was a slow process. Also, over time, with the help of Quinn, I learned that Charlie was the main culprit. Charlie and I had a love/hate relationship, especially when he started leaving me gifts of his poop to step over on my way out to wash clothes.

chapter 20

From the Village

When I finally had the majority of our boxes unpacked, it was time to make the house feel more like a home, so I called the embassy to arrange for someone to come and help me hang decorations. While we could do a few simple picture frames and such ourselves, the embassy frowned on us drilling holes into the walls DIY style. Instead, they offered a one-time service for one of their employees to come and do it for you to save on destruction and future repair costs.

That was when I met Edison.

"Why are you so friendly?" Edison was the affable Nigerian and lucky soul that had been directed to help me. Unfortunately for him, English was the official and dominant language of Nigeria, which made communication much easier for me. I didn't have to pause and think before speaking. I could just ramble on in my native tongue—albeit slightly adapted to account for differences in idioms and the Nigerian penchant for Pidgin. At that point, I had been happily following Edison around for the better part of an hour. I showed him where to hang items and then pestered him with questions about his homeland and my new country of residence. I laughed out loud when he stopped dead in his tracks and asked me about my sunny, yet inquisitive disposition.

"I don't know," I said. "I suppose I picked up the habit from my parents. They always chat with people from different places, different walks of life, asking them what their world is like." I told him that my grandparents had been the same way. "I just enjoy learning about the places I live and the people who live there. The world is too interesting not to."

Satisfied with my answer, he grinned. "You are very right." And then we continued with our work—or rather, he continued with his work, and I continued to follow him around.

His cell phone rang, and he answered. I couldn't help but eavesdrop. It was quite common for the embassy workers to take calls about other jobs they might have—most of them had some sideline gig—even while they were at their primary place of work. He began talking to someone about buying a very large quantity of yams. "Forgive me," he said when he ended the call. "It was my farm manager. I was instructing him to buy and plant five hundred heaps of yams," he explained. I smiled. There he was, a carpenter for the embassy who couldn't possibly be making that much money, yet he also had a farm and employed others to work for him. And now, unbeknownst to poor Edison, there was an agricultural connection between us. While well and truly piqued before, my interest was intensified, and I began asking him about his farm.

He told me that his small holding was his pride and joy. Located within the Federal Capitol Territory, it was about an hour's drive from Abuja proper. He said that his only crop was yams, that he had no interest in diversification. But I knew that a farm large enough to produce five hundred heaps of yams was big enough to generate a decent side revenue. A heap is the one-meter mound of earth where the yam is planted and when harvested, the quantity is measured by what is produced within each heap and called as such.

"Where do you sell your yams," I asked. "Near the farm? Or do you truck them to the fresh markets here in Abuja?" Seriously, I couldn't stop myself. The questions just poured out; the agriculturist and cowgirl in me were fascinated.

"Oh," he smiled, "I do not sell many. Perhaps 10,000 naira worth (about $24.) The rest I give away."

With that admission, I was now beyond fascinated. I was completely enthralled. "You give them away? To family?" I asked.

"Nah," he answered, "not just family. I give some to them, but I just give yams to whoever needs them. You know, people need food."

That shocked me. It went against the *mostly* accurate assumption that Nigerians were aggressive businesspeople, always looking out for themselves, always looking for a way to make an extra naira or two. A personality trait born out of a survival instinct, although many had gone beyond mere survival and ventured into full-blown corruption. But the point was, Nigerians rarely just gave things away.

"That is true," I told him. "And that's very noble of you to farm for the sake of others."

"Yes, but I just love farming. It shows I am from the village," he said with pride, touching his chest to emphasize. "That is important to me."

That was a sentiment I understood completely because I felt the same way about my ranching roots. I still embraced what little I could from my heritage because, with that same pride, I was from the country and the land was in my blood. In Nigeria, to say you're "from the village" meant the same thing. A certain pride accompanied that background, and with it a shared bond that transcended our cultures and languages. Upon telling Edison about my own tie to the land, our conversation became even more animated than before.

"Do you like to fish?" he asked with the excitement of a small child. "Most people that come from the village like to fish."

"I love to fish," I said. "My father taught me."

He flashed a big smile. "My father taught me too!" He exclaimed, laying down his drill to give me his full attention. "Do you know I once caught the biggest fish in my village?" And he told me the story of the day when his father, who was busy working, had asked Edison, then just a teenager, to go and fetch something for him up by the river. Upon reaching the water's edge, Edison's boyish instincts took over, and he decided to fish instead of completing his errand. To his surprise, he hooked a huge fish. He worked and struggled to bring it to the shore, discovering at last that what he had caught was actually a very large mud fish—similar to a catfish, especially in its unattractive appearance. No sooner did he finally haul it out of the water than his father appeared, having come to find out why his son hadn't returned. When his father saw the size of the fish—almost as tall as Edison, or so the story goes—he yelped with joy. His father was no longer concerned with the forgotten errand and ran off to tell others. "But that was many years ago, I was only sixteen at the time."

I was laughing, trying to discern whether his story had been just another "fish tale" or if it were true. In all honesty, it didn't matter because it was a good story. But I was left wondering exactly how old Edison was if the tale he told took place many years ago. To my eyes, he looked no older than his late twenties, perhaps thirty at most, but the age of men was difficult to determine in that part of Africa. Men tended to look young for a long time, whereas women, unfortunately, seemed to age faster.

"I am forty-three now," he said. "I have two grown children who are in university!" He went on to tell me about his children and their studies, the very epitome of a proud father. He fascinated me—a carpenter for the embassy who also maintained a farm and sent his children to university.

"Well," he said as he began to pack up. "I need my other drill to finish this job, but I don't have it with me and can't go get it today. I will come back soon." I walked him to the door. He extended his hand to shake mine. "I am happy to have met you. You are a good person, from the village, like me. I like talking to you because you want to talk to us," he smiled as he stepped outside. "I will see you soon."

As much as I just wanted to be done with our move-in, I found myself looking forward to Edison's return.

chapter 21

Driving Lessons

little over a month into our time in Nigeria we had
already had our share of ups and downs. We had had
mysterious, angry skin rashes—poor Quinn. Several
bouts of the usual upset stomachs as our bodies adjusted to
new water and the environment—poor all three of us. Our
house alarm had inexplicably gone off at two o'clock one night,
causing panic, racing hearts, and an impromptu test of our safe
haven. But we had also discovered the warmth of the Nigerian
people, with their friendly smiles and kind nature. We discovered places to eat and shop that would suit us well. And, at one
point, I looked out our window to see Santa Claus mowing my
lawn—well, not really, but the gardener was wearing a Santa
Claus hat . . . in 90 plus degree heat . . . in September.

One slight drawback though, was that we were car-less. Our
Jeep still hadn't arrived from Cameroon. Despite the fact that
Cameroon and Nigeria shared a border and had ports within a
day's sail of each other, our poor car was being shipped via the
embassy's transit system and therefore had to venture via sea
freight from Cameroon to Brussels, home to the State Department's regional distribution center, then back to Nigeria—and
that took months. So, with no car and no cost-effective rental
capability, my mobility was dependent on the generosity of
new friends and the embassy's motorpool. Although the friend

option was more fluid, I happened to enjoy motorpool because it gave me a chance to learn about my new home from a native—the embassy drivers being local nationals. Just like when Edison hung our décor, when the embassy drivers gave me a ride, I couldn't help but ask questions. Plus, it gave me an opportunity to learn the rules of the road from a seasoned veteran, a truly invaluable lesson in that part of Africa.

Stranded at the embassy one day with only two hours to get home before Quinn returned from school, I faced a transportation dilemma. Our friend, who had been schlepping me back and forth quite kindly, needed to stay at the embassy a bit longer, which would potentially put me home late for Quinn. Calling motorpool to see if they could give me a lift, I was told that on such short notice, it was possible so long as I didn't mind tagging along for a few other stops first. That was fine by me; a ride was a ride.

The black motorpool sedan pulled up to the front of the embassy where I was waiting . . . with three very large boxes of mail. A little bonus that I was sure caused the driver to cringe. But before I knew it, the driver—a short, slight man with a kind face—popped the trunk and hopped out of the car with a smile, politely helping me load my boxes. Then joined by another passenger—the original requestor—we set off into the city.

Driving in Abuja was not for the faint of heart. Quasi-established rules that weren't enforced meant that the only thing anyone cared about was their ability to get where they wanted to go, quite literally a case of every man for himself. On that particular day, the traffic was chaos. Cars sped past on both sides, horns blared, and pedestrians darted in front of us. Driving in Abuja was an assault on one's senses.

Dede, the motorpool driver, calmly navigated the relatively well-maintained motorway, chatting to the other passenger as he drove. A car darted in front of us and sounded its horn, a move that elicited no reaction from Dede. He just smiled and kept talking as if we were on a leisurely drive in the country with no one else around.

We took an off-ramp that dumped us into one of the busiest intersections in the city. A taxi—the notorious Kelly-green pseudocars they used in Nigeria—having picked up a fare just ahead of us, decided it was time to move into traffic. Despite the fact that we were most obviously right next to him, he began a left-hand turn toward us. Had we been in the United States, there would likely have been a general recognition of impending danger by the taxi. Perhaps he would've put on his brakes or honked his horn, and most likely a few choice words would have been uttered, but not in Abuja. From my backseat vantage point, I saw the face of the taxi driver. He showed no acknowledgment of our car—even though he was looking directly at us. It was as if we were invisible. And while he wasn't moving fast, he would certainly have hit us square in the front passenger door if he continued on that trajectory. However, Dede, who had noticed the taxi from the start, was trying to avoid him with the same calm, rational manner that he'd maintained the entire time. He did not cede way to the taxi; he just continued on his path for the right turn lane. But as the unweilding taxi's bright green hood came closer and closer to us, Dede had had enough. He lifted his left arm, placed his hand in the middle of the steering wheel, and put his full weight into the horn. His expression went from serene to agitated in an instant. "What?!" he exclaimed, looking the taxi driver squarely in the eyes. "What *is* your problem?!"

The taxi driver just stared blankly because any other expression would have admitted fault. With one fluid movement, Dede took one hand off the wheel, placed it behind his head, ran it up and over his hair until he came to his face, then mimicked pulling his face off and thrusting it to the floor. Anger sparked in his eyes. He had essentially just told the taxi driver that he was going to rip his face off.

The taxi jerked to a stop, and the offending driver looked at Dede with recognition of defeat. Dede continued into the turn lane, maintaining eye contact with the taxi driver a moment longer, and said, "Who does he think he is?" Then after making the turn, safely removed from the taxi's path, Dede returned to his former, happy self, all smiling face and pleasant chatter.

After dropping the other passenger off at his destination, Dede and I made our way across the city toward my house. Of course, I took that opportunity to ask Dede a few questions.

"How long have you worked for the embassy?"

"I've worked for you (the embassy) for eight years," he smiled proudly.

"Wow, eight years. That's a long time to be a driver. Don't you get tired of it? Of the hassle?" I asked, thinking of the altercation he just had with the taxi.

"No. This is a great opportunity for me," he grinned. "I've learned so much. I meet great people. I even get to travel. Once, they even sent me to be a driver in Iraq," he beamed. "This job is a great opportunity. I am lucky."

Just as sweetly as when he had picked me up, Dede helped me unload my mail, insisting on carrying the boxes to my front door. I thanked him, gave him a bottle of cold water for his troubles, and then waved goodbye until the next time.

As I shut the door, I made a mental note of that day's driving lesson: stay calm and enjoy the ride, but don't be afraid to threaten to rip someone's face off. I was pretty sure that would be a gesture I would use at some point in the future.

chapter 22

Reasons to be Thankful

As we began our life overseas in 2004, boarding a plane to England with an infant who refused to sleep for the duration of the eight-hour flight, the furthest thought from my mind was: *What on earth are we going to do about his education?* At that point, John and I figured we would move back stateside long before education became an issue. Of course, that didn't happen, and when Quinn began school while we were stationed in Germany, I found myself coming to terms with the same questions, fears, and expectations most parents have—*Will he be challenged? Will he get the right teacher? Will he fit in?* Yes, I was starting down the path of becoming a Tiger Mom—focusing on the minutia of the system to satisfy the bigger picture, falling prey to our cultural bias of trying to make sure everything was the best.

But that all changed when Quinn entered school in Cameroon and amplified when we moved to Abuja. As we prepared for our first Thanksgiving in Nigeria, yet another one celebrated overseas, I found myself thinking over and over again about the one thing I was particularly thankful for—Quinn's schooling, or perhaps more correctly, his rather quirky educational experience.

Quinn was in fourth grade that year, the age when kids really begin to notice the world around them and are still willing to share those observations with their parents. At the American International School of Abuja, much like his contemporaries in the States, Quinn had classes in reading, writing, math, science, social studies, physical education, music, art, technology, and library. However, unlike many of his contemporaries, he also had classes in French and Nigerian Studies. His formal education was the best we could hope for, but that wasn't the reason I found myself so thankful. No, I was thankful for the learning that occurred between the lessons and on the periphery of his school days.

I was thankful for his bus ride. Quinn's was not the big yellow school bus of my childhood but a rather posh white bus with curtains in the windows. During his daily commute, those windows gave him a view of the world he lived in. Quinn could tell you which sections of Abuja's roads were the craziest during commuting hours and at which intersections you could buy various items from hawkers, like books or energy drinks or cell phone chargers. He could tell you about the ads he saw on the billboards or scrawled in spray paint on cement walls. Plus, he had the added benefit of a driver that listened to one of the local talk radio stations. At dinner Quinn would regularly chat with John about the different presenters and the news skits they did, including their use of local slang and idioms. And I would be remiss if I didn't say I was thankful for the Nigerian police officer with the AK-47 who quite literally rode shotgun on the bus and for the police trail car that followed along behind—the aforementioned deterrents for the very real threat of kidnapping. Although Quinn never blinked an eye at the heavy security, it was all just part of the ride.

I was thankful for his school's bell ringers. In Nigeria, electricity was about as reliable as a habitual liar, so rather than use an electronic bell system to signal the end of classes, the school employed a few very nice gentlemen who sat at desks in the hallways with watches. When the end of a class or the end of the day came, these men got up and walked along outside the classrooms and rang old-fashioned brass handbells. As archaic as it seemed, the method actually made perfect sense. The kids who walked around with their cell phones and iPads thought nothing of the irony which the bells illustrated.

I was thankful for the school's non-traditional cafeteria. Since Quinn had never been a fan of school-provided lunches, it seemed rather an odd thing for me to be thankful for. Nevertheless, it made me smile. Myself, having grown up with a typical American school cafeteria of the time—tasteless, mass-produced food—I know I would have given anything for a cafeteria like the one at Quinn's school. With the multitude of cultures at the school, all with different dietary needs, a traditional cafeteria system would have been difficult to sustain. Instead, vendors from select local restaurants came into the school daily. You want Chinese cuisine? You got it. Lebanese? Sure. Nigerian? Of course. Even our favorite Indian restaurant sold food there. I kept telling Quinn that he should buy their samosas, which he adored when we went out to dinner, but he politely refused and continued to take his peanut butter and jelly sandwich. Nonetheless, I was still happy the option was there, just in case he changed his mind.

I was thankful for his physical education classes. Most days Quinn came home dripping with sweat—evidence that he had had physical education that day, in the afternoon and usually outside in Abuja's brutal heat. If that had been me at his age, I am sure I would've come up with some mysterious illness to be excused from participating, or more likely, just passed out, but the heat didn't seem to faze Quinn. Neither did the very crude dirt track they ran on that occasionally left some spectacular road rash on his knees. However, he didn't know PE as anything different and thought it was normal. It certainly helped him build character.

I was thankful for the uniqueness that surrounded him at school. Quinn's class covered a unit on family heritage, and I told him about doing that when I was his age. My class always ended up as a mix of British Islanders, Western Europeans, Scandinavians, and the occasional Native American or South American—a reality of where I grew up, where we were pretty much all mutts of the same type. That was not the case for Quinn. His class's origins spanned the globe—American, Nigerian, Lebanese, Israeli, British, Japanese, to name a few. He was surrounded by an incredible mix of humanity every day. That mini-United Nations was what comprised his friend-base.

I was thankful for his language lessons. Even though Quinn had been studying French since we arrived in Cameroon, he had been picking up bits and pieces of other languages, as one does when friends speak different languages. All of the kids in his class spoke English to some degree, but on the playground, when kids were being kids, native tongues were easier to use.

"Mom, do you know how to speak Hebrew?" Quinn asked me after getting off the bus one afternoon.

"Hebrew? No." I replied.

"But you have friends that speak Hebrew, right?"

"Yes, I do, but I don't speak the language."

"Oh," he said, giving me a slightly disappointed look, "because I learned the Hebrew alphabet from David today at lunch."

How funny, I thought, because the things I remember learning on the playground did not include foreign languages . . . unless you counted Pig Latin, which I never got the hang of.

On the days when I found myself drifting back to Tiger Mom tendencies—worrying about the micro issues of why the math homework seemed too easy or wondering why the social studies didn't include more information about our individual states— these fundamental bits of real-life education Quinn picked up on the fringes of his structured learning brought me back down to earth. There were moments of pure, unadulterated, beautiful wisdom not found in a textbook. For example, Quinn told me about a hand-clapping game that one of his friends taught him that resembled the one that he learned from a kid from a different country when we lived in Cameroon. This proved without a doubt that the world was smaller than we thought. Those were the moments when I was reminded that education wasn't always confined to a set curriculum.

His education also reminded me of my own situation. It brought to light the struggle I had with my identity, trying to fit into a mold only to realize that I was perfectly fine just being myself.

For those informal lessons, I was truly thankful.

chapter 23

Define Home

C hristmas was certainly different in Abuja. Despite being
far from cold or visibly different than any other time of
the year, Christmas was a season of celebration and
good cheer in that part of Nigeria, and the locals embraced it.

As stores erected over-the-top displays of holiday delight, the
rest of the city transformed itself in a way we hadn't experienced
in Cameroon. Apartment blocks and office buildings strung
lights in brilliant designs. With the brown, dying grass that accompanied December, even Millennium Park put up a large,
fake Christmas tree, visible to those passing along on Shehu
Shegari Way.

The city's street vendors got into the spirit, taking the opportunity to pander to those looking for holiday gift ideas on the
fly. Gangly, young men who danced in and amongst the traffic
slowdowns stepped up their usual sales game with seasonal fare
like Santa hats, fairy lights, and Christmas trees. The hawkers
that sold books? Well, they made sure they had a large selection
of well-known and highly sought-after titles that time of year—
whether or not they were the real editions or illegal reprints, one
could only guess. And, if you didn't smile at the sight of the guy
with the cowboy-style Santa hat balancing a two-foot, pre-lit
fake Christmas tree with one hand while weaving between cars,
then you were most certainly a Grinch.

But it also remained the time of year when we keenly felt our distance from home.

When we first moved overseas, we were only supposed to be gone eighteen months, and yet, we were still overseas in December 2013.

"Don't you miss home?" That was the question most often asked of us as we moved from one overseas assignment to another, and it was certainly the most difficult to answer. Did we miss home? Yes. And no. It was complicated. Nine years away in four countries other than our own. Where was home?

On that fateful, cold day in 2004, as we stood in the Providence airport waiting for our flight to London, John turned to me and said, "See honey, for our fifth anniversary, I am giving you an all-expenses-paid trip to England!" Yes, you see, that momentous move also happened to coincide with our wedding anniversary, and with every consecutive year spent overseas, John dusts off the joke, duly modified to, "See honey, I have given you an extended world tour for our anniversary!" Yes, I still laughed.

England. Germany. Cameroon. Nigeria. While none of those places were the United States, they had all been home to us. It was a very hard concept to explain to family and friends when they asked us about missing home or whether or not we ever got homesick. We understood what they meant and knew how they expected us to answer, but when they said "home," they meant America. And yes, we did miss America—we missed our family; we missed our friends; we missed the familiarity of our life there; we missed that version of home—but that home was only a notion. Home had evolved into something completely different and far more complex for us. Ours was not a temporary lifestyle, living outside of the United States had become a part of who we were.

There had been too many times to count when John and I found ourselves slapping aimlessly at a wall in our house like deranged lunatics, trying to hit a light switch that wasn't there. "Darn it!" we'd gripe, then laugh. "That was where the switch was in our first house in Cameroon!" Those were the tricks our memory played on us—somehow in our mind, for just the briefest of moments, we had been somewhere else, in some other home. There were mornings when I woke up and needed a moment to recognize where I was, mornings when I would think that I was in our home in Germany. Sometimes Cameroon. Sometimes my childhood bedroom. But every time, in reality, I was somewhere else. I would wake up missing home, but the home I missed could have been any place and not necessarily my country of birth.

There were also days when we missed the creature comforts of the United States. Certain restaurants. Certain stores. Yet, at the same time, there were occasions when we missed those creature comforts from England or Germany. When we couldn't access those things, we'd get frustrated. But usually, we would find something a bit similar wherever we were at the time and rejoice—one of those instances happening that first year in Nigeria.

"Let's go to Next," I suggested to John and Quinn one morning. Next was the new large and somewhat shiny store in Abuja. When Quinn asked what type of store it was, all I could think to say was that it was like a cross between Target and Costco, but with sky-high prices like 7-Eleven. I ended my description by telling him, "It's more like the stores we have back home."

"Define home." Quinn threw my choice of descriptor right back at me. He wasn't meaning to be funny or snarky; he just wanted clarification. What he wondered was if I was referring to England or Germany or Cameroon, because those were the homes he remembered. America, the United States, to him, was just a place where you went for vacation, where our extended family lived. It was not home, per se; it just happened to be his passport country. My use of the word home required further definition to make sense to him.

For Quinn, who left the United States at nine months old, bouncing from country to country was not a novelty; it was simply life. Home for him changed so often that it was more a state of mind rather than a physical location and had, as a result, become an abstract idea for John and me as well. Home took two forms: the physical and the emotional. Home was where our belongings were. Home was also our family and friends. Home was food. Home was a song. Home was a rainstorm. Home was a favorite vista. Home was becoming bigger and bigger the more we moved. Most of all, home was when and where we felt at ease . . . and at that particular moment, Nigeria was home.

Contrary to what some of our friends expected—that we would hate Nigeria, that I would pack up Quinn and myself and leave within the first three months of our time there, some even going so far as to make bets about it with John—I actually loved it. In fact, all three of us loved it. We were settled and happy. Yet, inevitably, homesickness struck because homesickness is a very real and normal thing.

That first November in Abuja, all three of us had been hit with a particularly acute case of homesickness for holidays spent in colder climates. So of course, that meant our Christmas decorations went up the day after Thanksgiving—a first for us. Still stuffed from turkey and pumpkin pie, we lit cinnamon-and-fir-scented candles, trying to block the smell of the Harmattan dust that seeped in from outside. We strung lights along the breezeway that flashed and glowed, a delight of red, blue, green, and yellow. We hung our stockings on the wall with care . . . because, well, we didn't have a chimney in Abuja.

Also, that weekend after Thanksgiving, we managed to score tickets to one of the most coveted expat events of the year: the annual German Christmas market at the Julius Berger Life Camp, the international yet still very German enclave supported by the Julius Berger engineering company. Every year the camp pulled together a feat worthy of their engineering skills—turning their housing compound into a proper German Christmas market, complete with crafts, music, and food. Being so homesick for our years spent in Stuttgart and its huge Weinacht's Markt, we jumped at the opportunity to experience the Nigerian version of it. And all I can say is that, well, it was a little different. Even though it was evening and the sun had gone down, we were soaked through with sweat, but that didn't stop us from stuffing our faces with grilled bratwurst. We purchased German-style Christmas décor with a Nigerian flare—like the lovely Christmas tree-shaped throw pillow made out of a piece of pale green Ankara fabric. We even attempted to brave the refrigerated shipping container, which served as the glühwein bar. We were transported to Germany for a brief moment, an evening that felt a lot like one of the homes we were missing.

As the festive season continued, we filled ourselves with holiday cheer, watched the obligatory Christmas movies, and ate our favorite holiday foods—no matter the cost of procuring them. Our bout of homesickness faded because our holiday season was merry and bright, and, most importantly, we felt like we were home again.

I know people will never stop asking us if we miss home, and we will never be able to give them a simple answer. Yes, we do miss home, and no, we don't. At that point in time, that Christmas, home was Nigeria. Yet, at the same time, a version of home was also 8,000 miles away, another 3,000 miles away, and yet another 800 miles away. Home was right where we sat. Home was just a memory that had no measurable distance. We missed home. And we also didn't miss it. We carried home with us always—that was the joy and the curse of our lifestyle—it was confusing and complicated because as Quinn said, "Define home."

That Christmas, our first in Nigeria, still ranks among our family's favorites.

chapter 24

Joy Ride

Almost seven months to the day after we left Cameroon, our Jeep finally arrived in Nigeria. It had been a ridiculously long wait, and I was more than ready to be a little more independent and not have to ask for rides. And, after my first drive in Abuja, all I can say is that I must have been a Nigerian taxi driver in a former life.

For me, the first drive in a new country has always been a nerve-wracking adventure. My heart pounds, my palms sweat, and I can literally feel my blood pressure rise. It was like I was sixteen again, getting ready to take the road test for my driver's license. But my first drive in Nigeria, even though I felt the butterflies multiply in my stomach as I grabbed the keys, was different. I realized that I was less nervous about this first drive than I had been on some of my other first drives, especially the ones in England and Germany—those still make me laugh. I remembered in England how John leaned into me as I put his side of the car closer and closer to a hedge, while trying to figure out how to center myself in the opposite lane that I was used to. Or in Germany, feeling the fear of breaking one of their driving laws, for which they had no fear of issuing tickets. Driving in Africa was a piece of cake compared to Europe or the United States, because the biggest thing you had to remember in Africa was to forget everything you'd been taught and just drive.

As I sat down in Cary—yes, our car had a name, it had been Betty, but Quinn changed it to Cary when we moved to Cameroon. She smelled clean; the scent of the lemon disinfecting wipes I'd used still lingered. The trip from Cameroon had taken so long and was so weather-stricken that her interior had developed a fine layer of mildew by the time she reached us. It took two days of scrubbing and airing out for her to be normal again.

I slid the key into the ignition, adjusted the mirrors, and thought, *Hello, old friend.* It was the same feeling I used to get when I sat down in my saddle after not riding for a while, the same familiar feel of the leather, the feeling of being with my trusted friend, but most of all, it was the feeling of freedom. Driving our car was as close as I got to that particular feeling anymore.

One, two, three . . . Her engine started without hesitation— no small victory considering the less than easy life our car had led and the fact it had essentially been sitting idle for seven months. All of the electrics and gauges worked. The air conditioning—an absolute must when you had to drive with your windows up for safety reasons—blasted cold air into the cab on a day that was rapidly approaching the century mark. Somehow it seemed that Cary was just as happy as I was to get out and go again. Strange to think that of a machine, but it was true. I made a quick swing around to the other side of the compound to pick up our neighbor. John and I had a rule of thumb to never make your first drive solo if you can help it, opting for a second set of eyes to help navigate. Co-pilot loaded, I was off and onto Abuja's roads.

Honestly, the roads in Abuja weren't all that bad. However, if you're picturing a driving experience similar to the United States or Europe, then you would be sorely mistaken. While the roadways in Nigeria were in decent condition, you needed to factor in the less than stellar local drivers or silly things like the absolutely bizarre manner the traffic flow had been designed. Thankfully, having spent half a year as a passenger, I had the advantage of observing the ins and outs of the roads before driving them. But just for fun, here is an account of what that first drive was like.

First, the fuel gauge was almost on empty—standard practice when shipping a car. I needed to get from where I lived at the northern point of the city to the embassy's fueling station at the southern point of the city on about an eighth of a tank of gas. There were many routes to get to the fueling station, but I opted for the ring road, Abuja's answer to an expressway. While getting onto the expressway's slip road was easy—despite the fact that I needed to dodge taxis, buses, and all the people trying to hail said taxis and buses—the real trick once I came to the merge with the ring road was that I had about a hundred yards in which to get my way across three lanes of traffic in order to make a U-turn to head south. Yes, you read that correctly, I said U-turn—there wasn't an overpass or an underpass, just a small opening in the center divider to make a U-turn in the middle of a very active expressway. The ring road U-turn was always interesting. The same space was used for U-turns out of both the northbound and southbound lanes, meaning that from either direction you had to exit from the fast lane onto a narrow-paved strip in the center divide, which was shared by those doing the same thing from the opposite side. Once in that divide—basically a bizarre version of chicken—you had to immediately turn and merge into the fast lane on the other side. If your engine was a bit sluggish, heaven help you. Thankfully, Cary had a lot of get-up-and-go.

Traffic moved fast on the ring road. Sixty miles per hour was the low side of average unless you figured in the times you had to slow down in order to:

a) not hit pedestrians running across the expressway

b) not hit trucks or cars doing forty in the fast lane, or

c) not hit the pedestrian who picked that precise moment to dart into traffic as you swerved among the lanes to avoid hitting a slow-moving truck.

I took a breath and deftly navigated the traffic, not slamming the brakes once, and exited toward the embassy's warehouse site.

Once fueled up and ready to go again, my neighbor and I needed to stop by the embassy itself to pick up our mail. To do so after leaving the gas pumps, I had the pleasure of making my way through one of the craziest roundabouts in the city. Think of the scene in *National Lampoon's European Vacation* where Chevy Chase gets stuck in a London roundabout, add more cars and no rules and that was what it was like. I wondered if I'd have to use the face removal gesture I had learned from Dede. As we entered the roundabout, I pretty much threw us into the crush as there was simply no better way to do it. Other drivers gave me a double-take. I guess it wasn't often that they saw an aggressive blonde woman driving herself and barreling between the other cars like a seasoned local. Their shock was to my advantage. I took their momentary hesitation and maneuvered in front of them.

Finished at the embassy, I made the decision to drive home via the city's surface streets. Even though I'd taken that route countless times as a passenger, I still had to think hard about which turns to take and which on-ramps and off-ramps were real. I didn't want to fall prey to the pseudo ramps that literally left you in the ditch—further proof that both the road network and Abuja were still very much works in progress.

I pulled up to an intersection where the turn lane went from its standard one-car width to three cars wide in the blink of an eye—not because it was actually designed that way, but because why should one obey road markings when they might miss out on the light sequence? The car to my left nosed toward my front right quarter panel, trying to sneak in ahead of me. I gave the driver the international sign for "what the heck"—aka, an arm thrown into the air with a nasty look on my face—and proceeded to block his movement, continuing on as the traffic cop waved me through. I swear I could see the cop give me a grin of admiration for my fine driving skills.

And that day, the roads were also full of drivers practicing the Abuja Drift, which was really nothing more than the complete lack of ability to keep one's car within its lane. On the final stretch of road home, two cars began to squeeze me from opposite sides—the Abuja Drift in action. I laid my hand firmly on the horn, causing both drivers to jerk awake from their slumber and return to their proper lanes.

As I finally pulled into our driveway, the journey over, my neighbor laughed and said, "Yeah, you're going to be fine driving here." I took it as a compliment. The truth of the matter was that I loved driving in Abuja. Despite the crazy drivers, lack of law enforcement, and poor road design, there was nothing to it.

chapter 25

A Normal Life . . . in Abuja

Our life in Abuja was, for the most part, normal.
Well, normal for Abuja.
Nigeria had its issues. You didn't have to dig very deep into its daily news to find a story about an internet scam or ethnic violence, or political corruption within the country. But for us, in Abuja, the biggest issues we faced were petty crime and security. As members of the embassy community, to mitigate that risk, our daily lives were restricted to a five-mile radius encompassing the central part of the city. We affectionately called this area the Bubble—an appropriate name for such an odd place.

The majority of Abuja's residents fell into three categories:
- Wealthy Nigerians, generally comprised of politicians and businesspeople
- Expats from all over the world, tied to multinational corporations and other businesses
- The very large diplomatic community, which was where we fit in.

Chances were if you didn't fall into one of those three categories, you didn't live in Abuja. Most local Nigerians who worked at the embassy and other businesses in the city couldn't afford Abuja's prices and therefore lived outside of the capital.

The exception to this was the residential house staff who occupied the boy's quarters—a term throwing back to Nigeria's British colonial days—that accompanied most every home. The separation of social classes that this created shaped the city and its culture, making it much more like someone's weird idea of utopia than the capital of a culturally rich country.

But what Abuja lacked in the normal thrum and hum of Nigeria, it made up for with its other quirks. Living there was like living in some combination of the Wild West and the Gilded Age. Rules existed but were never followed. Those of us sent there by our respective governments—solidly middle class back home—lived amongst the ridiculously rich and spoiled and had ringside seats to their over-the-top displays of wealth.

Quinn came home from school with an invitation to a classmate's birthday party, not someone he was overly close to. As it was still grammar school everyone followed the rule of thumb that if you invite one, you invite all. This celebration was for an afternoon of food and fun at the local cinema. The parents were renting out an entire theater for a private showing of a current movie, treating kids to pizza at the mall, then off to swimming at a local club. Of course, the transportation for all of this would be via a stretch limousine. Hesitating at the invitation and wondering what on earth you would give as a gift for a ten-year-old child who lived like that, I was thankful when Quinn said he didn't want to go because his best friend wouldn't be going.

Later, when talking to his best friend's mom, she said that particular invitation was nothing. Apparently another family had set the bar for over-the-top birthday parties—the parents had bought tickets for their soccer fanatic son and nine of his friends to fly to England to watch his favorite team play. Recounting this story to John and Quinn, I watched Quinn's eyes light up at the thought of flying to Manchester to watch

Manchester United play—I squashed his brief daydream quickly by saying, "Don't get any ideas; we're not made of money."

Such audacity was, of course, not limited to children's parties. It wasn't uncommon to hear a supercar of the German or Italian variety racing up and down Ibrahim Babangida Boulevard, the road that ran along the boundary of our housing compound. With a reasonably long straight stretch, the road turned into a test track late at night by the rich. The roar of their unbridled horsepower echoed through the air.

There was really no way for us to fit into the rarified strata of Abuja society, so we lived amongst them, coexisting. Like the time we walked out of our modest house, only to be momentarily blinded by the sun reflecting off the gold mirror-plated, circular house owned by a technology tycoon on the opposite side of the street. One could forgive the momentary blindness given that its reflected light cast a lovely golden tone over our compound.

But beyond the bizarreness of the city, the big thing that Abuja had going for it was John's job provided us with a breather from the breakneck pace we had during our final year in Cameroon.

While John and I still had representational requirements, they were limited to attending a handful of events and receptions. Thankfully, there was no in-home entertaining expected or required. So, for the most part, our day-to-day life was quiet and sedate, the best of both worlds, as we had the benefit of living and working in Africa without the stress of constantly being on the go or in the spotlight. As I told a foreign service friend who visited Abuja on assignment, "We love Nigeria. We needed a break after Cameroon, but we weren't ready to leave Africa." Our position in Abuja was a perfect fit.

Another thing that Abuja had going for it, and Nigeria in general, was a love of providing service at your fingertips and forward-thinking entrepreneurs. No, not the ones you read about in the news that pretend to be a Nigerian prince wanting to scam people out of money. But honest-to-goodness entrepreneurs who excelled at finding opportunities, carving a niche for themselves. In Abuja, if you wanted something and also wanted it to be convenient, chances were you could find it.

Need an internet provider who would install service quickly and also be prompt and attentive to issues? No problem. In fact, the best internet service we have ever had anywhere in the world was in Abuja. Need a mechanic? One that was trustworthy and would also make house calls? Sure, no problem. Wanted fruits and vegetables you couldn't find at the grocery store delivered to your home? Absolutely.

That service was a particular treat for me—having grown accustomed to the abundance of fruits and vegetables available in Cameroon, I was less than impressed with what Abuja had to offer. In the grocery stores, the selection was small, subpar, and stupidly expensive. If I wanted to venture into the open markets, I could have found more, but it would've added a lot of time to my shopping, and I would've been taking a personal security risk. So, you can imagine my glee when I discovered the services of Elliot. He was an enterprising young man from Kano and had figured out how to tap into the lucrative market of expats willing to pay for quality fruits and vegetables, abundant in variety and delivered directly to your compound.

Once a week, usually midmorning, one of the guards would go around and ring doorbells to let us know that Elliot had arrived. Grabbing a few large shopping totes and a fistful of naira, I would make my way to the main gate where Elliot would be parked just along the sidewalk, having carefully laid out that day's selection while his assistant set up an old-school scale to weigh our picks. Elliot's vegetable service was a breath of fresh air, bringing beautifully vibrant greens, deep purple eggplants, carrots still covered with the earth they were pulled from, and during the season, heart-achingly bright red strawberries. In the grocery store, a small punnet of strawberries cost almost $20, but a pound of strawberries from Elliot cost only $5. Elliot was like having a farmer's market set up especially for you, right outside your door.

And then there was Felak Meats. I admit that I am quite particular about buying meat because of the whole rancher's daughter thing. I fully understand that we can't always expect a product to be the same the world over, but I still wanted quality. In Cameroon, I had struggled with the fresh meat sold in markets. I often found it so tough that the only reasonable way of working with it was to run it through a grinder multiple times. But in Cameroon, we also had the commissary as back up that got frozen consumables shipments from the United States, bringing in the same beef, pork, and chicken products we would get in an American supermarket—that luxury didn't exist in Abuja. A few companies offered grocery shipments, including one from South Africa, but the prices were astronomical. I searched and searched for a solution, coming to land on a local supplier, Felak Meats. Founded by a Swiss German expat in the agriculturally rich state of Jos, Felak provided a large selection of meats and cheeses, with the vast majority of the items being produced with Nigeria-sourced product. With a simple email, detailing the type and amount of product desired, beef, pork, lamb, rabbit, cheddar cheese, mozzarella cheese, and local honey was delivered to the compound gate, by the always smiling, always affable, Mark.

"Good morning, ma! How was your night?" Mark greeted me while walking to the back of his old station wagon and lifting the hatch.

"Good, good," I replied. "And yours?"

"Very good, thank you," he said as he slid a large ice chest onto the tailgate. "Today you have a big order: ground beef, chicken thighs, minced pork, minced lamb, merguez sausage, mozzarella, and miango pepper. Do I have that right?"

I followed along on the piece of notepaper I had scribbled my order on. "Yes, that's right," I said, opening my bright blue Ikea bag, ready for him to hand me the items.

As we went through the order, I could hear the faint strains of music coming from his car radio—it was country music. I stopped what I was doing and looked at him. "Mark, are you listening to country music? *American* country music?"

"Yes," he smiled, as if hearing a country song on a radio station in Nigeria was the most normal of things—well, it very well may have been, but it was certainly a surprise to me.

I laughed, "Mark, that is the music I grew up with! I just didn't expect to hear it here of all places."

He returned the laughter. "Oh yes, it's popular here. I like listening to it while I drive. It tells stories with lessons about life and morals, kind of like how we tell stories in Nigeria." I pondered that observation, thinking of some of country music's more questionable messages, like infidelity and drinking. But, hey, there were also a lot of songs that were more realistic and grounded in morality. Especially the 1970s and 1980s variety which played on his radio.

I counted out the money I owed him, then added another 500 naira (a little over $1) to it. "Ma, this is too much," he said, trying to give me back the 500 note.

"No, Mark, it's for you. It's a long drive back to Jos. Buy a snack or a soda along the way."

"Thanks! May God keep you until I see you next time," he said as he climbed back into his car, Dolly Parton playing in the background.

I waved goodbye, then lugged my precious supply of meats and other goodies back through the gate of the compound and into my house.

chapter 26

Of Scooters and Emergency Rooms

Of course, it was only a matter of time before we were reminded that not everything in Nigeria was convenient or easy.

"Mom, I think I hurt my chin," Quinn calmly said as he walked toward John and me, visibly shaken. "I think I hurt my chin. I think I'm bleeding, Mom," he repeated. There was a slight tremble in his voice. The white swim shirt he was wearing had acquired a tinge of asphalt black mixed with blood, his knees and elbows dirt-laden—all of which we quickly learned was the result of a proper up-and-over-the-handlebars scooter accident.

It was a cringe-worthy moment.

As parents, we were always prepared for the bumps, scratches, and cuts that go with raising a child, but while living in Africa, accidents took on a whole new meaning. Each time we heard a thump or an "Ow!" we silently prayed that what we were about to see wasn't worthy of anything more than a Band-Aid or at least not so bad that the embassy health unit couldn't handle it. While we were lucky to have local medical clinics approved for our use in Abuja, we'd find ourselves on the next flight to the

US Army hospital in Germany if our medical problems were too serious.

Quickly closing the distance between Quinn and me, I saw a small but gaping hole in his chin, blood trickling slowly down his neck. I looked back at John, and we both sighed—it was definitely more than a Band-Aid wound.

"Yep," John said, "that's a trip to the doctor."

Normally a trip to the doctor meant our embassy doctor, but it was a Sunday evening, and given the severity of the wound, the on-call embassy nurse advised us to take him directly to the local clinic where she would join us as quickly as possible. *Oh joy.*

Throwing ourselves into our Jeep, we raced across the city. Halfway to the hospital, the sky went black and soaking, tropical rain began to pound down. The hospital's security guard, shrugging on a thick green rain slicker, came out of his shack to open the heavy entrance gate which revealed a steep, narrow driveway that led up to the main entrance. The place was old and decrepit looking, a fact not helped by the storm raging around us. The parking lot was so poorly lit that John had to guess at a spot but given that there were no other cars there, it didn't seem that where we parked would matter.

John hefted Quinn into his arms, and we walked to the front of the building. There were no bright ENTER signs one expected to see at a hospital, and no clearly marked arrows or color-coded lines to follow; instead there were just two sets of identical-looking frosted glass doors. The set to the left was very dimly lit, the set to the right only slightly better.

"Which way do we go?" I asked as if John would magically know better than I.

"I have no idea," he said. As the rain poured down and thunder crashed, we peered around and finally spotted a small piece of paper attached to the doors on the right that listed the clinic's hours. Figuring that was a good sign, I gave that set of doors a push—they opened, and we walked in.

It was as if the three of us had been transported into some creepy movie set. The place was nearly deserted. There was only one man sitting by himself in what appeared to be the waiting room. The floors and walls looked as if they were being prepped for renovation or perhaps demolition. Lights were few and dim. There was no sound or activity to suggest the building's true nature.

I could only guess the reception desk stood straight in front of us. I ventured that guess because of the surly-looking woman sitting behind it that eyed us warily as we approached.

"Yes?" she said dryly. Her demeanor did nothing to help the post-apocalyptic atmosphere.

"Our son has fallen and cut his chin. He needs stitches," I explained, even though it felt like I was stating the obvious.

She glanced at Quinn. "Um . . ." was all that came out of her mouth, staring at the three of us as if she didn't understand why we were there.

Frustrated and confused, I straightened myself to full height and repeated, my momma bear voice coming out in full force. "The cut is deep. Our son needs stitches," I said. Then resorting to the privilege afforded our position, I used my ace-in-the-hole. "We are with the US Embassy. Our nurse told us to come here. She will be meeting us soon." I wasn't proud of that, but I was a mom desperate to help her child. The receptionist continued her blank stare. It took everything in me to not reach across the counter and grab her by the collar. "And as for the cost," I continued, "if I cannot pay in full tonight, then the embassy will cover it."

Apparently, those were the magic words because her expression immediately changed. It was all about money in Nigeria.

Even in an emergency room, hospital admittance was only approved if you could pay right then and there. No money, no help.

"Okay," she said, dragging out the word to emphasize that she was doing us a favor. "Take him down that hall," she tilted her head, motioning to the left. "Then you," directing her eyes back to me, "come back and fill out the paperwork. The doctor will come shortly."

Down the dark hallway, we found the treatment room. Their use of the term seemed a bit grand, as the rural veterinarian's office my family's ranch used was in better shape than that small space. The bed—essentially a sheet of plywood with a thin mat and scratchy, ill-fitting linens—was pushed tightly into the corner as there was no other spot for it. An old desktop computer sat on a tiny desk, and there was a small cabinet on the wall behind it for supplies. Although visibly clean, everything showed signs of age and neglect. I was trying my best not to judge. After all, we were lucky to have a place to go, but still.

With Quinn settled on the bed and John holding his hand, I headed back down the hall to sort out the paperwork, which was only one small piece of paper that simply required our name and contact details. Then we waited. And waited. Proof that some aspects of the emergency room experience were universal.

The evening continued to be a surreal mix of stress and disbelief. Both the hospital's nurse and doctor were surly toward us, even toward our embassy nurse, who had appeared as promised to be our liaison. Quinn did his best to stay calm given the complete lack of bedside manner; the room was so small they were practically laying on top of him while they cleaned and treated the wound. And much to our surprise given that we were in one of the premier hospitals in Nigeria, they stitched his chin with prolene. The thick blue suture thread is often used for heart surgery rather than the thin, dissolvable thread commonly used for minor body wounds.

Patched up with the blue stitches and a thick padding of gauze, we nevertheless thanked the doctor for her help. John then reached over to help Quinn off the bed, but as he leaned forward to give Quinn his hand, the end of the makeshift bed angled sharply down and toward him in catapult fashion. Quinn's body lurched up violently. The attending nurse and I thrust our hands to the head of the bed to stop it from propelling him into the opposite wall. When we stabilized the table, John and I let out an involuntary laugh, which the doctor met with a scowl. She left the room without so much as a smile or a goodbye.

I returned to the receptionist, dreading having to deal with her again; and dreading the bill. An emergency room visit plus a round of antibiotics would surely cost at least a few hundred dollars. I glanced in my purse to see how much naira I had with me, knowing that if I didn't have that much, the embassy would have to pick up the tab, and I would reimburse them the following day.

As the receptionist raised her eyes to me, she said, "Yes, with the visit and medicine, that is 9,705 naira."

Before I could stop myself, I blurted out, "Pardon me?" Because surely, she hadn't said 9,705 naira. That was far too low. It had to be more.

"Yes," she answered, her tone bored and monotonous, "9,705 naira." I nearly laughed again but managed to stifle it. I easily had that much with me, because 9,705 naira was only about $25. I paid quickly before she could say she had made a mistake, even though she hadn't.

We walked out of the hospital, John once again carrying a now very exhausted Quinn in his arms. Thankfully the rain had stopped, but it was still eerily quiet and empty. Abuja was a big city, the capital city. There were always accidents and people getting sick—shouldn't there have been more people at the hospital? The entire experience had been bizarre. The best medical facility in the city, yet it looked old and neglected. Treatment was adequate, yet with prices so low, how could they possibly expect to improve themselves or have more modern equipment and supplies? Some locals had told me that the wealthy among them did not use these facilities. If they needed treatment, they either traveled to Europe or the United States. Those who couldn't afford it just went to a pharmacy to seek help. It also said a lot about the country itself and its love/hate relationship with the well-being of its people. How could they expect the people to care about themselves or each other or their country if their health wasn't a priority? It was bothersome and mind-boggling.

Regardless, Quinn had received proper, albeit antiquated, treatment without us having to hop a plane to Europe. He was now the proud owner of a Nigerian scar . . . which went along nicely with his German and Cameroonian scars. I was sure that someday he would use their stories to his advantage.

chapter 27

A Trip to the Zoo

"Wait!" I shouted, contorting my upper body on the seat so that I could turn and look behind us. "That's it!" I had been studying our street map, keeping my eyes peeled as we drove along the ring road searching for the Abuja Zoo; I had just realized we'd blown past our destination. The map, which had placed us in the general vicinity, did not account for the access road. Accurate maps and well-placed signs were not part of the African experience. You got used to making multiple U-turns in an attempt to reach your destination.

"Are you sure this is it?" John asked as he eased us onto the access road, having made a very long detour loop to turn around and head back.

"Yes, I think so," I said, looking for the sign that I had seen on our first pass, spotting it ahead of us on the pothole-infested road. White, approximately six feet tall and eighteen feet wide, it was old and completely blank aside from black block lettering far too small for the overall size that read: NATIONAL CHILDREN'S PARK AND ZOO.

John made a right and we found ourselves in a maze of concrete barriers. At the end of which stood an armed soldier sporting a badge which bore the image of a scorpion—the mark of Nigeria's presidential guard. The National Zoo happened to be right next to the presidential villa.

The soldier held up an arm, signaling us to stop. As we pulled up alongside him, he made a winding motion for me to roll down my window, but when I did, a look of puzzlement overtook his face—obviously, we were not the people he expected to see there on a Thursday afternoon.

"Where are you headed?" The question came out gruff and menacing.

I gave him my most winning smile. "We are going to the zoo!" Which came out a bit more like the village idiot than an innocent tourist.

His expression changed immediately to one of suspicion, staring at John and I as if we were up to no good. He motioned for us to roll down the dark-tinted back window. As it slowly lowered, he was greeted by a smiling Quinn, sitting in the back like a king. It caught the soldier so off guard that his face suddenly softened—the appearance of a child seemed to legitimize our destination. He stepped back and waved us on.

However, we should've asked the soldier for directions because actually *finding* the zoo was no easy feat. We headed straight down the tree-lined road in the direction of Aso Rock, coming to an unmarked roundabout in which each exit looked exactly the same. There were no signs directing us anywhere, let alone to the zoo. After twists and turns and wrong guesses, we finally stumbled upon the zoo's large car park, which was empty apart from one very rusty car and a large bus. "We're here!" John said brightly, turning off the engine and giving his best impression of Clark Griswold arriving at Wally World.

The trip to the zoo was a treat for Quinn. After the unfortunate chin incident, which happened to coincide with the beginning of his spring break, we thought he deserved a day out. The Abuja Zoo had opened in 2001 and was run for years by an expat. It had clearly been a beautiful place at one time, but in 2013 the zoo was returned to the Nigerian government, and in the year since, had fallen into a state of disrepair. Even though a special management committee had been established for it at the same time and had been given six months to assess and begin its rehabilitation, like many special committees in Nigeria, it was obviously just a ruse. Nothing had been done to improve the facilities. It almost looked abandoned.

Half a dozen men lazed on the ground near the ticket booth, none of them in uniform but all apparently employees. Aside from a group of local school children—the occupants of the aforementioned bus—we seemed to be the zoo's only visitors. After buying our tickets, one of the men jumped to his feet and hurried toward us. "Can I take photos for you?" he asked eagerly. He wore faded capri-length pants and a too-tight, equally faded button-down shirt. It was hard to say no to him, but we did—we had our own camera and didn't need to pay someone to take pictures for us.

We made our way along the paved sidewalk, riddled with deep cracks and crumbled edges, to the first animal enclosure, where a giraffe stood in the dusty, fenced-in field. As I raised my camera to snap a picture, I became aware of a man standing next to me, one from the group that had been camped by the entrance. I took the photo, then turned and smiled politely. "Hello."

"That's Princess," he said by way of a greeting, motioning his head toward the giraffe. "She's eight years old."

"Really," I said with feigned interest, because the same information was written on a sign attached to the fence in front of me.

"Yes, she's my favorite," he continued, going on to tell us more about Princess and her sweet personality, doing his best to show us that he knew more about her than just what was on the sign.

Nodding in appreciation, we moved toward the next enclosure. And the man followed us. Like the others, his clothes were old and worn-out but clean—a T-shirt, trousers, and flip-flops. Anywhere else, I would've tried desperately to lose his companionship. Still, something about him intrigued me, so I turned and asked, "What's your name? What do you do here at the zoo?"

"I'm Benjamin," he smiled, happy that I finally showed genuine interest. "I'm part of the security here, but I studied zoology at university, so I also work with the animals. I can tell you about all of them." It became obvious that he wasn't trying to con us. He just wanted to share his love of the animals with someone, and given the lack of guests there, how could I say no? So, I slowed my pace, allowing John and Quinn to walk on ahead, and I hung back with Benjamin.

The next enclosure was a small rectangular cage in the middle of a pool of murky water approximately eight feet long by six feet wide. "Our Nile crocodiles and their new baby," Benjamin beamed as he pointed toward the water. I peered in. There, nestled amongst a variety of trash strewn atop the water, were two crocodiles looking absolutely miserable. Happily floating near them was a tiny baby croc, no more than a foot long, entertaining itself with an empty Fanta bottle. "We are happy to have this baby," Benjamin said like a proud father. "He is growing rapidly." And I wondered how on earth all three would fit in the tiny pond when the baby became full size.

"Now I will show you the snakes," Benjamin said, turning to lead us forward.

Damn. Snakes. Again. In Africa, snakes tended to be very deadly, and if there were ones that weren't, I wasn't willing to seek them out. Plus, judging from the state of the other enclosures,

I wasn't sure that I wanted to see the snakes for fear that some might be of the free-range variety.

"We used to have a place for the snakes," Benjamin explained as we walked along a tree-lined path, "but it needed improvement. We have yet to build a new one, so for now, they are in the barn." I kept listening, trying to keep my face full of interest, but all the while my unease was growing. I became increasingly aware that I was wearing lightweight sandals and not my high-shafted cowboy boots. One rule growing up on our ranch, which happened to be in rattlesnake country, was never to wear sandals in the barn during snake season, as the buzzing buggers liked to hide in the cool of the building. Tough leather boots that covered your lower legs were much more appropriate in a place where one could conceivably be struck by a set of cranky fangs.

As we entered the zoo's small, cluttered barn structure, my imagination was running wild with ridiculous vicious snake scenarios. The place was dim. Cobwebs covered most everything—I just knew I was entering my own personal horror movie. "Ah, here we go," Benjamin said brightly, walking toward a shelf in the back. "They couldn't survive anymore, so I preserved them myself."

I let out an audible sigh of relief.

There on the shelf, much to my delight, was a row of bottles and jars that in their former lives had contained whisky and mayonnaise but bore the bodies of extremely deadly yet now very dead snakes. Benjamin beamed with pride, "I wanted to make sure that we still had them to show people and teach them." The specimens—mambas, cobras, and others—were in various stages of decay. Still, it was obvious that Benjamin had done the best he could with what meager supplies he had available. He told us all about their habitats and life spans, but I wasn't listening too closely because I was keeping an eye on the floor, making sure none of their live versions were lurking in the shadows. Despite my fear, I have to admit that his display was equal parts fascinating and depressing.

In total, there were less than a dozen animal species on display at the zoo. None of the live inhabitants, aside from the dead snakes, had come from Nigeria. Some of the species had existed there until recently, but with no true effort toward conservation, those species had vanished from the country. Beyond that, the zoo's most glaringly obvious problem was the lack of the promised renovation. There appeared to be no new work anywhere. "We wait for the government, but nothing comes," Benjamin said, a tinge of sadness in his voice as he led us to the final exhibit.

Quinn stood in front of the tall wire cage, looking up at its occupant: a solitary gray parrot. He tried desperately to get it to talk. "Hello," he said to the bird in a sing-song way. "Hello. Heeeelllllooo."

"Oh, he is too young," Benjamin said, squatting down next to Quinn. "He does not talk yet. We had one that talked. He talked all the time. But when the president came for a tour, he took the parrot with him for his private zoo at the villa." Benjamin had no idea how succinctly his explanation had summed up both the zoo and the country.

We thanked him for his time, gave him a handsome tip for the guided tour, and headed home, still bewildered and captivated by Nigeria.

chapter 28

All Change

Growing up on the ranch, we had good years, and we had bad years. Such was the way of the world when your business relied on such unpredictables as the weather and the open market. When the good years came, we enjoyed them. When the tide changed and the years were bad, we simply reverted to the stoicism that had always got our family through—putting our heads down to the wind, holding the course, and moving forward. I found out that our time in Africa was much like living on the ranch—it reminded me to accept uncertainty and live life. And just like those more difficult years on the ranch, life in Africa sometimes tested our mettle.

The morning of April 14, 2014 was pretty much like every other morning in our house—we got up, got dressed, and got on with our day. Quinn caught the bus to school, John drove to work, and I settled down at my desk to write. But what we had been unaware of as we sat down to our peaceful breakfast was that terror had struck only moments before, a mere ten miles away. Just as the morning's busy commute was beginning in Nyanya, a small town on the border of Abuja in neighboring Nasarawa State, a bomb had gone off. The explosion struck Nyanya's transportation center that had been bustling with commuters hailing motorbikes, three-wheel okadas, and buses, all trying to make their way into Abuja for work.

It was the closest terror had come to the Nigerian capital in years.

News of the blast had been oddly slow, not reaching us until later that morning, long after Quinn had arrived at school and John had reached his office at the ECOWAS building. Had we heard about it immediately, we may have altered our routines, John may have driven Quinn to school, or we may have kept him home, but we hadn't known. Perhaps it was because the attack hadn't occurred in the heart of the city; it happened far enough away from Abuja to not cause panic within the city's more privileged bubble. Eventually, when the alert came, a level of heightened danger was announced, but little more than that. As news reports trickled in, at least eighty people had lost their lives, and more were unaccounted for. The blame was attributed to Boko Haram, their first strike near Abuja since the 2011 attack on the United Nations building.

I had a business meeting on my calendar for midday. However, I wondered if the other woman—a Nigerian—still wanted to keep it. The embassy had told us to proceed with our lives as normal but to exercise caution. But, as I was new to those types of threats, I was unsure how others would react, especially the locals. I texted her, expecting her to delay, but to my surprise she said she didn't see a reason to cancel.

When I drove to the Hilton for the meeting, things were pretty much the same as always. Locals went about their lives as if nothing significant had happened—except that the Nigerian Army was inspecting every car entering the hotel's parking lot. Walking into the lobby, scanning for situational awareness, I took in the faces of businessmen chatting away and the privileged local women having lunch. But there was little else visual to interpret, their expressions no different than any other day. At the same time, I could sense the subtlest of changes in the air,

just underneath the surface, a hint of danger, of uncertainty . . .
but life in Abuja went on.

chapter 29

Should We Stay or Should We Go?

We had just over a year left in Nigeria, which meant it was once again time for us to think about John's next assignment.

Now at ten consecutive years overseas and two back-to-back tours on the African continent, we had really resigned ourselves to the inevitable and figured the only offers would be for jobs based in Washington, DC—thinking the navy wouldn't let us stay away from the flagpole any longer. We contemplated this monumental change with mixed emotions. Ten years was a long time to be away from home, to be so far away from family, but at the same time being in Africa—with John doing the work he had been trained to do—still felt right to us.

Despite growing political unrest in Nigeria and the stability of many African countries teetering on the knife's edge, in our hearts, we simply weren't ready to walk away from Africa yet.

"Okay, I've got something for you." This time John called me from work.

"Oh yeah? Whatcha got?" I smiled, honestly having no idea why he was calling. I was sitting at my desk, ironically working on an essay for a book about life as an expat.

At the other end of the line, I heard him take a breath and pause. I recognized that trick of his, a signal that he was about to say something big. "What would you think of doing another SDO/DATT tour after this?"

I stopped typing. "Another one?" The incredulity was audible in my voice. "Honey, the navy'd never buy off on that. Besides, where? I didn't think there were any jobs left for your rank in Africa since we already did Cameroon, and the only other one doesn't line up with our rotation date."

"Well, there isn't, but there will be," he said cagily. "What would you think about Djibouti?"

"Djibouti? Really?" I replied, stunned and puzzled. Djibouti had returned. On and off the radar for years, now it was back on. An outlier amongst Africa FAO jobs. Djibouti, with the only forward operating US military base on the African continent.

Our defense attaché office in Djibouti had been in a state of flux for quite some time. Originally served remotely from the office in Ethiopia, it opened in country a few years prior, with the army taking the lead for filling the top position. However, times were changing. The port of Djibouti had become more and more key to security operations in the Red Sea, plus our base there was run by the navy. Rumor was that the navy would be taking over the SDO/DATT position during a reshuffling of priorities on the continent. From John's call, I guessed that the rumor was hot again.

"Yes." He hesitated another moment, then he added. "And apparently, my name is the one making the rounds to fill it, so it sounds like it would be ours for the taking if we wanted." I had heard those words only two years before when the Nigeria job had come up. *Ours for the taking* apparently was the phrase that followed us around. Then he said, "After jumping through all the necessary hoops, of course."

"Okaaay," I said, drawing the word out as I absorbed that information. All of the emotions we had about potential jobs and convincing ourselves that we would be returning home flooded my mind at once. I had not expected another option. I had not expected the chance to stay in Africa.

John picked up on my silence. "Look, think about it, and we can talk tonight when I get home. I gotta get back to work."

"Okay," I said, barely above a whisper, and with that, he hung up. I was left staring at my computer, unable to concentrate on what I had been writing; my mind whirled from the adrenaline that comes with change.

At that point in John's career, we knew that if we stepped foot off the continent for a job getting back to it would be difficult. The door to our time in Africa had been slowly closing until that call, and now we had a chance to keep it open—if we wanted. We were happy in Africa. Quinn was thriving. And I was enjoying the person I had become. If we had to leave the continent, I wasn't sure what would happen to us.

That night we sat down to discuss the ins and outs of a potential job in Djibouti as a family. While we all wanted to remain in Africa, Djibouti would be no cakewalk. The thing was, agreeing to Djibouti would mean another consecutive tour overseas and another tour at a hardship post. At the same time, John and I talked a lot about our desire to ride out the Africa gigs as long as we could—it's what we were trained for, so much of who we were.

Compared to Nigeria and Cameroon, Djibouti was a different beast entirely. It was roughly the same geographic size as New Jersey and the epicenter of global military engagement in Africa. Everybody and their brother were opening a base or at least an office there. The job would be tough, and the pace would be brutal—a colleague had told John that in his two years there, he hadn't had a day off, except for a short trip home for R&R. But the opportunity was incredible, and after a relatively easy tour in Nigeria, we knew we would be ready for something more challenging.

However, on a personal level, some of the amenities we had taken for granted in Cameroon and Nigeria would not be available in Djibouti. Over the years, the French had turned it into a little haven. However, it was still tough with incredibly high temperatures and desert conditions. But the biggest challenge would be to Quinn—at that time, there was no international or American school in Djibouti.

"From what I can tell, schooling will be a huge issue. The French school is really the only option, although it's not highly praised," I said, having read emails and briefings on Djibouti. "Quinn, you would have to choose: French school, boarding school, or homeschool."

That was a blow to Quinn who thoroughly enjoyed his schooling experience in Cameroon and Nigeria. "I don't want to leave you! I won't go to boarding school. And I don't want to go to a French school."

"Well, then, if we want to move to Djibouti, you'd have to homeschool," I said. "I'd be your teacher."

He stared at me. That, in a nutshell, summed everything up. In order to stay in Africa—which was what all three of us wanted—we would have to make some big sacrifices. John would be tethered to the job. Quinn would have to switch to homeschool. I would have to balance the role of DATT's spouse with becoming Quinn's teacher. "I want to stay in Africa," Quinn said with a tinge of resignation. There was no joy for him at the thought of homeschool but staying in Africa meant more.

"I agree with Quinn," John joined in. "The job would be a tremendous opportunity for me, for us."

What could I say to that? And honestly, there was no question in the matter to me; I wanted to stay too. No matter what choice we made, there would be sacrifice. Do we choose a life stateside and closer to family at the cost of John's career? If we did, what would that choice mean for our own well-being? Or could we weather what lay ahead if we stayed in Africa?

While there was no easy answer, there was only one right answer—Djibouti—and we all agreed.

"Okay, then, I'll make our interest known," John said. "We'll see what happens."

chapter 30

Time Runs Out

As the spring of 2014 slid toward summer—visually unnoticeable in Nigeria except for marking days off on the calendar—Africa reminded us once again of its unpredictability.

In the waning days of 2013, Ebola had been discovered in Guinea, 1200 miles to the west of Nigeria. Over the next several months, cases of the brutal virus crept over borders, putting all of West Africa on alert, as the movement of people between countries was as fluid as that of Americans between states.

The threat of the Ebola virus was coupled with a heightened terror campaign from Boko Haram—which until that point in our time in Nigeria, had only lingered on the periphery of our life.

Early in April of 2014, Boko Haram gained global notoriety with the mass kidnapping of 276 schoolgirls in the northern Nigerian village of Chibok. That kidnapping sparked a worldwide uproar and the global social media campaign #BringBackOur-Girls, which was highlighted by the likes of Michelle Obama and Beyoncé. Emboldened by their new fame, Boko Haram continued to push toward the political heart of Nigeria. Later that same month was when they bombed the Nyanya transportation hub on the outskirts of Abuja.

With the Chibok kidnapping unresolved, the bombing in Nyanya, the looming threat of Ebola, and a national election on the horizon, security in Abuja continued to increase. Everyone became more cautious.

We felt the pressure in our daily lives. Rumors floated like falling leaves throughout Abuja. One rumor was that Boko Haram would use newspaper delivery vans to access the heart of the city. This resulted in a military crackdown on those delivery vans and the subsequent destruction of two days' worth of newspapers.

Still, our little family kept going, unswayed by the evergrowing elephant in the room, knowing we wanted to stick to our decision to stay in Nigeria, stay in Africa, and apply for the follow-on job in Djibouti.

On May 14, Boko Haram tried another attempt at breaching the capital city. Once again, the Nyanya transportation hub was hit. A car bomb was detonated while stopped at a security checkpoint, killing nineteen people and injuring dozens more. Life in the capital grew even more tense.

We started the ball rolling for the Djibouti position. Then ten days later, on the opposite side of the African continent, two suicide bombers blew themselves up in a restaurant frequented by expats in the heart of Djibouti City. It was the first time such an attack had happened in Djibouti, but unsurprising given the country's growing importance to the world's militaries. The terror group Al Shabaab took responsibility for the bombing. But suspected ties between al Shabaab and Boko Haram left John and me staring at each other, wondering what we were signing up for. Were we just leaving one frying pan for another?

Which brings us back to where this story began, back to June 25, 2014, the moment when our mettle was truly tested.

I had spent most of that morning digging out the suitcases we would need for our R&R trip back to the States. We would be leaving the following week for a month and a half of rest, relaxation, visits with family and friends, basically time off to reset our internal batteries.

At 3:30 p.m., while Quinn was happily playing with Legos on the coffee table near me, I sat down on the sofa to call my mom.

"I still have to get your bedrooms ready, Tiz," she said, calling me by my childhood nickname. Tiz, short for Tizzy, as in "to throw a tizzy fit" because apparently, I had a knack for throwing such fits in my early years. The name stuck and became the familiar moniker most used by my parents, so much so that I worry when they call me Julie.

"Oh Mom," I gave an exasperated sigh. "You don't have to worry about our rooms. We're not picky." We had been chatting about our trip, our family so excited to see us finally, as it had been a year since we'd been in the States. We talked about the plans for the Fourth of July, what restaurants we wanted to go to, and all the fun things we were looking forward to.

And that's the moment when Boko Haram finally made it to the center of Abuja. When the bomb at Banex Plaza exploded and shook the windows of our house. When our world spun and we were forced to confront the darker reality of our life in Africa.

In the minutes immediately following that explosion, after I had hung up with my mom and texted with John, I began working through the plan of what was next. I ushered Quinn up the stairs, then upon reaching the second-floor landing, locked the metal security gate of our safe haven behind us.

We went into my bedroom, and Quinn settled himself on my bed. I opened the closet where we kept our go-bags, grabbing them and tossing them next to him on the bedspread.

"Mom, what's going to happen?" Quinn asked, watching me methodically go through our backpacks that held everything we would need in case of an evacuation—passports, important papers, medications, and money, which included US dollars, naira, and euros. Our real-life was a less sexy version of a Jason Bourne story.

"Honestly, honey, I don't know." At least I didn't know yet. "We just have to sit and wait and listen for news and updates from the embassy," I told him. "But I tell you what, let's go into your room and pick out which stuffed animals you would want to take with you in case we do have to leave."

"But I don't want to leave," he protested. "And I want to take all of my stuffies with me if we do!" His anger flashed. "And what about the rest of my stuff? My books? My toys?"

His words hit me like a punch to the gut. Poor kid. I wanted to scream. I didn't want to put him through this agony, and what was worse was that I felt the same way he did. "I know," I said in the calmest voice I could muster at that moment. "I don't want to leave Abuja either. But, hey, we are going on vacation soon anyway, so let's just take a few extra stuffies along, that way, you have them. And if the embassy makes us evacuate, then you shouldn't worry because they will do their best to pack up our house for us and send our stuff to the next place." Those words did little to appease him, but I knew the most important thing was to be honest—lying to a child could have nasty repercussions, especially with regard to something so serious. "And honey, we have to remember that our safety is the top priority. Everything else is just stuff. Yes, it would be sad to lose them, but we can replace things—we can't replace us." That was the best truthful, yet shitty, answer I had to give him.

"I know, I know," he said as he scanned the stuffed inhabitants on his bed. At that moment, he sounded a lot older than ten.

I pulled him into a hug, doing my best not to cry. "Can I also bring a few favorite toys?"

"Yeah, but small ones, okay?"

"Okay." But I also knew that I would cut him slack and let him stuff his bag with whatever he wanted, placing anything else that overflowed into mine and John's.

In that moment, I had no idea what would happen: if the bombings would continue, if the embassy would go to ordered departure of families and nonessential employees, if we would leave and never return—things like that happened more often than people back home realized—embassies closed, families left, houses were placed in the hands of the local staff or abandoned completely. So I just kept checking my phone for updates and messages, triple checking that my embassy radio was on, and then began to rethink what needed to be in our luggage. The only thing I was certain of? I was not ready for our time in Nigeria and Africa to be over.

chapter 31

Rest and Relaxation

S even days after the Banex Plaza bombing, we stood in line at Abuja's Nnamdi Azikiwe International Airport, waiting to board Lufthansa's red-eye flight to Frankfurt, the first leg of our R&R trip back to the States.

I know I must have looked a sight—dark circles had taken up residence under my eyes in the wake of all that had happened, markers that I'd be lying if I said I was fine. And even though I kept telling myself I was fine, I really wasn't. Those last few months had taken a toll. Standing there, I looked like just another expat heading out of town for the summer. In my jeans and red cowboy boots, my sweater draped over an arm, and backpack slung over my shoulder, I looked fine but was a mess inside.

I was happy at the thought of stepping onto the plane, seeing our family, and enjoying the creature comforts of America. But I was nervous at the thought of leaving Nigeria; it rested on the knife-edge of chaos. I was worried about not knowing if things would get worse while we were gone, not knowing if we'd be given the "all clear" to come back. Most of all, I was angry to be placed in such a mental battle to begin with. I had been doing great the past few years, feeling like I'd found a sense of purpose, a home in Sub-Saharan Africa, and I didn't want to lose that.

All three of us were exhausted—I wasn't the only one sporting dark circles under my eyes. I battled a flare-up of stomach issues, my stress manifesting itself as acid within my body. There was a literal and emotional weight to it—the carrying of our go-bags and other important items—pulling us down.

Thirty-seven hours later, we finally reached California. Thanks to summer thunderstorms in the Midwest, a brutally long trip that played havoc with flight connections—the best we could manage for my family upon arrival was a zombie-like attentiveness.

But it didn't take long for us to tuck our reality away for a bit and enjoy California. We had arrived just in time for the Fourth of July and my mom's homemade ice cream—a staple in my family on the patriotic holiday. A few days later, we all piled into pickups and headed to the mountains to open my family's cow-camp for the season. We marked the day, as my family has for years, by writing the date and our names on the old bare wood cabinets. We also took a trip to the coast and went to the county fair. For those precious few weeks, we were almost carefree.

Almost.

John and I sat in the waiting room of the gastroenterologist clin-ic in my hometown. Thrilled to have found a local place that would accept our military medical insurance, something that was not always a guarantee.

It had been a month since the Banex Plaza bombing, and things on that front were relatively stable. In the meantime, though, Ebola had made its way into Nigeria via a man who flew from Liberia to Lagos, thus triggering a new and pronounced level of panic within the country. While we were enjoying our time in California, we were also monitoring the latest news from the embassy. There was talk of next steps in case the virus spread to Abuja, including sending non-essential employees and their families home. My body, not fully content with the concept of R&R, began bucking under the stress of that new information. No matter how hard I tried to relax, it just didn't work, and my stomach suffered, hence the trip to the doctor.

I was busy filling out the clinic's new patient survey when I paused at one of the questions. *Was I currently, or had I been recently under stress?* I turned the page to show John, and we both laughed out loud, which caught the attention of an older woman also waiting to be seen.

"What should I put?" I whispered to him, trying to regain my composure but still giggling. "I mean, I haven't really felt stressed out, but I've been under stress. I don't know how to explain it."

"Well, we have to tell him. I mean, that's probably part of what's causing your problem."

John was right. I circled yes, then where it asked for an explanation I wrote: I LIVE IN NIGERIA. Writing about the bombs and Ebola and stress from the thought of potentially being forced to leave Africa seemed odd and would've been too much for the space given.

A few minutes later, while sitting in the exam room, John and I watched as the doctor read over the form. He paused, then looked up, peering at us over his glasses. "You live in *Nigeria?*" Yes, even I knew that sounded odd, given that his office was in a small town in northern California. He was clearly doing his best to maintain a professional demeanor yet was obviously incredulous at what I had written.

"Yes," I said, then started rattling on about the fact that I came to him because we were visiting family in the area and that I wasn't really stressed, per se, but that we had had a fairly tense couple of months of late and that a bomb went off not too far from our house right before we left on vacation and how now there was Ebola in the country, and we didn't know if we would be able to go back.

When I was finally finished with my story, John and I looked at the doctor and waited for his response.

He sat there, unmoving, most likely processing what he had heard. "Alright, then," he said calmly, breaking the silence . . . and then looked back down at the form and continued on with the appointment.

Over the years, we've had people gasp or feign disbelief or simply laugh when we told them we lived in Africa, but hands down, the doctor's reaction—as if it were perfectly normal for his patients to talk about a bombing—was the best we had ever received after telling someone where we lived.

When we left California a few days later to head to New York to visit John's family, I felt better. I had a new treatment regime and a better bill of health.

chapter 32

Enter Ebola

I woke up as our plane was leaving the Sahara and entering the airspace over Northern Nigeria. The pleasant German flight attendant, whom I had noticed only briefly before closing my eyes, very kindly asked if I still wanted my lunch, there were only forty-five minutes left before we landed. "You've traveled a long way today I take it," she said, kneeling beside my seat. "You've slept since take-off. You're coming from the States?"

"Yes and no," I said. "We were visiting family in the States. Now we are heading home."

"Home?" Her expression quickly changed from a friendly smile to a mask of concern. "You mean Abuja is your home?" She was genuinely puzzled and asked me how long we'd lived in Nigeria. "Aren't you scared? Concerned about everything, about . . ." she trailed off. Saying the word Ebola had become akin to the uttering of "he who shall not be named" in the world of Harry Potter. On top of all the other nefarious things Nigeria was known for, now Ebola had been added to the list.

I smiled back at the flight attendant. While we returned to Nigeria with no fear of contracting the virus—the only known cases had remained isolated to Lagos—others, like the flight attendant, weren't so sure. But how do you explain to someone that the threat was minimal where they were headed when the media did its best to make it sound like doomsday was nigh? And then, because the question would have inevitably followed, how do you explain to someone that you prefer Nigeria over the security blanket of your home country? For most people, it was impossible to comprehend, so I opted for my standard simple response. "No," I said. "I'm not worried." I wanted to add that I was more concerned about further terrorist attacks than contracting Ebola, but I figured that was one trigger that didn't need to be pulled.

At the airport, the fear of Ebola was palpable. Like the height of the COVID-19 pandemic, but half a decade earlier—while not high-tech or rigorous, we were observed for signs of illness as we made our way to immigration. The temperature of every passenger was taken with a thermal temperature gun. Some arriving passengers were asked to fill out health forms based on where they had traveled from and their nationality. There was definitely less touching and more separation—odd in West Africa. Even the immigration official wore a paper face mask.

But despite it all, we were happy to have made it back to our home. Having gone through the roller coaster ride of "will we or won't we" get to return while in the States on leave, it was nice to finally be there. Back at our house, Quinn gave extra hugs to his stuffies that had bravely remained in Abuja during our absence.

Despite everything we went through the previous few months, life returned to its normal pace. We unpacked our bags, went to the grocery store for fresh food, and resettled.

August proceeded to fly by, and we were feeling pretty good about the situation in Abuja. Everything seemed to be calming down. We were still on a heightened alert for terror activity, but nothing too restrictive. And while Ebola was still an issue throughout West Africa, Nigeria had put decent measures in place to protect its residents. Yes, long before COVID-19, we had to have our temperatures scanned upon entrance to public places, hand sanitizer was everywhere, and shaking elbows instead of hands became a thing.

The first day of school was a particularly sunny morning. Quinn hefted his backpack onto his back, smiled for a picture with John on the porch, and then went to catch the school bus. It was the beginning of his fifth-grade year, and he was excited.

Life continued, almost as if normal.

And then the school closed.

When the first case of Ebola reached Nigeria in late July, their federal government made the snap decision to delay the start of the upcoming school year in order to prevent the potential spread of the virus. The theory was that delaying the start would give schools time to update their campuses with the virus prevention health standards that had been quickly established. Under these new rules, all schools would have to ensure their employees received Ebola recognition training. That there were sufficient steps put in place to prevent potential spread like temperature monitoring, good hygiene practices, and isolation capabilities. This was all to be accomplished and confirmed before the student body returned from summer break—which for local schools was mid-September, but mid-August for most of the international schools.

While not absurd, the new requirements were an uphill climb for many of the nation's public schools which generally suffered from at least some level of disrepair and left many to wonder where the money to make the upgrades would come from. For private schools like Quinn's, upgrade work began immediately, using the month they had before the start of the academic year to install sinks in every elementary classroom, hand sanitizer stations throughout the school, and conduct necessary staff training. Satisfied that everything was ready to go, school began for Quinn, as scheduled, on Wednesday, August 13.

The first week went great. Quinn was happy to be back—happy to be in the fifth grade, happy with his new teacher, and happy to be with his friends. Everything was going smoothly. Virus prevention protocol was being followed. Although some families had elected to stay on vacation a few additional weeks, school was back to normal.

Then the following Thursday, as we were getting Quinn ready for bed, my phone pinged with a message from the school: **School is closed effective immediately. Duration of the closure is unknown. More information to follow.** It was 8 p.m.

"Woo-hoo! Day off!" Quinn cheered as if he'd been toiling away for months rather than a week. "I get to sleep in!"

John looked at me with a puzzled expression, a mirror of my own. *Why was the school closing? Was there a case of Ebola in Abuja? A case at the school? A terror threat? Something else?*

An hour later we received a follow-up email from our principal, explaining in detail that our school was being closed by the government due to Ebola restrictions, despite having made the necessary upgrades. The principal assured us the school administration and our embassy would look into a possible waiver, but for the time being, the school would be closed, and instruction would be converted to online. Reopening status would be made on a day-by-day basis. Once again, Africa reminded us not to take anything, especially our routines, for granted.

A week into the closure, the principal announced that according to the national decree, it would remain closed for in-person learning until October 13, although they would continue to do their best to get that appealed. It was only right to appeal, given that the main reason for closing the schools had been to limit large gatherings of people during such a precarious time. Yet, churches and markets did not have to abide by the same rules—a ridiculous double standard.

As Quinn began his online schooling journey, I found myself stuck in the real-life version of *Are You Smarter Than A 5th Grader?*—and sometimes, that answer was no. I spent my days as our household's chief computer and internet technician, desperately trying to make sure that Quinn could access the learning portal, then making sure that our internet remained up and running. Everything that I had going on—articles waiting to be written, etc.—had to be placed on the back burner, but at least I had that luxury. In our embassy community, many dual-career families were struggling to figure out how to balance having their child home all the time. Even those with nannies couldn't rely on their help because most of them, while wonderful at watching the kids, did not have the basic education required to keep up with their schooling.

Those days did not pass all that quickly. And when John began traveling for work again, the days seemed even longer for Quinn and me.

"Can we go out?" Quinn asked as he sat working on a writing assignment. It was Thursday, September 11, a school day. We had been doing online learning for fifteen days, and at least if the rumors were true, we were one of the few families that actually made their child "attend" school. So, while I should have set a good example and continued to follow the rules, I instead looked him in the eye and said, "Sure. Why not?"

When I was Quinn's age, sometimes my mom would surprise me by showing up at school and signing me out for the rest of the day for "an appointment," our code for "playing hooky." The "appointment" being a trip to Sacramento where we would go shopping and have a nice lunch together. Those days rank high in my memories of childhood.

During Quinn's toddler years, we would often do a shopping/lunch day together, but that had stopped when he started school, especially when we moved to Africa and things were more complicated. But that morning, after so much uncertainty and stress, I knew it was time to play hooky . . . so we did.

Of course, our trip didn't take us far because of the current security restrictions. We decided on lunch at Dunes—our go-to grocery store/department store/restaurant not far from our house—and found a lovely table in their atrium. Bright sunlight shone down from the opening in the roof six floors above us. Quinn felt like a king, out in the middle of a school day, having lunch alongside businessmen and women, the only child in sight. He ordered his favorite, pesto pizza, while I opted for fish and chips. We sat and chatted and watched replays of soccer matches on the television next to us. Time—already slowed and stretched out by the current circumstances of our life—was gloriously expanded that day. We had chosen to stop and enjoy the moment and make the best of what could have been a very depressing situation. After our leisurely lunch, we walked through the grocery section to pick up a few things we needed, then headed home, where Quinn finished his schoolwork for the day.

Finally, on September 22, after a considerable amount of diplomatic negotiation, the school reopened. I made Quinn stand in our entryway as I snapped a "first day of school, part *deux*" picture. And even though he had enjoyed the less restrictive lesson time at home, he was happy to be returning to the classroom and his friends.

chapter 33

Brushes with Greatness

John and I entered the last quarter of 2014 with a renewed sense of purpose toward our time in Africa, happy to still be in Nigeria and happy with our decision to apply for Djibouti. As one friend—a career foreign service officer who had spent years in Africa—said to us over lunch, "Some people are just cut out for this life." He was not referring solely to himself; he meant us too.

And when the diplomatic reception circuit restarted in late October—having been stopped for Ebola regulations—we were ready.

Well, mostly.

Getting dressed for the postponed German National Day event, I felt stiff and uncoordinated. The process of making myself reception ready, something that usually took me no more than forty-five minutes, became a long and drawn-out affair as I stumbled through the motions of styling my hair and applying makeup. Finally, having pulled on black evening pants, a sleeveless black and silver top, and a pair of black heels, I glanced in the mirror and saw the tell-tale shadows of bags under my eyes. *Man,* I thought, *I am out of practice.*

Standing in the middle of the main reception area, I took in the scene. Tables loaded with imported German delicacies, the blooming lush gardens of the German residence, the golden glow of the lights, everything just so. I stood there alone, while John was off talking to work colleagues. I had been chatting with our ambassador's spouse until we pushed the acceptable time limit. In the diplomatic circle it is frowned upon to chat with your fellow countrymen at events. So, now I stood there scanning the crowd for another familiar face to talk to.

And then I saw him.

Opposite me, also standing alone at that moment, was a man—average height, older, with a great shock of white hair. A very familiar shock of white hair. I couldn't help but stare because surely it wasn't who I thought it was . . . *was it?*

Was that Wole Soyinka standing there, returning my stare with a shy smile? Soyinka, the Nigerian writer, a giant among authors, a Nobel Prize winner, a legend in his own right.

Surely not.

But maybe?

Throughout my life, I have had the dumb luck to meet several people who fall into the famous category. I have also found that in the diplomatic world you never know who you would meet. And while I am an introvert, if the time and setting are appropriate, I will muster the courage to say hello, because, well . . . because. But that night, standing there trying to figure out if it was really Soyinka or not, I froze in place. Wole Soyinka couldn't possibly be there yet, it looked JUST LIKE HIM.

Even though it would have only taken a moment to find out, cross the floor, introduce myself, and say hello, I didn't. I just kept standing there like a deer caught in headlights, trying to smile.

"Hey sweetie, want to get some food?" John had reappeared next to me, breaking my trance.

I turned to him, my eyes wide. "John, *do you see that man*?" I flicked my gaze to the left, in the direction of Soyinka, doing my best to be subtle. "That one, over there. Is that Wole Soyinka?"

John generally deferred to me for verification of whether or not someone was famous, but that night his eyes registered recognition. "I don't know. But it sure looks like him," he whispered.

"But it can't be, *right*?" I whispered back. "I mean, why would he be here in Abuja, at the German event?" It really made no sense at all. Perhaps if it were the British High Commission, it would have been a possibility, given his work with Commonwealth programs, but German National Day? Nah.

"You know as well as I do, strange things happen at these events," John said. "Maybe it is him? Maybe we should walk over?"

I nodded. Why was I so dumbstruck by the man? If it was him, I certainly didn't want to miss the opportunity. "Okay, you're right; let's walk over."

We turned to walk that way . . . and he was gone, swallowed into the crowd. I looked left and right, no sign of him. "Damn it!"

John laughed.

"It was him, wasn't it?" I said, more to myself than to John. "I mean, it had to be, right? No one else looks like that!"

"Absolutely," John agreed, although I wasn't sure if he said that just to amuse me. "Even if it wasn't . . ."

That was part of the wonder of Nigeria, of Abuja—its over-the-top personality made being part of the diplomatic corps an adventure. You never knew what you would see or who you would meet.

Later that year, for Christmas, John gave me a book of Soyinka's poetry as a token of my unconfirmed brush with Nigerian greatness.

chapter 34

Remember the Tooth

Six months left in Nigeria. I had so many mixed feelings. When we first received word that we were moving to Abuja, I began to read all I could about Nigeria and its people. I read anything and everything. I read countless articles and even more Achebe than I already had. But my favorite was a book called *Looking for Transwonderland* by Noo Saro-Wiwa. Part travelogue, part memoir. I was fascinated by Saro-Wiwa's account of a return trip to her homeland: a country she hardly knew after being raised in England, and also the country that robbed her of her father, the writer and activist Ken Saro-Wiwa, who was executed by political rivals in 1995. In *Transwonderland*, Saro-Wiwa brought to life a beautiful yet complex country, leaving me with one powerful thought: I needed to experience it for myself.

However, Nigeria had other plans, and after we arrived, it emphasized that point as only Nigeria can. From the beginning of our time there, security became the buzzword that superseded all the reasons why we couldn't experience the Nigeria I had read so much about. As if part of some weird inverse relationship, the more we wanted to explore, the tighter the restrictions became. At the start of 2015, we had only experienced the Nigeria that existed outside of Abuja's bubble, twice. Both of the trips had required full security details—armored vehicles, armed guards—and were so close to the capital that they only lasted a couple of hours in total. In the end, we learned to make do with the Nigeria that was afforded to us—the quirky, bizarre city of Abuja. However, even that bubble became more and more restricted toward the end of our time there.

Still, that being said, we had our hands full. On top of everything else that was happening in the country, Nigeria announced that it would hold a presidential election that spring—set to be the most-watched election in the world in 2015, given the country's history of coups and political violence. Because of that, Quinn's school faced another temporary closure. A development that, while necessary for security, caused many to wonder about the quality of learning the kids were receiving that academic year after the month-long upset due to Ebola. I spent a lot of my time going back and forth with Quinn's teachers and the Department of Defense's education office liaison to ensure he wouldn't have to repeat the fifth grade.

We were also jumping through the final hoops for Djibouti. Including another two-hour-long phone interview to assess our suitability for the job before we could be given the official yes to go. When they asked me what I felt John's biggest weakness was, I let out a loud, barking laugh. "You really expect me to answer that while he is sitting right next to me?" That got a return laugh from them. At the end of the call, apparently, all of our answers were suitable, and we accepted their verbal "congratulations." The wheels of another major move began to turn.

Given all that, you can only imagine how I felt one evening in late January when I bit down on a carrot during dinner and felt a sickening crunch that was certainly not the vegetable.

"Excuse me," I said distractedly, quickly pushing my chair back from the table and running into the bathroom.

Staring into my open mouth, I saw blood pooling around my bottom left teeth. I wiped away the blood with my tongue and saw the jagged remains of a molar.

Murphy's Law struck again.

"Son of a bitch," I mumbled to my reflection.

It is important to note, for us, only a few dental emergencies merited medical evacuation when no approved treatment was available; breaking a molar was not one of them.

Early the next morning, I sat in the doctor's office at the embassy health unit with my mouth wide open, pointing to what was left of my tooth. It was a bureaucratic formality to have the embassy doctor confirm the problem before I could seek further help. "Well, I am no dentist," she laughed, "but I can confirm that that is indeed a broken tooth." She then went on to tell me that I had three options: pay my own way to Europe or the United States and have it fixed at an approved dentist; wait to have it fixed in the States while in transit for our move that summer; or go to the only local dentist approved for emergencies by the embassy and see if he had the capability to fix it. Given the pain I was in—not wanting to spend a thousand dollars out of pocket for a European trip that wasn't a vacation—I opted to try my luck with the Nigerian dentist.

I do not suffer from dentophobia, but I will admit that I was more than a little nervous about pursuing the local dentistry option. Dentistry in that part of the world was truly a hit-or-miss situation. In Cameroon, there had also been only one dentist approved for our use, which we used when we were completing our medical clearances for Nigeria. The entrance to her office had been in a very narrow, unpaved alley. The interior was old and shabby but clean. She did the best with what she had available, but that wasn't much, which left me thankful that all we had needed for our clearances was a visual inspection. To say I was more pleasantly surprised by the dentist in Nigeria would be an understatement.

While not ultra-modern or fancy, the office was located in one of Abuja's more upscale malls, just down the hall from our preferred wine store and several high-end shops. It was obvious that he catered to a certain level of clientele.

"This is not too bad," the dentist said as he moved a gloved finger around inside my mouth. "You only need to have the remaining tooth ground down and a cap placed on it."

Well, that was a relief. Had he told me I needed the entire tooth removed or extensive surgery, I would've changed my mind. As I found out, this guy had trained in the United States, including advanced dental cosmetic training in Los Angeles. Surely anyone who learned how to do cosmetic surgery in L.A. could be trusted, right?

"Now, I can make the temporary crown here in our office during your next visit. But for the permanent one, I will have to take a mold and send it off to be made," he explained, swiveling his stool around so he could pick up something from the counter behind him.

Send it out? Good grief, knowing how much dentistry costs in general, I could only imagine what that would run. "Where do you send it? How much does it cost?" Because if it was over a couple of thousand dollars, I was going to seriously consider hopping a plane to Europe.

Turning back around, he opened a display box of various crowns, holding it at an angle so that I could see them from my reclined position in the dental chair. "Oh, we work with a company in China. The mold is sent express, and it takes about three weeks. They do a great job," he continued matter-of-factly. "They will even match it to the color of your surrounding teeth. These are top quality-crowns. I recommend the zirconium; it's the best—less sensitivity and very strong. Altogether, it will cost about $500."

Wait, what? Just like when Quinn's emergency room visit cost only $25, I couldn't believe what I was hearing. The dentist we used in the States charged $3000 for crowns. That couldn't possibly be all. "Okay, $500 for the crown. And what about for the rest, the office visits, etcetera?"

"Oh, no, it will be $500 total—the crown, my time, everything."

One month later, I once again gazed into my open mouth in the bathroom mirror. Reflected back was my brand-new Chinese tooth, having been expertly inserted by a California-trained Nigerian dentist. *Who knew?*

chapter 35

Desperation

As the days ticked by on the calendar, we did our best to soak in as much of Nigeria as we could, but sadly life in Abuja had taken on a less vibrant, more desperate feel in the run-up to the election. Locals seemed to live in a state of apathy, while many expats made the decision to fly home to their passport country until better times returned. And for the first time since moving there, we were openly harassed by those looking to make a quick naira. They attempted to take advantage of our outsiderness, hoping we would crumble under pressure.

While out to lunch on a Saturday, we decided we would stop by Dunes on the way home to pick up some groceries. Thanks to Abuja's bizarre road layout, to reach Dunes from the direction we were coming from we had to drive past it almost a mile and make a U-turn. With the election looming, the roads were empty. As was typical on the weekend, the traffic lights had been turned off, meaning that those left on the roads drove like maniacs with little care toward themselves or others. To avoid going blindly into one of the worst intersections in the city to make our turn, John opted to use the laughably wide pedestrian crosswalk that preceded it by fifty feet—legal, no, but it was a common move that everyone did and was ignored by police.

But not on that day.

No sooner did John complete the turn that a group of three policemen ambled out from the shade of a tree where they had been sitting. Stepping into our lane, one of them put his hand up in the air. The other two, both with rifles slung over their shoulders, physically blocked our path. Being stopped when you had diplomatic license plates, while not unheard of, was certainly uncommon and rarely boded well. We immediately knew that something was up.

"Quinn, sit quietly," John whispered toward the back seat. The cop that had held up his hand was now positioned next to my window on the passenger side. He motioned for us to roll it down, which we did, but only about an inch.

"Is there a problem?" John asked as cordially as he could.

The police officer cocked his head and smiled, giving him the appearance of a snake eyeing its prey. "Come on now, you know that's not right," he said in a low, menacing voice. "You can no make turn like that. Now, what are you going to do to make it right?"

It was a blatant shakedown. John looked him in the eye. "If I've done something wrong, then you can give me a citation."

The policeman made a *tsk-tsk* sound with his tongue. "You know I cannot do that. You're diplomats," the word coming out of his mouth in a creepy, sing-song way. "I cannot do anything to you. But what you did was wrong, so you make it right?" His one eyebrow arched as he asked the question.

My left hand was resting on the cup holder in the center console where our handheld embassy radio sat. I picked up the radio and waved it. "Look," I said as sweetly and innocently as possible, "perhaps you'd like to talk to our embassy security officer, I am sure he could help you."

The policeman straightened and backed up slightly. Still with a sly smile, he held his hands up, and said, "Come, come, we've no need for that. I can't give you a ticket." He hesitated, then added, "But you can give us a weekend."

And there were the words: *give us a weekend.* Times were tough and uncertain, and these men had gambled that perhaps this car of diplomats would cower in fear and hand over cash in order to avoid hassle and potential harm—which some did. That's why the shakedowns continued to happen because sometimes the gamble paid off.

"No," John said flatly. "I can't do that. Like I said, give us a ticket and we will pay it." To emphasize John's point, I waved the radio again.

We sat there for what felt like an eternity. Quinn was completely still. John and I remained unmoving and showed no emotion. I wondered at what point I should call his bluff and radio the embassy. Then one of the other two policemen just shook his head and moved out of the way, waving us off. We had won. But before John could accelerate, the police officer that had been harassing us made sure to get one final word in. "Okay, but what you did was wrong. You must respect our laws in the future!"

As we drove away, we shook our heads in dismay. Respect their laws? What laws? What order? And more importantly, at what point would the devolving situation in the city, in the country stop? Would we make it to the end of our time there without further incident? It was a rather depressing thought and one that we carried with us as we went ahead with our grocery shopping.

The checker, a sweet, young Nigerian woman I had made friends with over my numerous trips to the store, greeted us in her usual warm manner, but the expression on her face betrayed her. "You've not left yet?" she asked, clearly puzzled by our presence. "You are staying here?"

"I'm staying," I said as she rang up our items. "This is home, we live here." And it was home. And we felt at home, even though Nigeria was doing its best to upset our lives and test us. John and I had discussed it over and over—we would stay until we had no option. However, the incident with the police left us wondering if our time was running out.

The cashier smiled. "I am glad you are staying. Things are crazy, everyone is leaving, but this is our country. We have to hope for the best." Yes, things had changed. Many of her regular customers, she explained—both expats and Nigerians—had fled the country, leaving behind those who could not afford to do so.

"Have a good weekend," I said as I took my change from her. "And I hope it will be a quiet election."

"Yes," she smiled, "we all do."

That evening, John and I attended a cocktail reception where I struck up a conversation with an older British gentleman, an expat businessman who had spent most of his adult life in Nigeria. We had a long, colorful discussion about our love of Nigeria and Africa in general, about why we found it fascinating and frustrating at the same time. I told him about our run-in with the police earlier that day.

He shook his head sadly, "You should have been here a few decades ago, it was a different place." He told me stories of a Nigeria I wish I had known, just as beautiful and colorful as what I had read in Noo Saro-Wiwa's book. "But now, they have no respect, no drive! They either cheat their way through life or expect everything to be given to them. They say they want democracy, but it isn't our kind of democracy; it's only a shell that suits their needs." He took a sip of his drink, looking nostalgically into the distance. "It's just not the same place."

That conversation left me sadder than I had been in some time, both wishing I could've experienced the Nigeria of his memories and hoping for its future. Unfortunately, being hopeful was difficult. John was stopped the following week again on his way home from work, then Quinn's teacher was harassed at a checkpoint as she left school one afternoon. As we headed into the weekend of the election, all we could do was hold our breath.

chapter 36

A New Day

I sat by the edge of the pool, book in hand, watching John and Quinn splash around in front of me. Aside from their laughter and the slap of the water, the only other thing I could hear were the birds in the trees. We were only 100 yards from the compound wall and the road it obscured, but that day there was no sound of cars, no honking of horns, just silence. While I relished the peace, I kept my ears tuned, just in case.

It was Election Day, and we were spending it within the confines of our compound. If you weren't working as an election monitor, the Nigerian government had asked that you stay home. The election had been postponed slightly due to voter registration issues, and there was fear of violence. And if that wasn't enough, the incumbent, Goodluck Jonathan, was being challenged by Muhammadu Buhari. Buhari had been president in the 1980s, having seized power through a military coup only to be overthrown in another military coup two years later. Seriously, you couldn't have come up with anything better if you had tried to write a plot for a thriller about a shady African election.

The election ended up taking two days—you knew it wasn't going well when President Goodluck Jonathan's card didn't even scan correctly as he tried to cast his vote. As evening fell on the second day, the election commission announced, to the shock of many, that former president Muhammadu Buhari had won.

The country held its collective breath, wondering if the result would set off rioting and if Goodluck Jonathan would step down willingly. Quinn's school sent out a message saying that it would remain closed for the rest of the week out of an abundance of caution. John was told to work from home for another day at least. Everyone waited.

Then, that same night just before we went to bed, President Jonathan called Buhari and officially conceded his defeat, maturely offering congratulations to his successor. It was an ending no one could've predicted. Buhari, in turn, congratulated his opponent on a race well run. A seemingly changed man, he made a formal announcement saying that he expected all Nigerians to honor the results of the election, to honor democracy and anyone who chose violence would not be part of his people, his country. Quite different than his first foray as a president.

The next day, for the first time in almost a year, it felt like we lived in a bright and hopeful Nigeria. Sadly, though, it would be one that we wouldn't get to experience. The formal acceptance of our application for the job in Djibouti had come through. We would be leaving Nigeria in a few months' time.

chapter 37

Nowhere in Nigeria

The movers arrived the third week of June. It was an interesting pack out for us, being our first done during Ramadan, with the majority of the packers being Muslim. In the past, we had always set out tons of bottled water and snacks to keep the movers happy, but this time they maintained their religious fasting and worked straight through. John, Quinn, and I took turns hiding in our small pantry with the door closed anytime we wanted to have something to drink or eat, an attempt to assuage our guilt.

At one point, during the middle of the afternoon on the first day of pack out, I retreated to the pantry to feed my growling stomach. *How ridiculous*, I thought as I scanned the shelves for a treat. The men packing our things must have been starving by then, yet they portrayed no emotion. I, on the other hand, couldn't last another moment without a snack. Spying a nut-filled granola bar, I unwrapped it as quietly as I could and began eating.

Standing there in that small space with the door shut, I thought about how bizarre it was—a grown woman hiding in the pantry eating a snack during the height of the day in Ramadan. It was almost as bizarre as our time living in Nigeria, where everything I had wanted to experience was always just out of reach, where we lived restricted to the confines of the

Abuja bubble. And it made me think of Noo Saro-Wiwa's book and my quest to find Transwonderland.

Did I ever find Transwonderland? Well, yes and no.

There was actually a Wonderland in Abuja—not the same one from her book, but a similar amusement park, called Wonderland, that sat on the outskirts of the city, near Quinn's school. Throughout our time there, we kept saying, "Someday, we are going to go to Wonderland!" Of course, we knew it would be an iffy adventure, given that the park had been closed off and on for years, and we were pretty certain that the safety standards for the rides would be questionable at best, but we didn't care, we were going to go.

"We have to go," I said one day as we drove past it during those final months in the country, the park's Ferris wheel peeking above the trees. "It would be such a great bookend to our time here—reading about Transwonderland, then visiting Wonderland." John and Quinn both agreed. We had to go.

But, by now because you know that Murphy was always looking for an opportunity to throw his law in my face, you know how this will end.

Shortly after making our declaration to experience Wonderland in those waning days, we received an email from the embassy alerting us to stay away from certain local businesses due to their ties to the Lebanese terrorist group, Hezbollah. And yes, you guessed it, Wonderland Amusement Park was on that list. Thanks again, Murphy.

It had been the story of our time in Nigeria, another experience snatched from our grasp, the bubble ever confining. How could we say that we ever really knew Nigeria? Well, I guess we did in a way. Every time something was taken away, we witnessed the harsh reality of the country. Still, I couldn't help but feel that we were leaving just as there was hope of a new day. Such was life.

July 1, 2015 dawned, and we zipped up our suitcases. It was brutally hot outside. Our bags were filled with the clothes it seemed we were always in—lightweight, hard-wearing summer clothes—because we were heading to summer in the United States for a short vacation before transitioning to the always hot desert climate of Djibouti.

We were sad to be leaving Nigeria, but also excited as to what lay ahead.

As John and Quinn rolled the luggage out to the waiting embassy van, I took one last look around, making sure we hadn't forgotten anything before I locked the door to the house for the last time. It had been an experience, and despite everything, I was still in awe of the fact that I had the opportunity to call Nigeria home for two years.

I will miss this, I thought as I pulled the door shut.

PART FOUR

DJIBOUTI

chapter 38

Welcome to the Gates of Hell

The small Dash 8 airplane came to a lurching halt in front of Ambouli International Airport. It was August 17, 2015, the beginning of our time in Djibouti.

Before the flight attendant had even opened the cabin door, I could feel the heat seeping in from outside. Only 10:30 a.m., and it was already 102 degrees. While we had done hot before—West African heat was nothing to sneeze at—Djibouti would be different.

But it wasn't just the heat. I knew Djibouti was going to be different before the wheels had even touched down.

Our final approach to the airport had taken us out over the Gulf of Aden, a brilliant, shining cerulean blue oasis, and then back over the city, which was varying shades of dull neutrals. Gray, white, and faded buttercup yellow buildings, darker gray pavement, and lots and lots of brown in the form of dirt and sand. A sight that would give some pause as to the importance of the tiny country . . . right up until you landed at the airport, where the world's militaries shared the runway with commercial flights. As we taxied toward the terminal, we passed a US Navy P-3 leaving Camp Lemonnier on its way to takeoff. Any hint of normality or insignificance was a ruse—Djibouti was no normal place, and what I saw on that arrival told me everything I needed to know about why we were there. Perched at the tip of the Horn of Africa, Djibouti held the key to stability in the region, and everyone knew it.

Stepping off the plane meant entering another world and a markedly different lifestyle than we had had in West Africa. Our quiet years in Nigeria, the relatively calm time in Cameroon, well, those days were over.

The three of us were halfway down the plane's stairs when we noticed two men standing near the entrance to immigration, waving to us. Despite the size of flights in and out of the airport, there were no jetways. I turned to John, "There's your welcoming committee." Indeed, it was a first for us. We were met planeside by John's soon-to-be staff—people who had eagerly awaited his arrival since it was first announced months before.

"Sir," said the one that I would come to discover was his assistant attaché. "Welcome to Djibouti."

The other man introduced himself as our non-commissioned operations officer—the person whose job was to keep everything running smoothly. I smiled and stuck out my hand to him, "Hi, I'm Julie."

"Ma'am," he said, shaking my hand.

"Nope, I'm not ma'am, just Julie." I really struggled with formalities and titles and always preferred being called by my first name.

A smirk crossed his face. "Yes, ma'am." There was a distinct touch of humor in his tone. *Ah,* I thought, *so this is how it'll be. I think we will get along just fine.*

As we made our way from the airport to our temporary house, I tried desperately to take everything in. However, what resulted was more of an impressionistic blurry reminder rather than crisp clear memories—a turn here, a big store there, cars honking, people walking.

Quinn and I had climbed into our social sponsor's car for the trip, leaving John to ride with his staff and talk shop. Our social sponsor was another embassy employee who had been in-country for a while and was happy to help us adapt to life in Djibouti.

We had pulled out of the airport behind John and the other guys and followed their lead as they took a turn at the first intersection. "Okay," our sponsor said, "it looks like they are going to go down via Siesta Beach."

"Um-hmm," I acknowledged, doing my best to stay alert but fading fast.

We passed a small gas station and various other low-slung buildings. There were a few trees and lots of brightly colored bougainvillea. There were also layers of dust and sand everywhere. People walked very slowly along the side of the road—men in shorts and T-shirts, women more modestly dressed in *baatis* (a long, loose dress similar to a kaftan) and head scarves—the heat of the day set their pace.

A turn, then another, and another—it didn't matter, I would have been lost if asked to remember. "And that is the main supermarket, Casino," our sponsor said.

Ah, something familiar. Quinn piped up in the back, "We know Casino."

"Yeah, Casino was where we shopped in Cameroon," I explained.

"Good, then you'll know what to expect," she smiled. "Most everyone shops at Casino. There are some smaller, less expensive stores in the city, but Casino will most likely be where you find everything."

Another turn, but this time it appeared that we were skirting along the edge of the land—which we were. Out my passenger side window, the view opened to reveal a sandy beach, silvery-blue water lapping at its edge. "Look, Quinn," I almost whispered.

"Yep, that's Siesta Beach," our sponsor said. "A favorite spot for the locals, especially on Friday afternoons. It's off-limits for us, plus I wouldn't want to wade into the water given that they use it for all manner of activities if you know what I mean. But it's still pretty to look at."

And it was pretty, stretching along the edge of the city, the Gulf of Aden just beyond. Being midday on a Monday, it wasn't crowded. Still there were a few people scattered around, some swimming, some washing their clothes or themselves, some just standing and staring into the distance. On the opposite side of the road, the beach extended in a narrow strip where people took refuge in the shade of tall palm trees. Women sat tending makeshift food stands, selling the local version of samosas, and dispensing juice from large yellow Igloo-style coolers. Everything about the scene was in stark difference from the sparseness we had seen earlier on the drive—the beach was literally an oasis where the desert met the sea.

Then, as quickly as it had appeared, the beach was gone. We turned left and headed into a maze of narrow streets and roundabouts. Before we knew it, we were at the gate of our temporary house. I listened while we were given a quick tour and shown how to use all the necessities—oven, water dispenser, coffee maker—but in reality, I heard nothing. We had barely waved goodbye and closed the door before I sat on the couch and promptly fell asleep.

Since John's job had sat empty for months, we had to hit the ground running. So from the moment we woke up on our first full day in-country, we were working. It was like taking a big gulp of air and then breaking into a sprint.

Despite having been through an SDO/DATT tour in Cameroon, Djibouti would be a different game entirely. The embassy was small, but John's job was huge because of our military ties to the country and the importance of security and stability in the region. And that significance meant that I couldn't count on John to be around to help us settle in—that side of our life would be all on me.

For those first few weeks, whenever I left the temporary house, I lugged my backpack with me containing: my current war book, a blank notebook, various pens, my planner, and a clear plastic file folder to shove receipts, other important papers—oh, and a lightweight scarf because the embassy was way too air-conditioned for my taste. In those early weeks, I had also begun Quinn's homeschooling—truly a new adventure for us—and had to fit that in amongst everything else. One minute I would be sitting and listening to a list of upcoming events and responsibilities and going over the specs of the house we were meant to be moving into. The next, I would be making sure that Quinn, who tagged along with me while we worked on finding a nanny/housekeeper, had his schoolbook to read, remotely learning until home became a more permanent location.

We were looking forward to the house they had earmarked for us. While it wasn't the most beautiful house in the world, nor in the best location, it did sit right on the edge of the water—always a bonus for a navy family. We hadn't lived near the sea since England, and even then, it was a fifteen-minute walk, so to think that we would be able to wake up in the morning and have coffee on the second-floor verandah while staring at the Indian Ocean would be worth the wonky, small kitchen and too small entertaining space. And as it was the only house available, beggars couldn't be choosers.

Until the ambassador decided otherwise.

As I said, Djibouti was an important location for our government, and John's job was a key position in the military-heavy environment. So when the ambassador got wind of our housing option, he put his foot down and said no. He promptly told his staff that our residence needed to be big enough and nice enough to entertain on the level we were expected to entertain. He added that there had to be a house within the embassy housing pool that hit those marks, even if it meant rightsizing and moving people around. And while that sounded awful to me—no way did I want the reputation of kicking someone out of their house just so we could entertain—I knew it was the right decision. Thankfully for us, there was an employee who, having been there for a few years, was rattling around as one person in a very, very large house.

"I'll pick you up and take you to see the house, then you can let us know what you think," the housing coordinator said to me over the phone.

"Will that be okay with the current occupant?" I asked, not relishing the idea of traipsing around someone's place while they weren't home.

"Oh sure," she said. "He doesn't mind."

Sadly, the new, larger house did not have an ocean view. *So much for having my morning coffee by the sea,* I thought wistfully. We made our way down the very dusty side street on which it sat and waited for the gardener to open the compound gate. I glanced around, taking in the surrounding houses and the large empty lot opposite the gate that was covered with bits of trash and foraging goats. We were a mile from the airport and much nearer the embassy—logistically, I knew it was a better location.

The gate swung open to a large garden and parking area—a rarity in Djibouti, especially the garden. Having anything green in that harsh climate was more of a bonus than an ocean view.

Most embassy houses had only small, paved areas and no greenery to speak of. "It's in a bit of disrepair right now," the housing coordinator said, "but with the right gardener, and a bit of effort, it could be quite the place." She was right. The garden was a series of rectangular plots in varying sizes with a flagstone path woven in between. The shrubs and grasses had been left to their own devices for some time, but it was evident that the place would look almost showy if trimmed.

The house was a large, two-story French African colonial painted a warm buttercream yellow with white accents. We literally had to make a path to the door by pushing through a couple dozen feral cats that had claimed the marble-floored verandah as their own. Then opening the tall, carved-wood door, we stepped into the house's vast, white-walled interior. The space was huge and felt even more so by the fact that it was only sparsely furnished. Sensing my concern about filling the giant void, the housing coordinator said, "Don't worry, there is quite a bit of furniture set aside for your residence. Plus, you can always request additional if that is not enough."

I walked through the bedrooms, sitting room, pantry, and formal reception area—all more than adequate for our needs— but was completely underwhelmed by the kitchen. Yes, it was large for a kitchen in Djibouti. Yes, there were drawers in the cabinets, another rarity in the country. But it had obviously been built as an afterthought by someone who never had to prepare their own food, leaving that chore to staff. The cook in me recoiled. "Um, well," I started, as I accidentally bumped a hip into the countertop, only to watch the entire unit sway side to side.

"Honestly, this is the best kitchen I've seen in a while," the coordinator said. "It's twice the size of most and has functional storage. We can shore up the cabinets for you and make sure everything is stable."

I guessed I couldn't complain. I would make it work. "We'll take it," I said as if I truly had any say in the matter.

"Great." The coordinator jotted down a few notes about the cabinets. "Unfortunately, it will extend your time in the temporary house a bit. With moving out the current guy and then to make ready for you, we're looking at mid-September."

Three more weeks of living out of suitcases. *Ugh.* But we'd do it. We had to.

And then, of course, Murphy's Law came knocking.

Two weeks later, I found myself standing in the middle of a rather rundown warehouse near the Port of Djibouti. The place was cavernous and completely empty except for eight wooden shipping crates, all of which sported varying levels of damage. The crates were ours, the ones that we had shipped from Nigeria, the ones which held 90 percent of our worldly belongings. I stood there, surrounded by Djiboutians who, like me, stared wide-eyed at what was in front of us, a mess of unknown magnitude. Two thoughts went through my mind: *It's just stuff,* and *I should be at home eating pizza right now.*

The day had started out fairly regular, aside from restless sleep courtesy of a large thunderstorm that rolled through in the middle of the night—shockingly, Djibouti, one of the driest places on earth, occasionally received rain—beyond that, it was fairly normal. A typical Thursday, the Friday of the Islamic week, and, therefore, the end of our workweek. I began the day looking forward to its end.

Everything was planned out: Quinn and I would focus on homeschool for the first half of the day, then we would head to the embassy's pool for an afternoon swim, and finally, when John was finished with work, we would all head home together for our standing end-of-week family date night of pizza and a movie. Life had been slowly finding its rhythm, and that week had been the smoothest so far. We were a little over a week away from moving into our official residence, and our household goods were due to arrive in-country that very day. A bright light was shining at the end of our tunnel. Our months of upheaval were finally coming to an end.

"Before we head to the pool, I need to pop inside the embassy and check my email," I told Quinn as we heaved our swim bags into the motorpool SUV that picked us up just after lunch. Because our temporary house had no internet and data for phones was too expensive, I used the computers at the embassy a couple of times a week to keep up with email.

My inbox was full. A few emails from our family and friends checking to make sure we were okay. The standard notifications from accounts alerting me to bills that were due or documents to download and tons of miscellaneous items that could wait another week before I read them. I had just finished going through the most pressing items when John's operations officer popped into the room, a smile on his face, clearly pleased with himself. "Your household goods have already cleared customs," he said.

"What?" I wasn't sure I'd heard him right.

Our entire move from Abuja to Djibouti had been an exercise in pain, the worst we had ever experienced. The majority of that pain was due to half-truths about the shipping and arrival of our belongings. Normally, for a move like ours, we were allotted two separate shipments: one large one, containing the bulk of our personal belongings, plus a second, smaller express shipment that would arrive first, containing only the necessities to get started. When we had talked to the shipping department in Nigeria, they told us that an express shipment would not be necessary for this move because we were going to Djibouti. We were not leaving the continent, and the entirety of our household goods would ship immediately and directly to us, not more than two weeks after we arrived. We followed their advice . . . to our detriment.

When we arrived in Djibouti and filed the paperwork to start the movement of our goods, we were informed that Nigeria had been wrong. Our stuff had been sent to the central distribution center in Belgium and it would take at least a month to reach us. Yes, that meant that everything, aside from what was in our suitcases, was stuck in Europe, waiting for an empty sea container and space on a cargo ship heading south. With John so busy getting his feet under him in his new job, the responsibility to fix this mess fell on me. During those first days in Djibouti, I spent hours sorting through emails and notes, finding and forwarding every bit of hard evidence I had showing the horrible advice we were given and handing it over to John's operations officer so he could work with the personal property people to expedite our belongings. In the end, through sheer tenacity and the refusal to take no for an answer, we won: the folks in Belgium would be sending all our crates via an air shipment to arrive on the original promised date. However, knowing that clearing customs in Djibouti could be a very slow process, I had not expected our crates to be ready so soon—hence the look of confusion on my face.

"Don't worry, we can put the crates in the warehouse until next week," the operations officer said. "Then, once your house is ready for move-in, we will have them delivered."

"Sounds good," I said, both amazed and relieved. He left, and I returned to what I was doing, a smile on my face. In exactly one week, we would be moving into our permanent home and sorting through the boxes that comprised our life. *Yes*, I thought, *this is turning out to be a very good day.*

I was almost finished at the computer. I had already told Quinn to get our stuff together so that we could head to the pool. Then John walked through the door followed by the operations officer and the embassy's general services officer. I knew something was up because none of them wanted to look me in the eye.

John broke the silence by saying, rather dismally, "It's about our stuff." He wore a look of disbelief mixed with anger.

The poor general services officer, whom I had only recently met, had the appearance of a man who just drew the short straw for diffusing a bomb. He gave me a sheepish look and began to speak. "Well, the good news is that your stuff arrived last night on the midnight flight from Doha."

He paused, looked down at his feet, then back up at me.

"The bad news is that it rained last night—a lot—and your crates were left outside on the tarmac without cover." He paused again. "There has been damage."

There has been damage.

He continued to talk, explaining the unbelievable mess, but I tuned him out, my mind shifting to problem-solving mode, mechanically working through possible solutions to this waking nightmare. Then I heard him say, "I suggest we have the damaged items delivered to your new house immediately and store them in some of the completed rooms."

"Yes," I said more forcefully than I should have, grabbing my notebook and shoving it into my bag. "But right now, I want to go out to the warehouse and look at the damage, then I will determine what can be delivered today. I don't want someone else making that decision." Not one of them dared argue with me. I swung my bag over my shoulder, told Quinn that swimming would have to wait and to stay with John. And off I went to the warehouse with three members of the embassy's locally employed shipping staff.

As we drove along, I found it odd to think that our stuff had been damaged by rain. The only way you would have known that there had been a torrential storm the night before was by the ungodly humidity that hung in the air. The ground, for the most part, was already bone dry.

Being a Thursday after 4 p.m., the warehouse, owned by a local shipping company, was closed. Only the manager—now well high on khat, the legalized drug of choice in the region that left its consumers in a mellow, euphoric state—was left to let us in. I had been wearing a sweater in the over-air-conditioned embassy but stripped down to my tank top as we entered the massive yet stiflingly hot building.

When we lived in Cameroon, I had worked in the embassy part-time. My job included counseling people about their choice of whether or not to bring their belongings to a place where there was a very real possibility of having to evacuate quickly and leave everything behind. I would tell them that it's a very personal choice, and everyone has their own reasons for why they do or do not bring their items with them. For us, the sense of home our belongings provided—being the only things we owned since we had no permanent residence in the States, no house we would eventually return to—were what made a place ours.

Yet, there I stood, staring at our broken, water-logged crates, wondering if we had made the correct decision. Three of the eight crates appeared to have been crushed inward from the top and were visibly leaking water. Two more had significant damage at the bottom. One appeared normal at first, but upon further inspection, I discovered a giant hole in the bottom with clothes hangers angrily poking out, water dripping from their tips. Only two crates seemed to have survived unscathed. My mind was so deep into problem-solving mode that I wasn't panicking or grieving for what I saw—instead, I simply told the embassy staff to pry open the crates and to start off-loading the boxes inside onto the flatbed truck that had backed into the warehouse next to us.

It was late evening by the time we had off-loaded and moved the contents of the most badly damaged crates—two trips worth. Our poor house, which was still a week from being ready, proved not to be ideally suited for what was happening. The work crews were still making repairs to the interior, furniture was piled here and there, and dust and debris was everywhere. Yet, we were still shoving and stacking boxes into the two rooms we could sacrifice and that, more importantly, were able to be locked up. We opened boxes that were soaking wet or visibly damaged. Family photos, still recognizable but soggy, were spread out to dry on any available surface. John's briefcase, a beautiful buttery leather thing that I'd given him for Christmas years before, had to be literally wrung out and hung on the corner of a door. All of my evening gowns were strewn around as if on display in a shop and not simply drying. The two large battery backup systems we used for electronics were dripping with water when we opened them—we had no idea if they would ever work again. At that point, it had been such a long day that we were too exhausted and numb to care.

"Okay," I said, completely spent, "I think that's the worst of it. Let's call it a night." At 8:45 p.m., we locked the doors to the rooms and headed back to the temporary house.

After five hours of riding an emotional roller coaster, the three of us finally sat down on the couch to eat. Grilled cheese sandwiches had replaced the previously planned pizza because I just couldn't bring myself to do one more thing. We turned on the DVD of *Smokey and The Bandit* that we had borrowed from the embassy. I found myself laughing uncontrollably when

Jackie Gleason kept saying "sumbitch"—it was oddly soothing and relatable knowing the aftermath that still awaited us.

"How are you finding our country?" The question was posed to me by a senior Djiboutian military officer as he took a sip of coffee while chatting with me in the living room of our new residence.

It was our first official event in Djibouti. We'd finally moved in. Finally unpacked the rest of our boxes. We were settling in.

That day we had invited representatives from all branches of the Djiboutian armed forces over for a low-key hello to announce ourselves to the community. I had been floating amongst the guests, shaking hands, plying them with cake and cookies, making small talk, and stepping back into my role as Mrs. DATT.

"I find it fascinating," I said to the colonel. It was still my standard answer at that point.

"Really?" He said, visibly amused. "Fascinating? You are finding our country livable?"

"Well . . ." I started to say, then began to think about what the previous two months had been like. A rough landing to say the least, but no fault of the country. "Yes, I do find it fascinating," I said. "Now, I'll be honest—it hasn't been the easiest of transitions for us. But I think we'll do just fine here."

"Well, good. Djibouti can sometimes be very difficult. You know what we locals call this region?" He paused to see if I knew, then continued when I shook my head no. "The Gates of Hell," he said smiling.

Welcome to the Gates of Hell, I thought. *Yes, indeed.* And I smiled back and wondered what the country really held in store for us.

chapter 39

Those Who Came Before Us

Djibouti was flagrantly different from anywhere we had lived, and I truly did find it fascinating. From its appearance to its tone —equal parts desolate backwater and stunning oasis, fluctuating between quiet and chaos, living there was like living in a modern-day version of the movie *Casablanca*. Djibouti, an unlikely little country, was an epicenter of power. Right away, it was obvious that we were just bit players stepping into pre-established roles, the same as everyone else.

More importantly, though, Djibouti was becoming home.

Despite our rocky start, we had turned the new DATT house into the residence it needed to be, as well as our home. The damage that our household goods had received was far less in the end than it had appeared at first. We hung up our paintings, put our books on the bookcases, and made the space within the compound walls our own. Well, almost our own. We still had a feral cat that was stubbornly determined to remain a resident alongside us. Quinn christened her Cat Two, numerically named as she had been one of the seven original strays that had stuck around the longest. By October, she was the only one left, and we were okay with that. Not allowed in the house, she became the residence's mascot, spending her days stretched out on the cool marble tiles of the veranda. She also became the Cheshire Cat to my Alice—silently judging me when I'd walk by . . . and I swear, sometimes smiling.

A place becomes familiar and more homelike through its sounds, which eventually help build future memories. I know that through my own memories. Whenever I hear water flowing through a creek, I think of the ranch in the winter, when I would lie in bed at night and listen to the creek outside my bedroom window. Or when I hear a rooster crowing, I am transported back to the Bat House in Cameroon, where our neighbor's over-zealous rooster would begin crowing long before daybreak in his daily attempt to be the first to greet the day. Sounds become as much a part of a place as the physical items which inhabit it.

After we finally moved into our official residence, the repetitive sounds found there helped establish its familiarity. Like the garbage trucks that made their rounds early in the morning. A PA system similar to an ice cream truck, complete with the tinkly, tinny music announced their arrival and alerted people to bring out their trash.

Then there was the baguette man with his old-fashioned bicycle horn. Every morning and every evening, he would push his cart—fashioned from plywood and painted turquoise—down the roads of our neighborhood. He would honk his horn, reminiscent of Harpo Marx, to hawk freshly baked baguettes, which had been a staple of the local diet since colonialism.

There were also the very beautiful yet very loud rose-ringed parakeets. The brilliant lime-green birds were everywhere—including a large flock that considered our compound home. They would whoosh and alight either in our trees or on the outside of our air conditioners and squawk happily at the top of their little bird lungs.

We had the *rat-a-tat-tat* of gunfire from the French military's firing range, only a stone's throw from our front gate. And the airplanes. Always the airplanes. The consequence of living less than a mile from the airport. The constant comings and goings of international and military aircraft made for interesting times. While I did sometimes curse how loud the French Pumas were when they flew, it was cool to go up on our roof and watch the planes take off and land.

But, by far, the most atmospheric and memory-inducing sound in Djibouti was proving to be the muezzin from our neighborhood mosque. Over our years in Africa, we lived near mosques most of the time, so their melodic calls to prayer, five times a day, had woven their way into our life. The mosque just down the street from our house in Djibouti had the most melodic muezzin we had ever heard. This was something we were very thankful for when other friends in the city said that the mosques near them could do with a vocal upgrade.

Those were the sights and sounds of Djibouti that comprised our daily life, imprinting the country in our minds.

But the pace of our life in Djibouti was relentless. It made us truly thankful for the two quieter years we had in Nigeria.

For me, I realized that everything about my life in Africa had been a progression. In Cameroon, I was the wide-eyed ingenue, allowing Africa to seep in, to learn and then grow. In Nigeria, I had had time to observe and just be. But Djibouti was a different story entirely; my life was lived at a pace I hadn't experienced before, and I was on a run from the start.

On a given day, I would go from teaching Quinn about Mesopotamia to slipping into a cocktail dress and heading out the door to a representational event that extended late into the night. Our arrival happened to coincide with the rest of the diplomatic community's return from summer abroad. The *rent-rée en masse*, as the French call it, which ushers in the start of the diplomatic social season. It was not uncommon for us to have four or five social functions per week.

During those first official evenings, I found myself shadowing John through the assembled crowds. Not established enough to mingle on my own, I stood next to him while we met and greeted the people that would comprise our social set for the next few years. The noise levels at the events made it difficult for me to understand the French being spoken. So it was just easier in the beginning if I simply smiled, nodded my head, and laughed at the appropriate moments—or at least at what I hoped were the appropriate moments. I could tell that some of the other attendees, mainly the spouses, shared my pain as they also stood, smiled, and nodded.

Once home, I would pass out, physically and mentally exhausted from yet another day in the life of us, knowing that it would all start again in just a few hours.

In time, however, I began to learn the pattern of the invitations we received, which events I knew I was required to attend, and which I could pass. For example, while I would need to attend almost every cocktail party, the invitations for military commemorations were usually for John alone—which was fine by me.

One afternoon in early October, John called from his office to give me the rundown of the invitations he'd received that week. "I have a bunch of them for you," he said. "Have you got your calendar?"

"Yep," I said, putting down the art history book I was using with Quinn and opening my planner. "Fire away."

He started to rattle off dates and times of work dinners and receptions, including ones that only he had to attend because it was easier to just keep track of it all. For example, to know in advance when he'd be out and or to make sure he had the correct uniform clean and ready to go. "And then, on November 11," he added, "there is the British Remembrance Day Commemoration at the cemetery. And you'll need to go to that one, you're specifically on the invitation."

"Sure, absolutely," I said, flipping into November and penciling in the details. There was no doubt in my mind that I would go, especially because, after our time living in England, we had developed a special bond with our British counterparts; I never turned down an invitation from them. And as I knew that some of their fallen from World War II were buried at the local cemetery, it was the right thing to do.

"No," John continued, "you'll especially want to attend this one. There is an American buried with them."

I stopped writing. "What?"

"I don't know much about it yet, but there is an American who fought for the Brits and is buried at the cemetery," he explained. "I've been told there is a file on him somewhere here in the office . . ."

"I want that file," I interrupted. "Can you bring it home to me?"

"I don't see why not. I'll try to locate it today and bring it home tonight." I could almost hear the smile on his face when he added, "See, I knew you'd want to go."

In the short amount of time that we had been there, Djibouti had captured my imagination. It was such a harsh environment, one that would cause anyone to question living there. Still being so central in world politics, it hummed with activity. I was entranced.

For many Americans, their only knowledge of Djibouti stemmed from its strange name (along with the juvenile jokes it prompted) and from the fact that we had several thousand deployed service members at Camp Lemonnier, which was our forward operating site located adjacent to the airport. Lemonnier also was just down the road from where we lived. But what I discovered was a Djibouti that was a curious cross-section of the world I had been living in. An African country with which America maintained a strong diplomatic tie, yet deemed dangerous enough that our larger American military entity only sent its service members there without their families. My own family's exception being that we were part of the embassy mission, separate from our fellow military peers at the camp. Explaining to people back home as to why we were there and why Djibouti should matter to them often involved a lot of clarification—not the least of which was the fact that Americans had been part of the country's story for a very long time. From Civil War veterans who had joined up to fight with Egyptian military in the late 1800s to the establishment of Camp Lemonnier after the events of 9/11, Djibouti was a forgotten lesson in world history—a faraway country whose global role was bigger than its physical size.

When John said that we had an American buried there, an even stronger fascination began to grow within me. I had no knowledge of an American service member—whether they served with our armed forces or another's—being buried on the continent outside of North Africa. I simply had to know more. Who was he? How did he die? What about his family? Did anyone else know about him? If the people back home barely knew of Djibouti, did they even know that this man existed?

Keeping to his promise, when John returned home from work that night, he dropped the file for Pilot Officer Lawrence Maguire on my lap. There it was, a life condensed to a small stack of papers. I read through them with the same zeal as if it were a bestseller. The life of an all-American boy who had grown up with a strong desire to do the right thing. He had enlisted in the Royal Canadian Air Force because our own country had not yet joined World War II. He was a young man who was loved by his family and those who knew him. A young man that so eerily reminded me of John. A young man who served and continued to serve despite the dangers he knew existed. A young man shot down only a mile from where I sat, dying at twenty-three and buried in the desert country that claimed him. I ended up in tears. If Maguire only knew that we were there, all those years later. If he only knew . . . At that moment, I decided to make Maguire's legacy my mission. Over the next three years, he would become my constant companion.

That year, November 11 fell on a Wednesday. It was a very hot and steamy afternoon, as the cooler season that would eventually usher in dry winds and lower temperatures hadn't arrived. I was dripping with sweat as I got dressed despite the air conditioning that blasted in our house. I pulled my hair into a twist, combing it smooth in an attempt to control its natural curls and avoid frizz. The doorbell rang. Our friends had arrived to pick up Quinn for his weekly soccer practice coached by service members assigned to Camp Lemonnier.

"Quinn," I called down the hall as I slipped my feet into my heels, "your ride is here."

"Okay, I'm just tying my shoes," he answered from his bedroom. I found him there in his Bayern Munich soccer kit, dressed and ready to play. We walked downstairs together, grabbed his soccer ball, and headed to the door.

"Dad and I will come directly to Camp when we're done," I told him as I kissed the top of his head. He bounced out the door and into our friends' car. With a wave, they were off.

At a quarter to five, John and I pulled into the parking area for the cemetery. A couple of dozen SUVs were already parked there, having ferried ambassadors, military attachés, and other members of the diplomatic corps to the ceremony. I pushed open my passenger side door, an absolute beast because of the added armor, then stepped down into the deep, silt-like dirt. The sun had begun its daily descent, casting long shadows amongst the graves, but the heat remained—it was still like an oven. Attendees gathered into their places, all of us standing, as it was the only feasible plan. I left John at his appointed place beside our ambassador and walked to the edge of the crowd, finding a spot where I could still see everything. A strong breeze, the remnant of a recent cyclone that had passed through the Gulf of Aden, blessedly blew through the cemetery grounds and tugged strands of my hair from the confines of its neat coif. I didn't care about the stray tendrils; that breeze was the coolest I had felt in weeks. Judging by the expressions of those gathered near me, braving the heat in suits and full military dress, they didn't mind either.

A British bishop visiting from Ethiopia began the service. I did my best to pay attention but found my eyes and thoughts drifting to the side, just beyond the attendees, to the neat row of gravestones on the ground. There was Maguire. I had been reading about him and researching his story for over a month, but that was the first time I had been to his grave at the cemetery. It was closed to the public except on special occasions. The cemetery, a spot of high ground just off the road, had been his resting place for the past seventy years. I tried to focus on the ceremony—members of the British diplomatic corps were doing readings. The procession of wreaths, laid out by representatives of the various countries present. John and our ambassador took our own wreath forward and placed it amongst the rest. I quietly snapped a photo of the moment with my phone, not exactly adhering to protocol by doing so, but I felt it necessary. At the end, our friend, the British defense attaché, read Laurence Binyon's "Ode to Remembrance":

> *They shall grow not old,*
> *as we that are left grow old;*
> *Age shall not weary them,*
> *nor the years condemn.*
> *At the going down of the sun*
> *and in the morning.*
> *We will remember them.*

Tears welled up in my eyes. While I was normally touched with emotion at these types of events, this one carried new meaning and more weight. As soon as we were dismissed, I took a handkerchief out of my handbag, dabbed my eyes dry, and walked over to Maguire's grave.

Standing there by myself, I looked down at the freshly cleaned marble that bore his name. "I'm so sorry," I said quietly. "But I am glad to finally meet you." I took a photo of his headstone with the wreath of yellow roses lying beside it. Then I just stood there, lost in my thoughts. With the amount of stress and fatigue I had felt in the short time since we'd arrived in Djibouti, the reasoning of why we were there and why we were putting such strain on ourselves had been top of mind. Looking down at Maguire's grave, knowing all he had sacrificed, it became clear—I knew what our job was and why we had to do it, but now I also knew there was another reason for us to be there.

John appeared next to me.

"We have to do something, John," I said, not looking him in the eye for fear of my tears starting again. "While we are here, we need to honor him. We need to make sure he's not forgotten. Our country has been tied to this place for so long and it seems like nobody knows that. We need to tell them. And we can start with Maguire."

Standing next to me in his crisp whites, John looked every inch the naval officer Maguire had aspired to be when he had applied to the Naval Academy, prior to leaving for Canada. The eeriness was not lost on me. "Absolutely," John said, "we'll do everything we can."

With that, I said goodbye to Maguire, and we left to pick Quinn up from soccer.

chapter 40

Alice During Her Adventures in Wonderland

D ays and months passed by so quickly in Djibouti. It seemed that we went from unpacking into our house one day to marking the first anniversary of our arrival the next. Everything blurred and changed. Some things took distinct shape, others remaining abstract and intangible, much like Djibouti itself.

The city, Djiboutiville, was not a place you could count on looking the same way twice. Every month there seemed to be something new, which was quite a feat given how small it was. New stores popped up in what was once a quasi-empty lot of shacks and trash. Restaurants and cafes aspiring to mimic globally recognizable chains appeared almost overnight. Some made a decent go of it; others disappeared just as fast as they came. For us, personally, the biggest change that first year was the arrival of QSI Djibouti, an American curriculum-based school.

The school's arrival was the answer to the prayers of parents and kids alike. The dream of having a reputable English-language school in the country had existed for some time. In the world of foreign service, schools are a way to entice and attract

employees to a location. But establishing schools in some locales was harder than you might expect. Bureaucratic hurdles
and small student body size could ax an idea before it even got
off the ground. However, in our case, the misfortune of others
became our good luck. When political strife in nearby Yemen
forced the close of the QSI location there, the ability to simply
transport that school's supplies across the narrow stretch of the
Red Sea was just the opportunity we needed.

"I'm tired of Teacher Mom," Quinn had said after our first
six months of homeschooling. "I want Mom Mom back."

"So, if a school were to open here, an American school, you'd
want to go?" I asked.

"Absolutely."

Happily, it came to pass, and when QSI Djibouti opened in
August 2016 with a dozen kids in attendance, Quinn was one of
them.

On the first day of his seventh-grade year, Quinn returned
to an honest-to-goodness classroom in a school fashioned out
of an old compound that once housed the European Union's
military contingent. His desk had a glorious view over the Gulf
of Aden.

On my first day of Quinn's new school year, I sat at my desk
in our makeshift office on the second floor of our house and
sighed with relief at no longer having to be Teacher Mom. Being Mrs. DATT and Mom Mom was enough. I was finally able
to think back on the time we had spent in Djibouti so far. If I
had to sum up our life there in just one word, it would be: surreal. While our life in Cameroon and Nigeria had exposed us
to numerous new experiences, over time even those had become
common place. That was not the case in Djibouti. While some
things did become common, at the same time there were always

new things popping up or happening that made me feel like Alice during her adventures in Wonderland.

On the morning school run, I never knew what I would see. Would I see a goat herder walking his goats to their grazing area for the day? Would I see camels lazily strolling in the early morning heat? Would I see a French tank navigating the same roundabout as me? Or, better yet, would I see a French soldier walking from housing to their base in his desert uniform of tight short-shorts, short-sleeved shirt, combat boots, and a beret? One could never be certain what awaited them in Djibouti. But what I saw in December 2016 was the surprise of all surprises.

Occasionally I received my own invitations to events sans John. However, it didn't happen often and most of them I turned down because it would have only compounded our crazy schedule. But that December I received one I couldn't pass up. I had been invited to an honest-to-goodness fashion show.

Let me start by saying I have never been the type of person to be invited to fashion shows. There was one time, years before when I was in college, and our local cattlewomen's group put on a fashion show fundraiser. They even talked me into being one of their models—I had been hesitant about that but went along with it when I found out that I could wear my cowboy boots with the dress I was modeling, which made me happy. But aside from that very brief foray, I would never make it onto a best-dressed list. In fact, before we moved to Djibouti, I had enlisted the help of my cousin who is a fashion stylist to help with my wardrobe because I didn't trust my own judgment with those decisions.

Still, an invitation to a real fashion show in Djibouti was not something one received every day. Curiosity would kill me if I didn't go.

I sat at my desk, looking at the invitation in my hand that said: Dress code—silver and white. I rubbed the frown lines on my forehead. *Hell,* I muttered to myself. I had asked a friend about the event, and she had told me to expect a dress code, that the previous year it had been red and black. *Hey,* I thought, *that's easy.* I had plenty of mix and match items in my closet. Perhaps they would choose black and white or black and gold—that would be a cinch. But no. Silver and white. In a dusty place like Djibouti, those colors were notorious for keeping clean and therefore, not in abundance in my closet. Of course, I could've gone out and bought something, but the one or two places that sold dressy women's clothing were eye-wateringly expensive. So, on the night of the event, I put on a silver top and black evening pants and hoped the chic women in attendance wouldn't judge me too harshly.

Our group of invitees from the embassy arrived at the posh Kempinski Hotel very early. Americans are notoriously early in the diplomatic world—so we did the only sensible thing and stopped at the poolside bar to have a pre-show cocktail.

"Pernod, *s'il vous plaît.*" It was sticky hot that evening, so rather than join the others in a glass of red wine, I opted for the more refreshing Pernod, served in the French style over ice.

Gazing around while I sipped, I couldn't help but stare in bewildered fascination at the location of that evening's show—a rock and earth jetty that stretched out into the water. Water that was actively patrolled against terrorists and criminals, yet that night showcased an honest-to-god catwalk for a fashion show complete with tall scaffold lighting and a large backdrop at the back.

As the sun began to set, we queued to enter the seating area. On each chair was a swag bag containing: a can of Diet Coke—the local distributor was the main sponsor of the evening—a mirror compact, a paper fan, a CD of the music from the evening, and, thankfully, a bottle of water.

With everyone in their seats, the lights lowered and Jain's "Makeba" filled the air. The familiar, thumping French-Afro pop beat combined with the sudden darkness and a faint sea breeze gave me goosebumps. The lights came up, highlighting the stage and runway. Leggy models began their strutting walks toward us, wearing clothing that had been curated for the climate. The music boomed and changed, morphing from one song to another. The colors in the clothes flashed as the models moved their arms. I was transported out of Djibouti and into a big city fashion week.

Then the lights lowered again. A spotlight illuminated the middle of the stage where a woman stood, dressed in a white bodysuit and large, feathery angel wings. We watched as she danced down the catwalk to the music. Her ballet twists and turns were beautiful and graceful. While everyone's eyes followed her, including mine, I suddenly found myself thinking, *What on earth am I doing here? I am on a jetty at the mouth of the Gulf of Tadjoura in a country filled to the brim with foreign military bases. Eighty-five miles northeast is conflict-ridden Yemen! Yet, here I am watching women strut down a runway in clothing imported from France?* Of all the things I experienced during our years in Africa, that was the most surreal. And even though my eyes watched the show, my mind was lost in the ridiculousness of it all.

After the show, we were ushered to the obligatory reception, complete with champagne. I imagined it to be similar to the fashion week after parties in Paris, just on a much smaller scale. I stood and listened to women chat animatedly about the clothes, complimenting the coordinator—herself a French expat and former model—on her curated collection and chattering about which items they wanted to buy in preparation for upcoming social events. At the same time, less than a mile away, people lived on the streets, struggling to make enough money to survive.

Less than ten miles away, the Chinese were building a monstrosity that would soon become their first overseas base. And less than fifty miles away was the open and unforgiving desert. Yet, there we were, sipping champagne and nibbling on canapés, talking about clothes. I had a hard time maintaining enough of a smile to suffice as polite for the remainder of the evening. It was the first and last time I attended an event like that. My mind couldn't justify its frivolity with the realities of Djibouti and the work we had been sent there to do.

chapter 41

Julie in Djibouti

I was sitting on our small patch of artificial grass on a late Saturday afternoon in early February. There was a touch of humidity in the air, a sure sign that the cooler season was ending, and even hotter days were coming. I gazed around the garden. Sunlight filtered through the leaves of the big tree that dominated our compound, creating a dappled effect on the vibrant green AstroTurf. The pale yellow of our house and compound walls added even more gold to the golden hour glow, the jewel-toned bougainvillea looking like sparks of flame here and there. Cat Two was casually stretched out beside me, staring bemusedly at the rope toy we had bought her for Christmas. John and Quinn kicked a soccer ball back and forth in front of us. I loved our little oasis in the desert.

"You know, I think we could pull it off," I said to John as he booted the soccer ball, sending it diagonally across the turf to Quinn.

"Pull what off?" He asked.

"The iftar. I think we could have it here. I mean, I know it has to be a sit-down meal and that we have limited space inside the house to do that and prayers, but I think we could make it work. The inside could be solely for the meal, and we could use this as the prayer space," I said, waving my arm to encompass the area where we were. "It would be beautiful."

John nodded in understanding, kicked the ball again, then paused and glanced around, seeing the space as I saw it. "Well, we could definitely give it a try." Just then, the ball whizzed back past John and off the pitch, a sly kick by Quinn.

"GOOOAAL!" Quinn yelled in triumph.

John hung his head in mock shame—I had distracted him too much.

Yes, I thought as I looked around the garden again. *This could work.*

While we were always busy in Djibouti, our life had been non-stop since the previous Thanksgiving. Everybody and their brother—or at least every politician and their colleague—thought that the 2016 post-election period was the perfect time to visit Djibouti and show some love to our military personnel serving at Camp Lemonnier. One VIP after another descended upon us in those waning months of the year—the fallacy of such visits being that it meant so much to the people serving far away from home, yet no one talked about the sheer volume of work required to pull off these visits or questioned whether or not they were actually worth it. By the time Christmas arrived, John was exhausted and took a week of leave for the sole purpose of staying at home and not having to answer the phone or go into the office. But our week of quiet dissolved before our eyes when our ambassador unexpectedly announced that he would be retiring at the end of January.

The ambassador's departure meant that, in a country where our nation's relationship with the host government was crucial for maintaining our military presence, John's roll, while already significant, would become more important than ever. So, when we quietly rang in 2017 from our rooftop, we took a breath and braced for the chaos to come. But as I had learned growing up on the ranch, during the toughest of times it was best to just put your head down against the wind and keep going.

As 2017 began, and John's workload increased, I did my best to ease his burden when and where I could, taking over everything to do with events, from conception to execution. As a result, I got to flex my old professional skills more than I had in almost fifteen years. Our routine became that he would give me his schedule and tell me what was most important, then I would sit down and try to plan things that would complement his mission. John approved of the majority of my ideas—even when they seemed a bit grand for our limited resources (both financial and human), sometimes causing him to wonder if I'd lost my mind. "Go big or go home," I'd say with a wink when he'd raise a questioning eyebrow.

On February 1, I had just sat down at my desk when my phone rang; John calling from the office. "Hey, what time is your coffee today?" he asked. I could hear him shuffling papers and then typing something on the computer.

"Two this afternoon. I'm meeting her at the embassy. Why?" I was scheduled to have coffee with my cousin's step-sister-in-law—someone I had never met—who happened to be in Djibouti for work. Things like that, as strange as they seemed, happened more often than you'd think, because the world is an odd, small place.

"Great, that should work. I have a meeting that just popped up with someone I think you'd like to meet." Apparently, the religious affairs team from AFRICOM was in town and had requested an impromptu meeting with John. During our time in Africa, I became acquainted with many religious affairs teams. Besides ministering to the service members, they did a lot of cultural outreach. Given that the media vacillated between branding the military as heroes or warmongers on any given day, I found the outreach side of their work intriguing and wholly underrated. But the main reason John alerted me to this particular meeting was because one of the attendees was one of only two Muslim chaplains in the United States Navy. A significant fact since there are hundreds of navy chaplains. This particular chaplain was a bit of a celebrity, having had the confidence of previous US presidents and been the focus of several major news stories. To me, not only was he fascinating, but he was also the perfect fit for outreach in a country that was 95 percent Muslim.

It took me less than a second to respond. "Absolutely. When's the meeting?"

"Well, that's the beauty of being the boss," I could hear the grin in his voice. "It can be whenever I want it to be. How about 11? That way we'll finish just in time for your meeting this afternoon."

"Deal." I hung up, answered a few emails, grabbed a shower, and got ready. I had an idea brewing in my mind, and that meeting would be my chance to see if I could make it happen.

"Ma'am," the chaplain smiled.

"You need to call me Julie," I said, extending my hand and returning his smile.

Half a dozen of us were sitting at the small conference table in John's office—myself, John, the chaplain, and the rest of the religious affairs team. After listening to them brief John about the work they had planned during their visit in the region, John thanked them and asked if we could have a few more minutes of the chaplain's time. The chaplain happily agreed while the rest of the team made their way to another meeting.

"We have an idea," John said when it was just the three of us, pouring himself some more coffee. "What would be the possibility of having you attend an iftar here?"

In a country like Djibouti and positions like ours, the gesture of hosting an iftar was on par with showing the highest level of respect for the nation and its culture. During the holy month of Ramadan, Muslims went from sunup to sundown abstaining from water and food until the fast was broken after prayers with an iftar. In Djibouti, where at that time Ramadan occurred during the hottest months, the strength of their devotion to this practice was incredible, and iftars were very celebratory in nature. Throughout Ramadan, there were iftars everywhere—the equivalent of Christmas holiday parties—hosted by restaurants, families, friends, businesses, you name it. And among the diplomatic community hosting an iftar was common.

The year prior, John and I had talked briefly about hosting a small iftar of our own but now we had the weight of hosting one without a sitting ambassador. With the *charge d'affaires* leaving during Ramadan, we knew that we had to think bigger than just an intimate get-together if we wanted to do it properly. Ours would be the largest for our embassy that year. We had to get it right, making sure to not step a foot wrong.

The chaplain smiled again. "I think that's a very real possibility. I would love to be a part of your iftar."

"Good. I'll get an email to your bosses, and we'll get the ball rolling," John smiled in return. I could hardly sit still in my chair as we talked through a few ideas. It was what I had imagined—an iftar with a Muslim US Navy chaplain—now we just had to make it happen.

"Thank you," I said to the chaplain as he got up to leave, shaking his hand. "It was so great to meet you. I can't wait to work with you on this."

He returned my thanks and laughed, "And just think, how often can you say you had someone on the Jihadi watchlist in your home?"

Indeed.

Later that February, after the meeting with the chaplain and my sun-drenched afternoon revelation that our compound would be a suitable location, I sat at my desk staring at plate and napkin options on Amazon. Moments before, I had been working on the details of a coffee we were hosting in a week but had hit a mental wall and decided to switch gears, focusing on simpler tasks like ordering supplies for other events. While many embassies had loaner items for representational purposes—dinnerware, silverware, and linens—Djibouti did not. The responsibility fell on us to provide whatever was needed. My china was limited to a table setting for twelve, so we often opted for upscale disposable plates and cutlery when hosting larger gatherings. Since diplomatic mail often took more than a month to reach us, I had become used to ordering supplies well in advance. A real fear was not receiving things in time evidenced by the mug we had ordered for John the previous October in anticipation of Christmas. Sadly it did not make it to us until the end of January having been missent to our embassy in Ireland.

I browsed through color and quality options, clicking on napkins in the navy blue and gold synonymous with our service institution. Plates and cups were added in bulk. Within the next three months, we would host over a dozen events at our house, and I'd burn through everything in my virtual shopping cart. I hit the Order Now button.

We had decided on the theme "A Celebration of Cultures" for our iftar, taking the opportunity to highlight the similarities our cultures shared, particularly those of my agricultural background. Given that during the busiest times of the year on the ranch, my family would go most of the day without stopping to eat—strikingly similar to fasting at Ramadan—it seemed an interesting parallel. For our iftar, I would serve a meal based on what my family would have had after a long day working cattle, while throwing in traditional Djiboutian favorites to round out the menu. One thing that furthered the cultural connection was that dates were the preferred treat to officially break a fast. It just so happened that my home state of California was one of the largest date producers in the world. Even though I knew it would be an extravagance, since dates were easily available locally, I wanted to further extend the hand of cultural diplomacy by offering them their familiar delicacy but from my home. Reaching out to ag friends back home, I found a date farm that intrigued me. Navigating away from Amazon and the napkin orders, I pulled up the date farm's website. I scanned their selection and stopped at the big, fat Medjool dates stuffed with California walnuts. *Yes, those will do nicely,* I thought. I quickly emailed their customer service department explaining what I was doing, how many dates I needed, and when I needed them by, then hit send. It never ceased to amaze me how fast I could spend money.

As the calendar days flew by, it increasingly felt like I was running on fumes. Our house became a constant swirl of activity as if we had a revolving door instead of a regular one. That pace, combined with the change of seasons, was taking a toll on me. I went to sleep thinking about all I had to do. I woke up thinking about all I had to do. Every day, the bags under my eyes grew. And my nose was constantly stuffed from dust and other pollutants in the air. And given the increasing number of headaches I had, I began to wonder if I needed to get my eyes checked. Frankly, I was a mess. And Liya, our indispensable housekeeper, noticing the deterioration of my health, started taking matters into her own hands.

Shortly after John and Quinn had left one weekday morning, I sat at my desk taking a first pass at the iftar guest list. I wore a hoodie with the hood pulled up to keep my congested head warm and had a large cup of coffee sitting by my side. I must have looked a sight. I had my "work" playlist blasting loudly, doing my best to power through instead of admitting defeat and going back to bed. So I didn't hear Liya come up the stairs—in fact, I didn't hear her until she was right next to me.

I hit pause on the music. "Good morning, Liya."

"Morning," she replied, then promptly moved my coffee, setting it on the table behind me and replacing it with another steaming mug of her famous hot orange juice. "You are too tired. Too sick," she scolded. Even though she was only a couple of years older than me, Liya acted like my surrogate mother during those years in Djibouti. Despite the fact that she was built like a bird and only stood five-foot-nothing on a good day—much like my own mother—you didn't mess with her, especially when "Dr. Liya" appeared. Instead, you found yourself doing whatever she commanded. That day she obviously had enough of my degraded state and had taken it upon herself to stop by the fresh market on her way to work and buy oranges. Her go-to cure for fatigue, colds, allergies, and everything else in between, was squeezing the green-skinned, ultra-sweet oranges into a cup, heating it in the microwave, and creating a warm burst of tangy vitamin C. As much as I didn't want to admit, it helped.

"Thank you, Liya. This is just what I needed," I told her, trying to smile but knowing that I looked like death.

"You need rest," she scolded again. "And you drink too much coffee." Seriously, it was as if my own mother were standing there.

"I know. I know." I didn't want to look her in the eye. "But we have too much to do right now."

I could tell she didn't buy my reasoning for pushing through, but still, she understood. "Tomorrow I make shiro and gomen for you, so that you don't have to cook." Her final word on the matter was to insist on cooking our family dinner to lighten my load. Of course, I didn't mind, I could eat her Ethiopian home cooking any day.

"Thank you," I called as she walked back down the stairs. "Make sure you grab money out of the can to pay for the ingredients." She had a habit of treating us to dinner, but I did my best to make her buy the ingredients with our money, although it was like convincing my mom of the same thing. Mothers—even surrogate ones—were the same the world over.

Later that day, with my hands covered in chocolate, my phone vibrated to life on the countertop next to me—John was calling from the office. I gingerly tapped the screen to answer it and then tapped again to switch it to speaker, doing my best not to smear it with the chocolate. "Yep?" I concentrated on pouring the melted dark chocolate into the plastic mold in front of me— once cooled, it would turn into submarine-shaped lollipops.

"Sorry, did I catch you at a bad time?" he asked.

"Well, I am doing my best to not screw up these submarines. I am not sure the guys at Naval Reactors would approve of my work," I laughed. I had to make six dozen of the chocolate lollipops for the US Navy's Submarine Force's birthday reception we were hosting the following week. Despite having the air conditioner on, the morning's heat was not an ideal environment for working with chocolate, but I was doing my best. I thought to myself, *If I was back in California, this wouldn't be a problem; it's still cold there.* At that point, I had lived in the perpetual summer of Sub-Saharan Africa for over half a decade.

"Oh, I'm sorry," he apologized. "Listen, I won't keep you. How about tomorrow you come in, and we can go over the calendar?"

"Sounds good."

"Okay, then, see you later," he said. Then added, "Mwah!"

It was a good idea to go in the following day. We had a dinner in two days, then the submarine birthday party, and to top it off, the secretary of defense was coming, which didn't directly involve me but took all of John's bandwidth—so we needed to make sure we were on the same page.

The next day, the two of us ate lunch in his office and went over what lay ahead. I loved those days when I sat across the desk from John and we worked together as a team. Chaos may have surrounded us, but for an hour or two, everything was calmer, easier. We were true partners, meeting our challenges together.

"What about Memorial Day?" John asked as he finished his sandwich. "I know it's close to the iftar, but the details need to be squared away. Are we going to do anything beyond the commemoration this year?"

I put away my lunch bag and pulled out a travel mug of fresh coffee. "So, I had an idea about that," I said as I poured us each a cup and then dropped a handful of foil-wrapped chocolates between us. "I know it's going to sound crazy, but what if we hosted a short reception at the house immediately following it?"

The Memorial Day commemoration was my baby, from start to finish. We used it as a chance to honor and remember Pilot Officer Maguire as well as all Americans who had given their lives in service of their country. The year before, we had conducted the service first thing in the morning. Still by the time it was over, it was so blazingly hot that we were wilted with sweat and could hardly make it through the rest of the workday. This year I decided on an evening ceremony, just before sunset, to make it a bit more palatable to all involved. Wanting to host a small cocktail party after would primarily be as a thank you to those who helped me pull it together because it was the right thing to do.

"That's two days before the iftar—do you think you can handle both?" John asked, unwrapping a chocolate.

I took a sip of coffee. "I think so. It wouldn't have to be a full reception, just some cold drinks, and cookies. Truly, I just figured it would be a nice thing to do for the guys from Camp who helped pull it off, a chance for them to be outside the wire for a minute more. And the layout for the reception would be simple. Liya and I can get it ready that morning, then while we are at the cemetery, she can lay out the food and drinks. She knows the routine, easy peasy."

"Alright, I trust you on this. What about the new DCM's arrival? That will be the day in between the two events." Our new deputy chief of mission—and *charge d'affairs* due to the absence of an ambassador—would be arriving with his family the day after Memorial Day and a day before the iftar. John and I were acting as their official sponsors, which meant that we were responsible for the following: making sure their temporary house was ready, including having sheets on the bed and towels in the bathrooms; stocking their temporary house with enough grocery basics to get them through a few days; scheduling their meetings throughout the embassy for their check-in; meeting them at the airport upon their arrival, and then escorting them to their temporary house and showing them how everything worked. During a normal week, it would be a lot of work, but during the week that they were arriving, it was going to be a ton of work. "Can we handle it all?"

I sighed, "It's not whether or not we can handle it all; we have to. There's no choice."

"Okay," John said, spinning his chair and running his hands through his hair. "Hey, we can't forget to schedule a meeting with our guys to talk about the cultural aspects of the iftar. Let's do that now."

The small conference room was stupidly cold, as were many of the spaces in the embassy. I wore a long sweater that I would have to strip off as soon as I went back outside, but in that room, I needed it and the hot coffee I had in front of me to keep from shivering. John and I were meeting with his Djiboutian staff members—men who worked for the office for years, providing an invaluable conduit between us and our host nation—to further discuss the iftar. John wasted no time and turned the meeting over to me. I explained how we had decided to host an iftar at our residence that year. It would be for senior Djiboutian military members, senior US military members from Camp Lemonier and CJTF-HOA, and our guest of honor—the man presiding over the prayers that evening—would be the Muslim navy chaplain. My idea was met with enthusiasm, but they reminded me that I needed to make sure we got the local cultural aspects correct. I assured them we would because I trusted them to be my cultural advisors—which was apparently the right answer because they began eagerly telling me what we would need to do. I smiled and jotted down a list of questions in my notebook that I would need to mull over. WHICH LOCAL ITEMS DO WE ABSOLUTELY NEED? WHEN DO WE NEED TO PROCURE THEM? SHOULD I HAVE MY SANITY CHECKED FOR WANTING TO PULL THIS OFF?

Two weeks before the iftar, I took Roble—one of the aforementioned cultural advisors from John's office—on a walk-through of our house and compound. While he approved of the turf-covered area for prayers, he suggested that we get a new coat of paint on the compound walls. Jeremiah, our gardener, who was making the rounds with us, heartily agreed and added that he would replace a few old plants with new ones. Sure, I told them both, agreeing to it all and instructing Jeremiah to only pick the best plants he could find. Quality plants were not always a given in Djibouti, but Jeremiah was particular and took pride in his work, so truly, I needn't have worried, but at that point in time it seemed like worry was all I did.

Inside the house, Roble looked around our formal reception area and said, "We will need to move all of this furniture out so that we can fit enough tables in for the night."

Ugh. Just *ugh.* While I had anticipated that suggestion and knew it was the correct thing to do, I cringed at the thought—two days before the iftar was the Memorial Day event, which would use our existing furniture, therefore, the deconstruction and reconstruction would need to be a quick turnaround. "Okay," I sighed.

Roble, sensing my growing stress, said, "Don't worry, madame, I will work with the warehouse staff and take care of it for you."

"Thank you, Roble," I smiled. "You're a lifesaver." *It will all be worth it,* I thought and silently reminded myself to take some deep breaths and perhaps fit in some yoga that evening.

A few days later, I sat in the heart of Djibouti City, gazing at the sky far above me—that day a dusty shade of pale blue. It stood in stark contrast to the neutral walls of the buildings that rose up around me and the glass of bright coral pink juice that sat in front of me. It was a beautiful tableau, like a cross between an exotic bazaar and a café in Paris.

I wanted to stay there all day, but that wasn't going to happen. *Well, at least I can enjoy it for a moment or two,* I thought.

I was sitting at a juice bar belonging to Roble nestled down-town, in the old part of the city, full of character and life. It was another steamy mid-May day, and I was grateful for the ice-cold glass of mango and melon blended into a smooth, frothy drink. Even though I always packed a water bottle with me wherever I went in Djibouti, sometimes water just didn't cut it. The juice not only quenched my thirst but also satisfied it with its pulpy substance. It was easy to see why the locals loved it.

We had already spent an hour at a restaurant, sampling the local delicacies they were going to provide for the iftar. Then we went to a florist to order the bouquets we needed for Memorial Day. Time was passing both slowly and quickly. The air felt like soup. It seemed like we had just sat down with our juices when it was once again time to go. I peeled myself off the plastic chair, my so-called rugged outdoor pants sticking to my thighs like a wet swimsuit.

We drove through the gate of Riyad, the city's sprawling fresh market and our final stop for the day. Entering Riyad reminded me of entering an old-fashioned fairground—stalls and build-ings laid out in a maze-like pattern on well-packed dirt. While you could park and walk around if you wanted, you could also just drive, literally pulling up to your desired vendor and rolling down the window to order—Djibouti's version of the drive-thru. I had been to Riyad several times and could easily get to my pre-ferred watermelon seller right inside the main gate, but beyond that, I struggled to remember how to navigate the narrow paths, so I was only too happy when Roble offered to drive.

We wound around the market, taking a right turn here, a left turn there. Had I needed vegetables or flour or new pans, I could've had them, passing those stalls and their owners, watching us eagerly, wondering if we were there for them. One final right turn and we were in the meat market. The stalls, to my untrained eyes, had no markings to distinguish them from

one another and there were so many that it was confusing—
were they all one? Where did one end and the other begin? We
slowed to a stop about halfway down the alley and Roble rolled
down his window. The stall owner nearest us smiled in recognition and walked over. They greeted each other in Arabic, then
Roble turned to me and asked, "How many kilos do you need?"

"Six," I answered and then added, "Can you have her run it
through the grinder twice?" From the front seat of the SUV, I
watched as the woman walked back to a fresh quarter of beef
hanging in the corner of her stall. She pulled out a knife that
looked like a cross between a sword and a machete and started
carving pieces off, laying them onto waxed paper next to her. Eyeing the mound of beef, she weighed it—of course, right on the
mark—and proceeded to feed it into an ancient grinder. There
was no refrigeration. The meat was brought in daily. Having
worked with some of the best butchers in America, I wondered
what they would think of this, although I am sure they would have
found it just as fascinating as I did. And while I knew a lot of my
fellow countrymen balked at the local meat in Djibouti, worried
about hygiene and getting sick, as I watched the beautiful bright
red beef pile up on the paper, I knew I had no need to worry—it
was Roble's butcher. He was particular about what he bought and
also knew that I was serving this to some of his country's most
high-ranking and influential people. He wasn't going to take a
chance; he had just as much riding on the event as I did.

With thirteen pounds of ground beef sitting in a bag by my
feet and seven large watermelons in the back, we made our
way straight back to my house, where I spent the rest of the
afternoon in the kitchen. I cut the watermelon into chunks and
blended it into juice, carefully strained and poured it into large
Ziploc bags, then stacked them neatly on the bottom shelf of
one of our upright freezers. I took the ground beef and made

Budgie burgers—an old family recipe—patting out seventy-two patties and freezing them. Finally, as evening dropped and with everything tidied up, I went through my to-do list and crossed off what I had accomplished that day. While I had made a significant dent in things, there was still a lot of work to do—so I sent John and Quinn to our favorite burger place to pick up dinner, and I collapsed on the couch for a moment's rest.

On the morning of Memorial Day, Liya and I were doing the final furniture arrangements in the house for the reception that evening, pushing the side chairs back a bit, reorienting the dining room table, and making sure everything was clean and dusted. My phone pinged—an email from our operations officer with the final RSVP list for the iftar. Our Djiboutian contacts were notorious for not responding to invitations until the last minute. I had purchased and prepped food in anticipation of seventy-five attendees, and the email confirmed that I hadn't been that far off with my estimation—I would have at least sixty in the house that night. I say at least because there were always those who didn't RSVP but showed up anyway. I hit reply and thanked him and asked him to confirm that we would have enough additional security guards for the event. Then I returned to the Memorial Day preparations; I still had to fold the programs we printed the previous day.

At 4:30 p.m., John, Quinn, and I left for the commemoration. We had spent the previous Saturday cleaning the cemetery with a group of national guard volunteers from Camp Lemmonier. It had been hot, sweaty, dirty work. The end result was very evident when we arrived on that afternoon: all the weeds had been removed from amongst the gravel, and the graves of Maguire and his crew had been cleaned and freshly painted. For all the craziness that I had been surrounded by for the past six months, the sight brought tears to my eyes. Before anyone else arrived, I walked over to Maguire's grave and looked down at it. "Hello, old friend," I said to his gravestone. "I hope you like your spruce up."

Two hours later, dripping with sweat, we were back at the house with a majority of the guests who had attended the graveside ceremony. The door to our house was opening and closing so much that Cat Two sneakily tucked herself behind a planter. She was delighted to seize a moment when we were preoccupied to dart between legs and run inside the house. Having caught the eye of one guest, who pointed Cat Two out hiding behind a chair in the entryway, I just shrugged and let her be. There was no way she'd truly get in the way, being too scared of strangers for that, so I figured she was better off staying right where she was until everyone left.

The visiting religious affairs team, including the Muslim chaplain, had arrived in town early enough to be at the Memorial Day commemoration and stopped by our reception afterward.

"Your place is beautiful," one of the team members remarked as I greeted them.

I laughed. The house was beautiful, but sometimes I forgot that because it was also just our house. "Oh, thank you," I said. "But the house comes at a price. You have to sell your soul to live here." No sooner had the words left my mouth than I realized what I had said bordered on blasphemy. What I meant was, the house came with the job, and the job exacted a heavy price on those who did it. Oh well, I was only being me and at that moment, exhausted from the day, I literally felt like I had sold my soul to the devil and was wondering if it had been the right decision.

Morning, on the day of the iftar, came all too soon. I dragged myself outside first thing, cup of coffee in hand, inspecting the garden and making sure that all of the small American flags I had put out for Memorial Day were still in place. By 8:30, I was once again standing in the kitchen, up to my elbows in prep work. My fingertips were bright red, visually screaming in pain because I didn't have time to allow the potatoes I was peeling to cool. There wasn't a moment to spare, not even to save my fingers the agony of the steaming heat. I had to get the potato salad made, and in the refrigerator so it could chill. I opted for a cold potato salad to accompany the burgers, because it was what we traditionally served on the ranch after a long day of hard work and partially because the ambient temperature that day was predicted to hit 120 degrees.

There was still so much to do and seemingly little time in which to do it. John had dropped Quinn off at school and would then pick him up at the end of the school day and come straight home to help with the last of the prep work. The two of them were doing the best they could to lighten my workload.

By midafternoon I was pretty sure that my trusty stand mixer was dying. It was desperately trying to whip egg whites for my cupcake frosting but was making the most horrible sounds. Granted, it was fifteen years old and had spent half of those years running at the wrong frequency via a voltage converter. I hadn't realized that I was talking to it, trying to coax it along, until Liya came in the kitchen and found me saying, "Please don't die. Please don't die. Please just make it through today." She shook her head and laughed.

The formal reception area had once again been transformed. As promised, Roble had come through. Gone was our furniture—the couches, side chairs, and end tables—having been replaced with eight large rectangular folding tables, each with eight chairs. We had borrowed tablecloths from the ambassador's residence—easy when there was currently no ambassador—and Liya ironed them and put them in place. John and Quinn had set out miniature flag stands in the center of the tables—one tiny American flag and one tiny Djiboutian flag in each. On either side of the flags, we placed two plates of the specially ordered Californian dates, ready for the moment when that day's fast was broken.

An hour before our first guests were set to arrive, I took the burgers outside and put them on the grill. The predicted 120 degree temperature had held true, and rivers of sweat ran down my body. I kept chugging from a bottle of ice-cold water to keep from passing out, thinking, *Wouldn't that be great, for me to have a heat stroke right before this thing starts?* But thankfully, I powered through without fainting. I took the burgers back inside, wrapped them tightly with foil, and slipped them into the warm oven. I had just enough time to grab a quick shower and get ready.

By the time the first of our Djiboutian guests arrived shortly after six, I was freshly made up and smiling, standing next to John on the verandah. The guests walked through the gate and into our newly painted compound, approaching the house via a path flanked by American flags. John and I shook their hands as they passed into the house.

After a very brief welcome by John, the chaplain led our Muslim guests outside to the turf lawn where we had laid out dozens of brightly patterned prayer rugs. As much as I wanted to watch, to see the beauty that I'd envisioned unfold, I stayed inside out of respect but could still hear their prayers faintly through the walls. Once the prayers were over, everyone lined up to fill their plates, then sat down to a much-appreciated feast.

John and I stood in front of the gathered guests. "This evening was all Julie, from start to finish," he told them, causing my cheeks to burn in embarrassment. "While the meal is a combination of our two cultures, it goes further than that," he continued, explaining about my ranching background and how food played an important role after a long day's work and how, it was in a way, similar to their fasting during Ramadan. I stood there, modestly dressed but wearing my bright red cowboy boots. I marveled at how far I had come—the simple country girl from northern California standing there as an unlikely diplomat in the Horn of Africa.

The evening was a hit. The chaplain's speech was beautiful. A senior Djiboutian general, one rarely seen on the diplomatic circuit, was in attendance—a true win for John. Before he left, the general went out of his way to find me and thank me for what he called "such an enjoyable evening." And it truly was—an evening where people from different walks of life came together and shared a meal, eating and laughing and being human.

Three days later, the house was finally clean, and the furniture had been put back in its usual place. It was then that John and I sat enjoying the first quiet Saturday morning since early February. Years before, when John proposed to me, he said he didn't just want me as a wife; he wanted a partner. Those words had never been truer than during those crazy months in 2017. Unlike his years in the submarine force, where there was a good portion of his life that I knew nothing about, there was very little about his current job I wasn't privy to. We were a team, the partnership he had hoped for when he slipped the diamond ring on my finger, and we had just proven how well it worked.

Over cups of coffee and newspapers, we relaxed and chatted. It felt great. However, we couldn't see what lay ahead. We didn't know that that quiet Saturday was one of the few we had left during the remainder of our time in Djibouti.

Nor did I know that my cowgirl roots would be used by others to get to my husband, placing me in a situation that made the iftar pale in comparison.

chapter 42

The Cat Who Came to Stay

I began to feel like Schrödinger's Cat—not the part about being both dead and alive, but a feeling of being both there and not there at the same time. Actually, I think Lewis Carroll summed it up best in *Alice in Wonderland,* when the Cheshire Cat told Alice, "You may have noticed that I'm not all here myself." Yes, that's what I felt like exactly.

The end date of our tour in Djibouti was no surprise: July 2018. Even though our orders had originally been written for two years, we had extended for an additional year, pushing the limit of what was allowable. We also knew where we were moving: Naples, Italy. Shortly after John's name appeared on the promotion list for captain in spring 2016, we were informed that he would be taking the job in Italy as the head of Africa engagements. No options, no debate. It was a natural progression for his career and the appropriate move for his new rank. Were we thrilled? Not especially, but not disappointed either. Mainly we were numb at the thought of leaving Africa. At least this time, there would be no wondering about what was next, as the decision had been made for us long in advance of the end.

At that point, with so many consecutive years on the continent and the grueling non-stop years in Djibouti, we were hitting a wall. Deep down, we knew that we needed to move on. But for me, it wasn't so straightforward. Those days my brain was not behaving in its most rational sense, and I found myself in a constant struggle between wanting to move to Italy, back to Europe and its quieter pace of life, and also wanting to give every last ounce of my energy to the job in Djibouti. Needless to say, that fight was taking a toll.

Days, weeks, and months passed. Time seemed to move even faster than before. We hosted events and attended events. We ticked the various boxes of our life: Quinn's school performances, birthdays, even the most mundane of life's experiences. I smiled, laughed, and cried where appropriate, but still felt like something was missing, something I couldn't quite put my finger on.

When the holidays arrived that year, everything blurred. It was as if there was no longer any difference between our work life and our home life. So many visitors of the VIP level set their eyes on Djibouti, that we no longer had any real blocks of free time. Our family time was measured out in minutes and hours. And it eventually wore me down with regard to one particular issue: Cat Two.

As our lives became busier, all three of us found reasons to go outside and pet our compound's feline mascot. Falling prey to her purrs that lifted our spirits like magic.

Up till then, we, okay it was mainly me, had maintained that Cat Two would remain an outdoor semi-pet. We would allow her to stay on the compound, but she wouldn't be ours because ours meant ownership. While I had grown up with pets, I wasn't keen on having one while we lived such a crazy lifestyle. Sure, a lot of people we knew from the military and embassy world had pets that traveled the globe with them, but those people also had a fair amount of horror stories. Tales about the hoops they had to jump through to get their pet from place to place, the lack of veterinarians in certain locales, the stress to the animals, the list went on. Even though I was an animal lover, I wasn't sure that I could do that to a pet or myself—I mean, just look at what we went through to get three humans to Cameroon originally. Why would I want to add a pet into that mix? I had therefore maintained a staunch No Pet Policy in our household over the years.

Until then . . .

Until that darn street cat purred her way into my heart.

And melted it.

"Mom," Quinn would say sweetly, staring at me with those big brown eyes of his. "You know you want a cat. You *need* a cat." He tried this tactic with me every time he fed her—yes, we were feeding her. I had actually said that we could feed her shortly after moving into our house. She was a thin stray that hung around every day, and I couldn't stand seeing her there with bones jutting out; I wasn't a monster.

"No, Quinn, I don't need a cat."

"But you do!" he'd protest. "And she loves you." This as she head-butted me for a scratch by the ear.

John and Quinn had been won over for ages, but I continued to protest, maintaining that it would be impractical to have a stray in the house when we had to entertain all the time. How would I keep the house ready for guests while teaching her to use a litter box?

But then, as Thanksgiving 2017 approached, my resolve weakened. All three of us were just so beat down from everything that Cat Two proved to be the brightest spot in our life. That tough little Djiboutian street cat made us smile and laugh— and when life gets you down, what more could you want?

When November began, as we waded through multiple VIP visits and other work commitments, we toyed with the idea of owning the rather cantankerous feline. I still wasn't entirely sold, knowing that the bulk of her house-training would fall on my shoulders since I was the one who was home the most. Would I be able to handle my normal workload and stress with an un-trained cat added to the mix?

Our Thanksgiving was small and low-key because our sec-retary of the navy (SECNAV) and his spouse were arriving that night for a visit. John and I were on tap to help with their arrival and also their tour of Camp Lemonnier the next day. Less than twenty-four hours later, the SECNAV's whirlwind visit was over, his plane was wheels up, and we were beyond exhausted. It was Friday afternoon. Quinn and Cat Two had been at the house, holding down the fort all day. We had allowed him to have her inside temporarily with the agreement to let her out if she need-ed to use the bathroom. Dragging ourselves through the door, the two of them greeted us with smiles—okay, Cat Two was in-different, but still. Quinn had been eagerly awaiting our return, as we had promised him we would decorate for Christmas that night. So, after changing into comfortable clothes and enjoy-ing some Thanksgiving leftovers, John and I poured ourselves drinks, turned on Christmas music, and put up the tree with Quinn. By the time night had fallen and the twinkle lights were reflecting off the ornaments, Cat Two was still in the house—and I was too happy and too tired to put her out. I watched her enjoy herself as we decorated like she had finally found the home she had been looking for. That night was a trial run. If it worked, we would go out the next day and buy a litter box.

It did, so we did. Cat Two stayed in the house from then on.

A few weeks into her new life, Cat Two discovered the arm-chair next to my desk upstairs and claimed it as her own.

One morning before Christmas, while sorting through re-ceipts, working on our reimbursements for the previous month's entertaining, I glanced over at her. She was awake and watching me. "Well," I said, "you've sure settled into your new life."

She stared, her green eyes cutting right through me, and purred as if responding to my observation. It made me feel calm and happy. There she was, a little street cat who had somehow survived in the harshest conditions, the physical embodiment of not giving up—in a way, a mirror of myself. Why had I waited so long to agree to let her fully into our lives?

I reached over and stroked her head. She purred in contentment. I felt less scattered, more centered. She was the missing piece we hadn't known we needed.

And just like that, we were four.

chapter 43

Impending Loss

"I will miss this," I said to John as I gestured toward the vast horizon.

The sun was setting in the weird slow-fast way it did in Djibouti—slowly at first, like it was taking its time to show off, then suddenly disappearing below the horizon, sending the world into darkness. It was like that all along the equator. You had to make every effort to enjoy a particularly beautiful sunset while you could.

It was spring break, and instead of going off the continent for a few days, the three of us decided that we'd take one last adventure trip in Africa prior to our upcoming move. We had decided on Lac Abbe, the large salt lake that straddled Djibouti's southwestern border with Ethiopia. We were staying overnight at Campement Touristique Lac Abbe, which sat on a hill overlooking the lake. Fashioned after a traditional Afar camp, complete with their distinctive half-dome huts to sleep in, it was rustic but authentic. John and I sat near the main building, which served as the camp's kitchen, enjoying a cup of tea, a welcome treat after a full day's travel, most of which had been on very bumpy desert roads. In the valley below, young girls herded goats home for the night. To the other side, we saw a man walking a group of donkeys. And a single cow—a typical African breed, scrawny by western standards but hearty for the desert—wandered into the camp, only to be chased back out by one of the boys who lived there. But aside from the herding and a few clangs coming from the kitchen, it was silent. Gloriously silent.

"I know what you mean," John responded, staring off into the distance.

"I think what I'll miss the most is the wide-open feeling," I paused, looking out over the vista. We sipped our tea, served in the local way—a rich combination of black tea, spices, and sugar. Quinn was at the far side of the camp area, perched on a large rock, reading a book in the waning light. "And I'll miss the work," I continued. "I feel like I matter here. I feel like I belong here."

John smiled a sad smile, pouring more tea into my glass. He knew how I had struggled over the years and how important our time in Africa had been for my sense of purpose and sense of self. We sat there quietly until the sky turned a deep midnight blue, the lake's limestone chimneys now black silhouettes in front of us. It looked like something out of a science fiction movie.

The next day, after taking an extended look around the chimneys and the region's fauna— warthogs, dik-diks, camels, and all manner of bird species—we set off back home.

Once we had cleared the mountains that separate the lake from the basin on the other side, the driver, Moussa, shifted the SUV into high gear. Moussa was a local Afar and knew exactly where he was going, even when no road was visible. At one point, I glanced at the dashboard and noticed the speedometer read 100 miles per hour.

Garat, our guide, turned to say that Moussa wanted to make a stop ahead. He explained that it was Moussa's village, on the outskirts of As Eyla, and that his cousin had invited him to bring us to his place for tea. I looked out the window, while we weren't in the middle of the desert anymore there was still very little around, an Afar hut here and there, a baby camel grazing on what vegetation it could find. *Where was this village?* I wondered. But, also, *how could we say no?* It would have been rude to refuse such a generous offer.

Still in the seemingly middle of nowhere along the faint tire tracks in the sand, stood a man. Moussa slowed. When we were close, the man trotted up to our approaching SUV and hopped up onto the running board without waiting for us to stop. He and Moussa began chatting animatedly in a local dialect. It was Moussa's cousin. "He's going to guide us to his place," Garat told us, translating the conversation. "It's just over this way," he said as Moussa eased the SUV off the tracks we had been on and headed out across the dry, scrubby land.

We stopped next to a hut. The door to get inside was a small opening, very low to the ground. Moussa, his cousin, and Garat easily entered with the grace of rabbits. However, unused to such a low door, the three of us, ended up on our hands and knees, crawling in. I can only imagine how it looked to them as I did my best to be graceful, knowing full well that I was anything but.

Garat explained to us that Moussa's cousin didn't speak French or English, so our visit there mainly consisted of polite small talk, then just sitting and smiling. That was fine, as I was happy to simply take in the moment. Despite the heat outside, inside the hut it was mild and surprisingly airy. About twelve feet in diameter, in the center the ceiling was still not high enough for me to stand up fully. Only Moussa and his cousin could stand, their heads almost touching the woven reeds that gave it its shape.

The cousin set out lovely glass cups and poured us tea, the same kind as we had been served at the campsite. Its beautiful shade of amber looked so elegant in the very humble setting. We sipped and nodded and smiled over two cups each. Hospitality is an oddly universal experience, even if no words are spoken.

Thanking Moussa's cousin for his generosity, we climbed back into the SUV and continued toward Djibouti City and home.

"I amend my answer," I told John as we drove along. "*That* is what I will miss about Africa."

chapter 44

Shall We Dance?

The loud ringing yanked me out of a deep sleep. I opened my eyes to darkness. I had no idea what time it was, especially since it felt like only moments since I had turned out the light. The bed moved slightly as John scrambled to grab his phone off the nightstand. He gave a groggy "John Tully" as he got out of bed, then quickly adjusted the tenor of his voice into full work mode.

I caught a bit from the other end of the line. "I'm sorry to call so late, sir . . ."—they always apologized, never relishing the fact that they'd woken us. John's face, highlighted by the glow of the phone, changed, clouding with concern while he registered what he was hearing. "Thanks," he said and hung up. The call had lasted less than a minute. He walked around a moment more, allowing himself time to absorb what he'd just heard, then crawled back into bed and stared at the ceiling.

"Something wrong?" I asked.

"No," he sighed heavily, laying an arm across his closed eyes. "Just more of the same."

My heart sank. Yes, more of the same but still urgent enough to call him in the middle of the night. I let out my own sigh, turned over, and went back to sleep. Unfortunately, though, my sleep was invaded by the reality of what had been happening for months around us. That night I didn't have a nightmare, or at least not exactly. Rather the dream was just a twisted version of my waking hours, intense but not far-fetched, enough to rattle my nerves but not scare me. It was no wonder that lately, when friends and family asked how things were going, I found myself telling them white lies, shielding them from the truth they didn't need to be burdened with. There was little that was funny or cute in our life. In fact, it had been bordering on the bizarre and teetering dangerously close to terrifying.

Things were changing rapidly in our part of the world. History was being written with each passing day. Djibouti was carving out its role on the global scene. While it purportedly wanted to become the Singapore of Africa, it had already firmly established itself as a hub for international militaries, the likes of which the world had never seen. The Djibouti of early 2018 was not the Djibouti we had moved to in 2015. In 2018, it was not only home to the United States' only base in Africa, but now also to China's and Japan's only military bases outside of their homeland. Throw in the French and Italians, sprinkle in the European Union, add the persistent rumors of others, and you can understand why that tiny country had become the physical embodiment of the saying: *"May you live in interesting times."* Call our life what you like—walking the tightrope, living on the tip of the spear, a balancing act—that is exactly what it was as we rapidly approached the end of our tour.

That night's phone call was just one in a long line of such calls. We had been hounded by the repercussions of incidents that had occurred over the previous couple of months. A few weeks before, we—the United States—were conducting an exercise in Djibouti called Alligator Dagger when a series of unfortunate events brought everything to a head. During a routine takeoff, one of our marine corps Harrier jets had crashed on the runway by Camp Lemonnier—the same runway used by the international airport and the other militaries based in Djibouti. While the pilot ejected and was up walking around before the fire trucks arrived, the plane had been reduced to a burning wreck, causing the airport to cease operations. Only hours later, a CH-53 helicopter that was part of the same exercise had a hard landing—a minor crash—at a site just outside of the city. While both were horrible incidents in their own right, they coincidentally happened on the same day as another CH-53 helicopter crash in California that claimed the lives of its four crew members and also the day before one of our Air Force F-16s had crashed in Nevada. Given the number of accidents the American military had suffered in a two-day period and the fact that two of them occurred in Djibouti, it came as no surprise when the Djiboutian government asked the United States to suspend all air operations in their country, ultimately leading to our commanders cancelling Alligator Dagger completely. Due to the international nature of the incidents and their potential repercussions, the official handling of it fell directly into John's lap.

On top of that, there were also growing tensions between the Chinese and us. Seriously, having bases so close to each other and operating in the same area together, was unprecedented and always a bit touch and go. John became the mediator when things got heated. It was a situation that never ceased to create new and interesting headaches.

It had been a tense couple of months, and that phone call only brought more unsettled sleep and hazy mornings that had become part of our life. Days became marathons, and there never seemed to be enough coffee anymore. Especially when John and I were invited to the birthday celebration for the People's Liberation Army at the Chinese base.

I have to be honest and say that I had been really looking forward to going to the event. When John brought home the invitation, I had given an enthusiastic yes, because I was wildly curious about stepping foot onto their base more than for the event itself. We had been to many Chinese events before. Most of them had been little different than events hosted by other countries—except for the one when the Chinese sailor played Wham's "Careless Whisper" on his saxophone. That was just plain ol' bizarre. But this event would be a chance to go inside the cold, monolithic military base that I had only previously seen on maps and from the water during a boat trip out into the Gulf of Tadjoura. I was almost giddy with excitement.

Until I became the focus of their attention. Somehow, I seemed to have become their favorite American.

In the year leading up to that night, the commanding officer of the Chinese base became a regular in our circle of diplomatic "friends." Yes, those are air quotes, because in the diplomatic world, while some people become honest-to-goodness friends, others become another version of the word friend. These are people you are friendly with and spend a lot of time chatting to, but they can never truly be a friend because of their national affiliation and political and ideological leanings. Does that make sense? Yes? Good. No? That's okay. It's all about the fine art of diplomacy.

Anyway, the Chinese base commander had become a regular at our house and a regular in my life. Even when I went grocery shopping. "I saw you in Casino with your son," he said to me one evening. *Yes, I know,* I thought. I couldn't escape our "friendship," no matter where I went.

But that was the name of the game.

John and I walked across the large, square courtyard of the Chinese base—sterile gray and somewhat intimidating. The base commander, who was welcoming guests at the top of the stairs leading to their gymnasium, saw us and smiled a big smile.

In contrast, his colleague's face—the senior political advisor standing next to him—was void of emotion and remained as frozen as an ice sculpture.

"Welcome," said the base commander as he bowed to me. "I am so glad you could make it."

"Thank you for the invitation," I replied, handing him a gift-wrapped bottle of wine. He had recently been at our house for a reception and had gifted me the Chinese alcohol baijiu in a bottle shaped like a missile. "See?" He had said that night as he handed it to me. "Rocket fuel!" And he broke into laughter—a rather dark joke when thinking of how our militaries viewed each other, but one that I nonetheless thought funny. Therefore, I figured it was only right to return the favor with a truly delightful red wine. It was made by friends from my hometown, named after the town's former, rather ominous moniker, Hangtown Red. I could do jokes too.

Descending the stairs into the gymnasium, which looked oddly like it was decorated for a high school prom, we were met by a group of young Chinese sailors who spoke excellent English, because, of course. And that was also when it became immediately apparent that I was one of the only spouses in attendance. So, while John talked to colleagues, I was interrupted at every turn, constantly being stopped by the young Chinese sailors (of the male variety) who wanted to pose for pictures with me. It was like being a minor celebrity.

After enjoying a lovely buffet, listening to the requisite speeches, and watching the obligatory propaganda video—I'm not calling them out on this, everyone shows propaganda videos at such events, even us—their band began playing.

"You'll really like this next song," said the base commander, who had suddenly appeared at my side, seemingly more interested in talking to me than to any of the hundred or so high-ranking guests in attendance. "It will remind you of home."

"Oh?" I said, wondering what American song they were going to haul out to impress me, but nothing could've prepared me for what came next. When the opening strains of the song began, the band seemed clearly familiar with it, as did the majority of the Chinese sailors who turned their attention toward the band, preparing to sing along. I was dumbfounded. I couldn't believe what I heard. Bobby Bare's "500 Miles," a song I hadn't heard in decades—a song from my childhood, a song that even die-hard country music fans would consider obscure in today's day and age—was being performed by Chinese sailors in Djibouti. I felt confused, completely out of time and place.

My host smiled. "Ah, yes, you know this song." My face had betrayed me.

The song was such a sentimental tug at my heart that I was struck with emotion and tried my best not to show it but failed. I turned to him and said, "Absolutely."

"It's a very special song for us," he explained. "They play it at our graduations. It makes us homesick."

Homesick. Yes, that I completely understood, because as soon as I heard those familiar lyrics, I had become homesick too. I stood there, listening to the sailors sing along, wondering where their homesickness took them. I was suddenly a child in the northern California mountains 8,000 miles and forty years away. *How could the base commander have known that it would strike that chord in me? Or was it just a lucky guess?* The song ended, the remaining chords faded away. I was fully back in Djibouti, my composure regained—however that was the moment when the base commander turned to me and said, "And now you will dance!"

"What?!" I tried not to spit out the champagne I had been sipping.

"It's a tradition for us at these events," he said, "and it's a dance you'll know."

The band struck up another song. The young Chinese sailors in their dress whites filled the floor in perfect formation. I cringed.

Line dancing.

Ugh. Not again.

Yes, I grew up on a ranch. Yes, I was a cowgirl. Yes, I wore cowboy boots. Yes, I grew up listening to country music. But the one place where I didn't fit the country girl personification was this: I hated line dancing. It just wasn't me. Yes, I had done it for the flash mob in Cameroon, but I considered that a one-off, a favor to Uncle Sam, and certainly not something I wanted to repeat.

"Please," the commander said as he waved me toward the dance floor.

"*Um,*" I stuttered. "I don't actually know how to line dance." I was grasping for straws, trying not to offend. But what I should've done is kept my mouth shut.

No sooner had I uttered that admission than the commander snapped his fingers, and one of the dancing sailors came off the floor, snapping to attention at my side. The commander spoke quickly to him in Chinese. The young man nodded sharply then turned to me and said in heavily accented English, "Come, I show you how to dance."

What I should make clear is it was *only* the Chinese sailors dancing, along with two other young international attendees. All of the other attendees, and I mean *all* of them—the other militaries, our Djiboutian friends, our American counterparts from Camp Lemonnier, our fellow attachés, literally a couple hundred other people—were just bystanders. They watched the dance but made no move to join in. I handed my glass to John in defeat. My cheeks flushed with fire as I stepped onto the floor in full view of the guests. My young dance instructor began showing me steps. Immediately, this caught the attention of his fellow sailors on the dance floor who then gleefully joined him in coaching me.

One. Two. One. Two. Side. Side. Back. Forward. Back.

I did my best to keep the diplomatic smile on my face while I counted the steps in my head, moving my feet in time with the music and my partner/instructor.

Forward. Back. Forward. Back.

It was hilarious, really. There I was begrudgingly dancing on behalf of my country once again and thinking, *Why don't I get paid for this?* While I loved the work I got to do alongside John, I felt more professionally fulfilled than I had in years, and yet, well, there were nights like this when I thought, *Really? Really??*

I looked out into the crowd to see the base commander standing next to John, who had taken out his phone to film my misery—I wanted to scream at him and jam the phone where the sun didn't shine. John's deputy stood behind him, trying his best to not double over in laughter—I made a mental note to punch him in the arm later. No matter how embarrassed I was, there with my two left feet, I literally couldn't betray my game face for the sake of diplomacy, I had to appear as if I was having the time of my life. Somehow, yet again, I was left taking one for Uncle Sam's team.

The song mercifully ended though it seemed like it lasted an eternity. I smiled as brightly as I could to my dance teachers, bowed slightly, and said, *"Xie xie."* Thank you—one of the few phrases I knew in Mandarin Chinese. Then, I made my way off the floor and wished to disappear into a quiet corner for the rest of the event. But, once again, the base commander magically appeared at my side. "Now, we need to cut the birthday cake."

Gee, that's nice, I thought, not grasping the inflection in his words. I thought he meant he would go cut the cake, and I could finally fade away, my humiliation on the global stage over for the evening. But I was wrong. I didn't catch his emphasis on we because as I began to move toward John—who was still stifling a laugh at my expense—the commander stopped me. "Come, you'll help me," he said, taking me by the elbow and escorting me to a long table holding two massive birthday cakes. John tagged along behind.

I should note John and I were far from the most senior or most important attendees at the event that night. *Why on earth would he use me, us, when he had a global ensemble of generals and admirals in the room?* Of course, I also wasn't that naïve. John and I were the diplomatic faces of the American military, and I was a spouse—a rarity in Djibouti. The Chinese had been doing their best to play nice in public with us. But while I intended to go to the event that night for sheer enjoyment, I hadn't expected to be played as the pawn.

As the knife we jointly held sliced into the cake, I was blinded by the sheer number of camera flashes going off. Film crews were videoing it. It was insane. *HOW ON EARTH DID I END UP HERE?!* thundered in my head.

In those brief moments, as John and I smiled and posed with the base commander, everything that weighed on me for the past decade came to the forefront of my mind. *What on earth have I become? How did I get to this moment, this place?* I was equal parts fascinated and exhausted. Yes, the events of that evening were a shock, but I still held my own and knew how to play the game. Yes, I enjoyed the work we did, but never once in a million years did I believe that I would end up as this person. I finally let my smile fade a little, as the cameras refocused their attention else-where. I was exhausted.

An hour later, after they had managed to make John and I dance together—that made me laugh, seeing the fear in John's eyes as we were pulled onto the dance floor—we made our way home. We were silent for a moment as we drove off their base. Then I burst out in almost a maniacal laugh, which prompted John to do the same.

"Well, how was your evening at the *Julie Tully Show*?" We laughed all the way home.

chapter 45

Fair Winds and Following Seas

"Please enjoy," our host, the Japanese ambassador, said as he smiled and lifted his spoon, signaling for the rest of us to begin.

I was sitting directly across from him, staring down at a skillfully hollowed-out eggshell that rested in a bed of straw nestled inside a champagne coupe. Inside the eggshell was a dollop of fluffy pale-yellow scrambled egg topped with gold leaf. *Real* gold. I really, *really* wanted John to snap a picture of it with his phone but that would have been uncouth. Rather, I had to etch the image into my memory instead.

Besides the absolutely amazing display of craftsmanship and edible precious metal in front of me, when I remarked about the precision of the cut of the eggshell, the ambassador quipped in jest that the chef had done it with a Samurai sword. I laughed. What struck me most was that this crazy and impressive meal had been made to honor John and me. Seriously. Of all the incredible meals I had had over the years, I had never had anything to that scale. Certainly not one prepared specifically for me. I ate every bite of what was placed in front of me that night, in awe of its artistry and the thoughtfulness behind it. I was also in awe of the fact that it was still Djibouti, a land where I had learned that such extremes were just part of the total package.

Two days later, at eight in the morning, the harsher reality of our pack out had replaced the gold leaf. John and I took a final walk-through of the house before the movers arrived. The pictures and decorations were off the walls and waiting to be wrapped up. Even though the furniture was still there, the place felt empty. It was eerie. The echoes of the parties and dinners we had hosted in that room filled my head. I could picture the cast of characters who had graced the space: ambassadors, generals, admirals, military officers from around the world, our rotating cast of office staff, friends laughing, family. But this was the end. When the packers arrived, our life would be carefully boxed up and placed into plywood shipping crates and sealed up for the voyage to Italy.

It seemed only fitting that we were leaving Djibouti in the heat of the year, given that we had arrived in the same weather. As the Djiboutian colonel had said to me three years before, about it being the Gates of Hell—well, I suppose now I could say that I had been to hell and back and survived to tell the tale. I was a different person than when I arrived, and for that, I would be forever thankful.

I planted myself next to John, our dining room chairs pressed together against the wall, a cup of instant coffee in my hand, trying to stay out of the way of the packers, just watching. There went our plates, our glasses, our life. John's replica of the *USS Tucson*, his first submarine, was carefully covered with three layers of bubble wrap. My chinks and spurs. Quinn's books. I was numb. I was grieving. We were closing up shop, a gig we had been playing since we first stepped foot in Cameroon all those years before. I was not crying. I was beyond that. I had cried the week before when John took the first picture off the wall, and the reality of what was coming hit me full force. Bab-el-Mandeb is the Arabic name for the strait of water that abuts Djibouti, the English translation of which is Gateway of Tears. I couldn't have picked a better name myself. That tour so interesting, so incredible, and so heart-wrenching. I was leaving because it was time, but I would not forget Djibouti, nor would I be forgotten because I had added my own tears to its collection. It seemed a fitting end to our time in Africa.

JUNE 24, 2018. PACK OUT, DAY TWO. I. HATE. MOVING. I wrote in my journal.

On a positive note, though, the French moving company we'd been assigned knew how to do it right. The day before, they showed up at eight-thirty in the morning, took only an hour for lunch, then left right on time at four-thirty, having completed two-thirds of the house. Pretty impressive compared to some of our previous moves.

But I still hated moving. Moving was a long, involved, and tiring process. That morning I had woken up with some sort of sinus issue or head cold. My nose was simultaneously running and stuffed up. By the end of the day, I felt like I'd developed a stress disorder from the sound of packing tape being pulled and torn. That evening I jotted another note in my journal: THANK GOD FOR GIN.

A week later, on the night before we departed, the three of us went out for one last time with our ambassador and his wife, an intimate meal at one of the local restaurants. We sat outside, despite the sweltering heat, dining on camel meat and drinking gin and tonics. While our time with that ambassador had been short, as he had only arrived at the beginning of the year, ours was a quickly formed friendship and tremendous working partnership. We would miss them terribly.

On the drive back to our house, John, Quinn, and I laughed about the progress of Djibouti in the three years that we had lived there. We joked with Quinn about making one last stop at the new mall, which had opened the previous year. We *oohed* and *ahhed* at the colorful lights that still decorated the roundabouts after Djiboutian National Day. It felt like a different place from the one we had arrived in, like everything was moving forward according to plan . . . until we came to an unexpected and unmarked road closure. John had to drive up onto the sidewalks for one last time, but then the car in front of us stopped suddenly and tried to back into us. We laughed until our sides hurt. Things had changed, but perhaps not as much as we thought.

Djibouti had been an experience, a fitting bookend to our time in Africa. Such a small country, yet such an important place on the global stage. There hadn't been a moment when living there wasn't interesting. Okay, sometimes it was just plain ol' bag of cats crazy, like when goats would stumble down our street, high on the discarded khat leaves they had found. Djibouti had changed so much during our time there; I could only imagine what it would look like in the years to come. In a way, I was sorry that I would miss that, but most of all, I would miss the complete unexpectedness of Djibouti. And of Africa.

Reversing the process of our arrival, we loaded our bags into the office car and made the short drive to the airport. Endings are always strange. I sat in the back of the SUV with Quinn, silent and resigned, ready to leave. John was placing our house keys into a Ziploc bag and starting to turn his phone off for the last time when it rang unexpectedly. Out of habit, he actually answered it, even though he was no longer the SDO/DATT. It was someone from the Chinese base, asking if we were available for dinner that night with the base commander.

"I'm sorry, we can't. We are on our way to the airport right now. Our flight is at seven o'clock," John told the caller. It happened more often than you'd think, having to leave a place without saying goodbye to people—once the clock started ticking, you had to go, with or without certain farewells. He listened to the caller's response on the other end of the line, nodding his head. "Okay, okay, thanks." He shook his head in amusement as he hung up, then turned the phone off and placed it in the Ziploc along with the keys. The job was over. We parked, unloaded our small collection of suitcases into the 115-degree weather and made our way toward the terminal.

The check-in area of the airport was ridiculously small given the size of flights that went in and out of Djibouti. The ticketing process was laughably slow. By the time we had our boarding passes in hand, we were only ninety minutes from departure. It was time to get our passports stamped one last time.

We turned to walk to passport control and came face to face with a Chinese sailor in his pale blue digital camouflage uniform. "Hello," he said in heavily accented English. "I am with the Chinese base commander. He is on his way in. He wants to say goodbye." We stood there dumbfounded. The scene summed up our time in Djibouti perfectly—surreal had been the theme of the last three years, so surreal obviously was how it had to end.

Through the line of people waiting to check-in and airport security strode the Chinese base commander, the man with whom John and I had become . . . friends? There's that word again. But was there another term for our weird relationship? We couldn't technically be real friends with him. That was just not possible in our respective worlds, yet we had been together so often, carrying on in the manner that would befit the word friend. Beyond the boundaries of work and the complications that came with it, we laughed with him, shared our respective cultures, shared pictures of family, and commiserated about a life lived far from home. Hell, he'd even got me to line dance. What had we been, if not some strange version of friends? And there he was, coming to say goodbye, a sign of respect for us, one more time.

"My friends, I had hoped to see you before you left," he said sadly, explaining that he had been on leave and only just returned. He said he had hoped to host us for a farewell dinner, but that never materialized. "So, I had to come say goodbye. You have been good friends."

People stared at us—other passengers, the Gendarmerie, American service members heading home from a tour at Camp. Some of them probably wondered who this little family was that had merited such a visit. Many others knowing full-well who we were but stayed silent about it. The commander presented us with a bag of gifts. John posed with him while I snapped a picture. He shook our hands and said a heartfelt *adieu*, then turned, and walked out of the airport and we headed upstairs for our flight.

Yes, that was Djibouti. A modern-day Casablanca, but for us, *l'histoire est fini.*

Farewell, Djibouti.

Farewell, Africa.

epilogue

Would you tell me please which way I ought to go from here?
—Lewis Carrol, *Alice in Wonderland*

It was still pitch-black outside when we got into our car, coffees in hand. Two-thirty in the morning on Labor Day weekend, we were on our way to Rome to pick up Cat Two. After initially trying and failing to get her out of Djibouti when we had left, a friend kindly offered to escort her to Italy once she was officially cleared to fly. They were arriving that morning on the red-eye flight from Ethiopia.

The autostrada was nearly empty as we skirted the Apennine Mountains and headed north. Quinn, half-asleep in the back seat, asked, "Can I play DJ?" The used car we had bought upon arrival in Naples didn't have a working radio, so I said sure and handed him my phone. He deftly shuffled through his favorite playlist and maximized the volume. The opening strains of Arcade Fire's "No Cars Go" filled the cab—a song that seemed oddly fitting as we zoomed along the dark, open road.

Before leaving home that morning, I had known we were in for a heck of a trip. Our friend had texted me from Addis Ababa to tell me that he and Cat Two were fine but that it was not going to be a fun flight to Rome as she had already peed all over him prior to leaving Djibouti, causing him to change clothes, and then proceeded to yowl all the way to Addis. I felt so bad. But was thrilled that Cat Two was coming home to us, where she belonged. We had had a rough transfer, emotionally drained and suffering from culture shock. Then we ended up in the base hotel for two months before finally moving into our apartment only the week before. Everyone in our family—us and Cat Two—needed a win at that point. We needed to be back together to start the next chapter of our lives.

We stood at the arrivals area in the airport, keeping our eyes peeled on the door. I kept thinking the worst, that perhaps the immigration officials would find fault with her paperwork or some such glitch. But then John said, "Do you hear that?" From behind the sliding glass doors came a familiar mournful yowl: Cat Two protesting her predicament. The doors opened and there she was. Our friend, a marine who looked as if he had just been through a battle, held her carrier out toward us and said, "Here she is. I'm going to my hotel." Apparently, she had really given him a run for his money on the final leg of their trip—escaping from her carrier and making her way from their last row seat to the business class section. Twice. I thanked him profusely, and then we parted ways, Cat Two staring in silent wonder at our faces, amazed that it was actually us.

On the drive home, only Cat Two and I were awake—John and Quinn had given up the ghost and went to sleep. From her carrier in the backseat, she let out the occasional quiet yowl to remind herself and me that it wasn't a dream. As I drove along, watching the landscape go by and the sun rise, I wondered yet again, *How did I end up here?* Not Africa, yet still so far away from where I began. Life was a weird and wonderful thing.

Almost three months after we left Djibouti, I was still an emotional mess and once again feeling at a loss. One day we had been in Africa, doing the work that had become like breathing to us, and then the next day, we weren't. We had no transition. No break to allow time and space to separate us and our minds from the previous eight years. It was as if we had been wearing a Band-Aid then had it suddenly ripped off, as if that would somehow lessen the pain. Well, it didn't. We were back with big navy, a place we hadn't been in fourteen years, and it no longer felt like home. For me, I was dropped back into a world that I no longer fit into. I had been a navy wife for almost two decades but then realized I was no longer the wife our navy and its community expected. My demons of self-doubt began to return.

It had not been some grand plan on our part to spend three consecutive tours on the African continent. It's just how it had worked out for us. Our stars had aligned and allowed us to stay in the region where we felt we belonged, where we felt we did the most good. Had it been the best idea? Most certainly, both professionally and personally. Did it end up complicating the rest of our lives? Absolutely. A fact never more apparent than during our reentry to big navy in Italy. I felt more foreign during those first few months in Naples than I had felt at any time in our life overseas.

I would try to make small talk with someone, especially those who were also new arrivals to Naples, and the conversation would naturally turn to discussion of where we had come in from and where else we had been stationed. I would overhear some spouses chattering, "Oh, you just came in from Mayport? We were there two tours ago. Do you know so-and-so?" Sometimes they would laugh in surprise, having run into someone they knew a decade before. Then it would be my turn, "Hello," they would say, "Where were you prior to here?" I would tell them that we just came in from Djibouti. "Oh, really," they would respond. "Are you active duty as well?" No, I would tell them, explaining that we had been there as a family for three years, that we had been at the embassy. While some found it interesting, the majority politely nodded while looking at me as if I were lying. In their mind no navy families lived in Djibouti, let alone Africa. Unsure how to act, they'd make an excuse and then fall away to talk to someone else. I never even attempted to tell them my adventures because I doubted that they'd have believed me.

At first these reactions stung, but then I was reminded how I'd grown while I was in Africa. I remembered that I could just be myself and could rely on myself to get through anything. I could do anything. That was what drove me forward during those first difficult months in Italy. With that knowledge and my family at my side, I transitioned into our new world.

I still dream of Africa most nights. In those dreams, I am once again sitting on our verandah in Cameroon, watching an afternoon thunderstorm roll through. Or I am shopping at the grocery store in Nigeria. Or I am attending another reception in Djibouti. Then the morning comes, and I wake up to our life in Italy, a relatively easy life. Yet I am struck with a sense of sadness, much the same as when I left the ranch and California for the first time. The French have a term for it, *mal d'Afrique*, which is the sickness of one's soul in reaction to their time in Africa. No pills can cure it. Time will not heal it. It's part of who I am now.

Mornings are when my thoughts wander most. Where the me from before joins the me that is now. The call to prayer no longer wakes me as it did during our years in Djibouti, which took some getting used to. Just as years before when the barking of our ranch dogs, begging to be let out of their pens after a night's sleep, no longer started my day. My days still begin before dawn, but with new rhythms and sounds. I get up, make my way to the kitchen, and pour a cup of coffee from the pot that John made before heading out for a run. I look out the window at the Apennines as the sun turns them a deep royal purple and the sky above a dark fuchsia. It's almost silent. The only sounds I hear these days are the low mewing greetings from Cat Two and the occasional call and response of the cadence of a command run on the road near us. It is during this time, when the world is waking up, that memories flood back. I am reminded of the strange, wonderful path that my life has taken . . . and I smile.

I am no longer worried about what is next or where my life is headed. Those years in Africa brought back the me from before, the me who faced the world unafraid of other's opinions, unafraid of not fitting neatly into a cultural box. Africa brought back the cowgirl and then some. Africa opened its arms and welcomed me, no matter how different I was. That amazing continent and our job there showed me that I could blaze a different path. It made me a different kind of military spouse—and I love this new version. Different is good. Different is great.

I am like Alice when she returned from Wonderland, forever changed yet still Alice. How powerful that is.

So now, with each passing day, I smile as I pull on my cowboy boots, moving forward . . . and my story continues.

about the author

Cowgirl-turned-nomadic navy spouse, Julie Tully writes about life, culture, and the places where they intersect. Julie's writing has appeared in *Legacy Magazine, InDependent,* and *Your Teen for Parents.* Her quirky lifestyle has taken her around the world, from rural Northern California to Europe and Africa. Now, after spending the past eighteen years overseas, Julie and her family prepare for an even greater adventure—returning to the United States.

julietullywriter.com

Printed in the USA
CPSIA information can be obtained
at www.ICGtesting.com
LVHW040944070524
779566LV00002B/338